ROUTLEDGE LIBRARY EDITIONS: PHONETICS AND PHONOLOGY

Volume 3

PLANAR PHONOLOGY AND MORPHOLOGY

PLANAR PHONOLOGY AND MORPHOLOGY

JENNIFER S. COLE

LONDON AND NEW YORK

First published in 1991 by Garland Publishing, Inc.

This edition first published in 2019
by Routledge
2 Park Square, Milton Park, Abingdon, Oxon OX14 4RN

and by Routledge
711 Third Avenue, New York, NY 10017

Routledge is an imprint of the Taylor & Francis Group, an informa business

© 1991 Jennifer S. Cole

All rights reserved. No part of this book may be reprinted or reproduced or utilised in any form or by any electronic, mechanical, or other means, now known or hereafter invented, including photocopying and recording, or in any information storage or retrieval system, without permission in writing from the publishers.

Trademark notice: Product or corporate names may be trademarks or registered trademarks, and are used only for identification and explanation without intent to infringe.

British Library Cataloguing in Publication Data
A catalogue record for this book is available from the British Library

ISBN: 978-1-138-60364-6 (Set)
ISBN: 978-0-429-43708-3 (Set) (ebk)
ISBN: 978-1-138-60830-6 (Volume 3) (hbk)
ISBN: 978-1-138-60831-3 (Volume 3) (pbk)
ISBN: 978-0-429-46657-1 (Volume 3) (ebk)

Publisher's Note
The publisher has gone to great lengths to ensure the quality of this reprint but points out that some imperfections in the original copies may be apparent.

Disclaimer
The publisher has made every effort to trace copyright holders and would welcome correspondence from those they have been unable to trace.

Planar Phonology and Morphology

Jennifer Cole

GARLAND PUBLISHING, INC.
New York • London
1991

Copyright © 1991 by Jennifer S. Cole.
All rights reserved.

Library of Congress Cataloging-in-Publication Data

Cole, Jennifer S.
Planar phonology and morphology / Jennifer S. Cole
p. cm. — (Outstanding dissertations in linguistics)
Includes bibliographocal references.
ISBN 0-8153-0165-0 (alk. paper)
1. Grammar, Comparative and general—Phonology. 2. Grammar, Comparative and general—Morphology. 3. Autosegmental theory (Linguistics) I. Title. II. Series.
P217.C655 1991

414—dc20   91-8451

Printed on acid-free, 250-year-life paper.
Manufactured in the United States of America

Acknowledgements

I have been greatly inspired by the many insightful comments provided by my teachers, Morris Halle, Donca Steriade and Jim Harris. I thank them for the time and encouragement they generously gave me during my graduate studies at MIT. A special thanks also goes to Jay Keyser for his kind support. My fellow graduate students at MIT contributed in many ways in providing the stimulating and supportive environment in which this research was conducted. My research has benefitted from the comments and ideas of many people, and in particular I thank Steve Abney, Diana Archangeli, Mark Baker, Ed Barton, Ellen Broselow, Andrea Calabrese, Nick Clements, Ken Hale, Ewa Czaykowska-Higgins, Harry van der Hulst, Nigel Fabb, John Goldsmith, Richard Hoberman, Hyoon-Sook Kang, Beth Levin, Juliette Levin, Mary Laughren, Steve Marlett, John McCarthy, Janis Melvold, David Nash, Glyne Piggot, Betsy Sagey, Brian Sietsema, Peggy Speas, Richard Sproat, and Loren Trigo.

This research was supported by a National Science Foundation Graduate Fellowship and by an IBM Graduate Fellowship, for which I remain very grateful.

My appreciation goes to Linda May and her LaTeX wizardry for copious technical assistance in preparing the revised document that appears here.

For continued nurturing and support, I thank my husband, Gul Agha, our children Leila and Eva, and my parents, Theodore and Sandra Cole.

I dedicate this book to my mother, who always understands, and to the memory of my son, Sachal.

Table of Contents

Acknowledgements v

Table of Contents vi

Preface viii

1 Introduction 1
   1.1 The Nature of Assimilation 5
   1.2 Theoretical Background 7
   1.3 Non-Linear Models 9
   1.4 Underspecification 15
   1.5 Harmony in Multi-Dimensional
       Phonology 17

2 Blocking in Parasitic Harmony 21
   2.1 Parasitic Harmony 22
   2.2 Menomini Height Harmony 24
   2.3 Maasai [ATR] Harmony 30
      2.3.1 General Harmony 30
      2.3.2 Dipthong-induced Harmony 34
   2.4 Conclusion 37

3 Consonant Symbolism 38
   3.1 Consonant Symbolism as Assimilation 40
   3.2 The Morphological Analysis 45
      3.2.1 Floating features as assimilation
           triggers 46
      3.2.2 The complexity argument 47
      3.2.3 Restricting the power of
           phonological rules 48

4 Morphologically Governed Harmony 53
   4.1 The Morpheme Plane Hypothesis 53
      4.1.1 Semitic morphology 53
      4.1.2 Morpheme planes
           and anti-gemination 56
   4.2 Harmony in Coeur d'Alene 61
      4.2.1 Glottal Harmony 62
      4.2.2 Faucal Harmony 70
   4.3 Wiyot Anterior/Continuant Harmony 82

4.4 Warlpiri Labial Harmony 94
    4.4.1 Progressive Harmony 94
    4.4.2 Regressive Harmony 100
4.5 Mixtec Nasal Harmony 103
4.6 Locality Conditions on Phonological Rules 111

5 Plane Conflation 116
5.1 Evidence for Plane Conflation 117
    5.1.1 Plane Conflation and Harmony 117
    5.1.2 Plane Conflation in McCarthy's
         Analysis 124
5.2 Lexical Phonology and the Bracket Erasure
    Convention 130
5.3 Counterexamples to the BEC 138
    5.3.1 English Derivational Suffixation 138
    5.3.2 Seri 140
    5.3.3 Ci-Ruri 150
    5.3.4 Sekani 155
    5.3.5 Discussion 156
5.4 Adjacency in Phonology and Morphology 158
    5.4.1 Adjacency in Morpho-phonological
         Parsing 159
    5.4.2 The Adjacency Constraint 160
    5.4.3 The Adjacency Constraint and Plane
         Conflation in Ci-Ruri 165
5.5 Floating Features and Morpheme Planes in
    Tonal Phonology 168
5.6 Summary 175

6 Case Studies in Planar Phonology 177
6.1 M-Adjacency in Fula and Malayalam 177
6.2 Fula Consonant Mutation 178
6.3 Malayam Nominal Derivation 183
6.4 Dakota 185
6.5 Hausa 191

Bibliography 200

Preface

This book presents my 1987 M.I.T. doctoral thesis, incorporating a small number of changes made to improve the exposition, while leaving the essential analyses intact. In my thesis, I investigate the proper treatment of harmony processes in phonological theory. The data I examine lead to a formulation of morphologically governed harmony processes which involves multi-planar representations. I draw on McCarthy's (1981) Morpheme Plane Hypothesis to explain a set of counterexamples to the analysis of opaque segments in harmony systems. The analysis of multi-planar harmony leads into a discussion of Plane Conflation and Bracket Erasure in Lexical Phonology.

In the three years since this thesis was written, phonological theory has continued to undergo rapid expansion and revision. One recent revision is particularly relevant to the analyses I present here. McCarthy (1989) undertakes a careful examination of the Morpheme Plane Hypothesis from which he concludes that "The effects of the W(eak) MPH follow from the observation that planar segregation means nothing more than the lack of inherent linear order relations and from elementary considerations of linear order among separate morphemes in nonconcatenative morphological systems." (McCarthy 1989:87). In other words, McCarthy denies that the MPH is an axiom of phonological theory, and derives its effects from the representation of linear order in the cases of floating features and non-concatenative morphology.

The ramifications of McCarthy's recent arguments are explored in Chapter 4, and though the treatment of Coeur d'Alene is consistent with McCarthy's findings, several other systems mentioned in Chapter 3 are not (see especially the analysis of Wiyot). The problem is that McCarthy's recent interpretation of morpheme planes will provide multi-planar representations only when a morpheme introduces a floating feature; yet not all of the harmonic features discussed in this thesis are underlyingly floating. Clearly, the question to be addressed in future research is to what extent do harmony systems display unexpected transparency, and what linear relations are required between stem and affix features in such systems.

A second area of recent development concerns the theory of distinctive features and their organization. This thesis adopts the version of feature geometry presented in Clements (1985) and modified in Sagey (1986). Predictions are made about which segments will block harmonic spreading on the basis of the adopted model of feature geometry. However the precise formulation of feature geometry continues to be debated, particularly with respect to the relationship between features that specify vowels and those that specify consonants (Archangeli & Pulleyblank (in press), Clements (1989)). If we are led to adopt a different model of feature geometry, then it is possible that the predictions concerning transparency and opacity in harmony systems will also change.

Bearing in mind recent changes in the theoretical framework, we may turn our attention now to the data investigated in the following chapters, which remain as interesting and challenging to phonological theory now as they were when I began this research.

Chapter 1

Introduction

The development of Autosegmental Phonology, or more generally, non-linear phonology, has lent great depth to our current understanding of long-distance phonological processes like harmony. In particular, these theories have provided a formalism in which we can express harmonic assimilation and the situations in which assimilation is blocked. We begin by examining the explanation of blocking phenomena in a non-linear theory of phonology. I argue for a theory in which blocking is not a primitive property; rather, the blocking behavior of a segment in a given harmony system is derivative from the phonological representation and constraints on the association of harmonic features. This analysis depends heavily on an adjacency constraint which prohibits derivations that create crossing association lines, as in (1). In this example, the adjacency constraint prohibits the assimilation of $[\alpha F]$ from x_1 to x_3.

1) $\alpha F \quad \beta F$

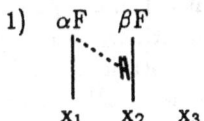

$x_1 \quad x_2 \quad x_3$

The adjacency constraint prohibiting crossing association lines has generally been assumed to be an inviolable principle of Universal Grammar. I present data from the harmony systems of several languages that seem on the surface to violate the adjacency constraint. In these harmony systems, a harmonic feature $[\alpha F]$ spreads 'over' a segment that is specified as $[\beta F]$. In a configuration like (1), these harmony systems seemingly allow $[\alpha F]$ to spread across x_2 and onto

1

x_3. While it would be possible to accommodate such harmony systems in the non-linear theory by rejecting or weakening the adjacency constraint, I present a different solution. I maintain that the adjacency constraint is universal, but that the situations in which a $[\beta F]$ segment fails to block $[\alpha F]$ harmony involve phonological representations that assign the harmonic feature $[\alpha F]$ and the blocking feature $[\beta F]$ to separate *planes*, as in (2).

2)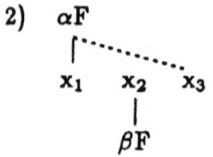

Assimilating $[\alpha F]$ to x_3 does not result in the crossing of any association lines; in particular, assimilation does not involve crossing the association line linking $[\beta F]$, and therefore the segment specified as $[\beta F]$ will not block harmony.

My analysis of these unusual harmony systems does not license the unconstrained use of multi-planar representations. The multi-planar analysis I present is adopted from the work of McCarthy (1981, 1986), in which it is argued that every morpheme in a word is represented on a distinct phonological plane, and new phonological planes are created only as the result of morphological affixation. I refer to McCarthy's proposal as the *Morpheme Plane Hypothesis*. I claim that only morphologically governed harmony processes will license representations as in (2), and therefore only this class of harmony processes will display the unusual lack of blocking phenomena mentioned above.[1]

In both my analysis of harmony systems and McCarthy's (1986) analysis of syncope, there is a distinction between phonological processes that apply to multi-planar representations, as in (2), and phonological processes that apply to uni-planar representations, as in (1). Following McCarthy, I argue that uni-planar representations are derived from multi-planar representations by a process called *Plane Conflation*. Phonological rules can be ordered before or after Plane Conflation. I address several questions concerning the nature of Plane Conflation, and conclude that the evidence at hand supports order-

---

[1] But see Chapter 4 for discussion of the proposal in McCarthy (1989) which rejects the Morpheme Plane Hypothesis in favor of a more constrained proposal in which morpheme planes are licensed by the existence of syllable templates, as in Semitic, or morphemes consisting only of a floating feature, as in Coeur d'Alene Glottal Harmony.

ing Plane Conflation at only one juncture in morpho-phonological derivation—between the word-level (lexical level) and phrase-level (post-lexical level) of morphological and phonological rule application.

In the discussion of morphologically governed phonological rules, we encounter several processes which involve a dependency between two morphemes, or a morpheme and a phonological segment, which are not adjacent in morpho-phonological representation. I discuss the role of adjacency in constraining morphology and phonology, and propose an adjacency constraint which limits non-adjacent dependencies to a very narrow class. The formulation of this constraint involves both linear adjacency in phonological representation, and a c-command relation in morphological representation.

The thesis is organized as follows: the remainder of Chapter 1 contains an introduction to non-linear phonology, and a discussion of the analysis of harmony within non-linear theory. Various assumptions which underlie the analyses in subsequent chapters will also be laid out. These sections can be skipped by the reader already familiar with non-linear theories of feature geometry and the analysis of harmony within such theories.

Chapter 2 is a short excursus on blocking phenomena in harmony systems. I introduce the notion of a *parasitic* harmony process in which harmony spreads from a trigger to targets that share some contextual feature. Parasitic harmony can be blocked in two ways: (i) direct blocking by a segment specified for the harmonic feature, and (ii) indirect blocking by a segment which fails to meet the contextual condition on harmony. I present data from Menomini High Harmony and Maasai ATR Harmony, and argue that an analysis of these systems as parasitic harmonies allows us to characterize the blocking phenomena they exhibit without invoking any ad-hoc filters or diacritic devices. This analysis is taken as further support for the constrained theory of harmonic assimilation that is adopted in Chapters 3 and 4.

Chapter 3 examines the phenomena of consonant sound symbolism, as observed in the Native American languages of the northwest. I argue that the complex range of consonant alternations seen in such systems is best explained by analyzing consonant symbolism as a kind of consonant harmony. The alternative analysis is shown to require a type of phonological rule which allows morphological structure to govern non-local phonological changes. I formulate an argument against this alternative based on the empirical observation that morphologically governed rules always operate locally. The locality condition on morphologically governed rules is taken up again in Chapter 5. Chapter 3 also introduces two of the harmony systems that are discussed in Chapter 4.

Chapter 4 investigates the special properties of morphologically governed assimilation processes, which differ in significant ways from non-morphologically governed assimilation. Morphologically governed harmony processes lack some of the blocking phenomena seen in non-morphologically governed harmonies. These differences can be explained by invoking the Morpheme Plane Hypothesis, under the assumption that morphologically governed rules apply to multi-planar representations, while non-morphologically governed rules apply after all morpheme planes have been collapsed.

Chapter 5 examines the process of Plane Conflation, which collapses the multi-planar representations created by affixation into a single phonological plane. I discuss the relationship between Plane Conflation and the Bracket Erasure Convention of Lexical Phonology, and argue against a theory in which Bracket Erasure applies internal to the word-level (lexical) derivation. I examine the role of Bracket Erasure in constraining the accessibility of morphological structure in morphological and phonological processes, and argue that the constraints on these processes derive from considerations of morpho-phonological parsing, and not from the Bracket Erasure Convention. I conclude that were Plane Conflation to be equated with Bracket Erasure, then it would also be prevented from applying internal to the word-level derivation. Although the data is not yet clear on this question, there is reason to think that in some cases, Plane Conflation can apply internal to the word-level derivation. Chapter 5 also addresses the question of how morpheme planes are conflated when they contain floating features. It is seen that precedence relations must be established between elements on separate planes, even if those elements are not linked to the skeleton, which otherwise mediates the precedence relations between all planes. Data from the tonal phonology of Tiv is presented in this discussion.

Chapter 6 presents a morpheme-plane analysis of morphologically governed phonological rules in four languages: Consonant Mutation in Fula, /i/-Insertion and /y/-Insertion in Malayalam Nominal Derivation, Coronal Dissimilation and Degemination in Dakota, and Suffix Tone Spreading in Hausa.

1.1 The Nature of Assimilation

A large portion of this thesis is devoted to explaining the properties of harmony systems in several languages. We can begin here by defining harmony as a type of assimilation, and noting the parameters by which assimilation processes can vary.

An *assimilation* is any process in which some segment x comes to share some of the properties of another segment y in the course of phonological derivation. The segment which undergoes the assimilation, x, is called the *target*, while the segment which conditions the assimilation, y, is called the *trigger*. The sharing of a phonological property between two segments is sometimes referred to as *agreement* in phonology.

Almost every language exhibits some kind of assimilation phenomenon. In many cases, the assimilation is of a low-level or phonetic character: for example, in English, vowels which precede a nasal consonant take on a nasal coloring; however, there is not a meaningful or *phonemic* distinction between plain and nasalized vowels in English. In other cases, the assimilation process is of a more phonological character: for example, in English the prefix /in-/ actually surfaces as [il-] before a stem beginning with /l/, as in *illogical*, and it surfaces as [im-] before a stem beginning with /p/, as in *improbable*. Here, the assimilation process creates a meaningful, phonemic distinction between the surface forms of underlying /in-/; all of the surface segments /n, l, m/ are distinct phonemes in English.

Low level, phonetic assimilations usually operate on segments which are adjacent in the linear representation of a word. In contrast, phonological assimilation processes can affect two segments even if they are not string-adjacent. For example, in the Polynesian language Chamorro, the presence of certain prefixes containing a high front vowel cause the vowel in the initial syllable of a stem to undergo a front assimilation. Consider the following forms (from Chung (1983)):

3) nára   'mother'   i nána   'the mother'
    káta   'letter'   ni kátta   'the letter (obl.)'
    húŋuk   'to hear'   inhíŋuk   'we (excl.) heard'
    púgas   'uncooked rice' mí pìgas   'abounding in
                                         'uncooked rice'

The affected stem vowel is not adjacent to the prefix vowel; in all cases at least one consonant intervenes between them.

Another way in which assimilation processes may differ is in the boundedness of assimilation. Processes like the Chamorro assimilation described above are *bounded*—they affect only one segment. Other processes cause a sequence of segments to undergo assimilation. For example, van der Hulst & Smith (1982) report a nasal assimilation process in Capanahua which nasalizes a sequence of vowels and glides that precede a word-final deleted nasal, as in (4):

4) poyan ⟶ põỹã "*arm*"
   bawin ⟶ bãw̃ĩ "*catfish*"
   ci?in ⟶ cĩ?ĩ "*by fire*"
   boon ⟶ bõõ "*hair*"

The Capanahua assimilation process is unbounded, but it affects only segments that are string-adjacent.² We also observe assimilation processes that are unbounded and affect segments that are not string-adjacent. Examples of this type of assimilation are the familiar *vowel harmony* systems found in many languages. For instance, Turkish displays a harmony system in which all suffix vowels in a word are uniformly back or non-back (with few exceptions). In this language, vowels assimilate the backness feature of the last stem vowel, as shown in the examples in (5) (from Clements & Sezer (1982)).³

5) | | *nom.pl.* | *gen.pl.* |
   |---------|-----------|-----------|
   | "*rope*" | ip-ler | ip-ler-in |
   | "*face*" | yūz-ler | yūz-ler-in |
   | "*girl*" | kIz-lar | kIz-lar-In |
   | "*stamp*" | pul-lar | pul-lar-In |

As is readily observed, the vowels undergoing this back assimilation process are not adjacent to one another or to the triggering vowel; consonants intervene between trigger and targets, and are thus said to be *transparent* to harmony.

Finally, many kinds of unbounded assimilation processes are blocked when a segment from a certain class is encountered. For instance, in the Capanahua nasal harmony system, nasalization is blocked by all consonants except glides; only a contiguous sequence of vowels and

---

[2] I am using the term *unbounded* in a non-technical sense here, to refer to assimilation processes that operate on a sequence of segments. In Chapter 4, I formulate a technical definition of *boundedness* which explicitly refers to the mechanism by which this multiple assimilation is effected.

[3] The vowel /I/ represents a back, high, unrounded vowel, and is represented as a /ɨ/ in Clements & Sezer (1982).

glides preceding a deleted nasal get nasalized. Another example is seen in Mixtec, which has a process of unbounded nasal harmony that is always blocked by the presence of a voiceless consonant (see discussion in Section 4.5). Several of the African languages that have [ATR] harmonies exhibit blocking by certain vowels that are invariably [−ATR]. Segments that block harmony are called *opaque* segments.

A theory of assimilation must address many questions, among them the following:

1. Are all *agreement* phenomena in phonology best treated as assimilation? Are there typological distinctions differentiating agreement phenomena?

2. How is assimilation expressed in the formalism of phonological theory?

3. Can any distinctive feature potentially assimilate, or is assimilation limited to a subset of distinctive features?

4. What are the class of domains in which assimilation processes operate?

5. What is the formal distinction between bounded as opposed to unbounded assimilation, and between assimilation that operates under string-adjacency as opposed to assimilation that skips over segments?

6. What are the conditions under which unbounded assimilation is blocked, or prevented from applying?

All of these questions will be examined, to varying degrees, in the chapters that follow. In the next sections, I will review the analysis of assimilation that has resulted from the development of *Autosegmental Phonology*.

1.2 Theoretical Background

In their seminal work, *The Sound Pattern of English*, Chomsky & Halle (1968, hereafter SPE) propose a formal theory of phonology that provides the critical first measures towards our current understanding of the nature of assimilation. First, they adopt from Jakobson the idea that phonemes are comprised of bundles of distinctive features, where each distinctive feature refers to a property of the segment, such as *back, high, round, coronal, etc.* Phonological processes can affect these distinctive features individually or in groups. Second, phonological processes themselves are given a formal representation as *functions* which map distinctive feature matrices onto distinctive feature matrices. This mapping may involve the insertion, deletion, or alteration of distinctive features. Given the SPE formalism, a rule of assimilation takes on the form seen in the representation of English Nasal Assimilation in (6):

6) English Nasalization:

$$\begin{bmatrix} +\text{syllabic} \\ -\text{consonantal} \end{bmatrix} \longrightarrow [+\text{nasal}] \; / \; \_\_ \; [+\text{nasal}]$$

The rule in (6) states that a segment bearing the features [+syllabic, −consonantal]—a vowel—gains the feature [+nasal] whenever it precedes a segment that is itself specified as [+nasal].

While the SPE formalism does allow us to characterize the essential change caused by a phonological rule, it does not serve to relate the property of the structural change to properties of the segment conditioning the rule. Referring back to (9), this statement of nasalization does not capture the significance of the fact that the conditioning segment is a nasal and the phonological change is the *nasalization* of vowels. A rule of pseudo-nasalization which nasalizes vowels when they precede voiceless segments, as stated in (7), is formally equivalent.

7) Psuedo-English Nasalization:

$$\begin{bmatrix} +\text{syllabic} \\ -\text{consonantal} \end{bmatrix} \longrightarrow [+\text{nasal}] \; / \; \_\_ \; [-\text{voice}]$$

Both rules (6) and (7) involve the same number of distinctive features. Thus, adopting the evaluation metric proposed in SPE, both rules would be equally valued by the grammar of English. Therefore, the theory proposed in SPE cannot account for the fact that phonological rules like English Nasalization (6) are indeed much more common than phonological rules like the pseudo-nasalization of (7), which are exceptionally rare at best.

The functions used in the SPE model face additional difficulty in expressing assimilations which operate at a distance, as in the case of

Introduction 9

harmony. Recall the process of Back Harmony in Turkish, described in Section 1. The SPE format would encode Back Harmony as a feature insertion rule that inserts in every suffix vowel matrix the value of [back] that is identical to the [back] feature of the final stem vowel of the word. Greek variables are used in the rule to express this dependency. Any number of consonants and vowels may intervene between the two vowels referred to in the rule, so another variable is introduced. The Back Harmony rule is stated in (8).

8) Turkish Back Harmony:

[+syllabic] ⟶ [αback] /αback] (C) + (CV) __

The descriptive power of the SPE formalism is greatly increased by the introduction of variable notation required to express long-distance agreement processes like harmony. This increase in power results in a decrease in the explanatory adequacy of the theory, and represents a major weakness in the SPE model.

1.3 Non-Linear Models

Developments in phonological theory of the past ten years have contributed significantly to rectifying the shortcomings of the SPE analysis. Foremost among them is the idea that distinctive features are actual objects in linguistic representation—objects that are independent of feature matrices and which can be associated with segments, and manipulated by phonological rules. In the SPE model, phonological rules are technically operations on feature matrices, where matrices are characterized by the features they contain, but rules do not strictly operate on distinctive features as independent objects. Williams (1976) and Goldsmith (1976), in their work on tonal phonology, proposed that certain distinctive features are represented on tiers which are separate from, and run parallel to the linear string of segments. In the diagram in (9), tonal features are represented on the *tone tier* and segments come to bear tone specifications by being *associated* with tones—where association is represented by drawing a vertical line between the segment and the tone.

9)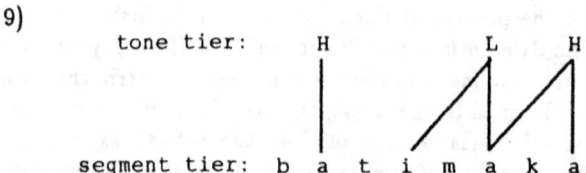

Also indicated in (9) is the fact that associations between tone features and segments can be one-to-one, one-to-many, or many-to-one. These associations are constrained by the well-formedness condition given in (10), which prohibits structures like the one shown in (11).[4]

10) Well-Formedness Condition: Association lines cannot cross.

11)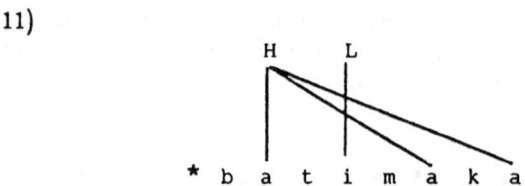

Any distinctive feature or phonological property which functions independently of the phonological segment, as do the tone features in (6), is termed an *autosegment*, and this non-linear approach to phonological representations is referred to as Autosegmental Phonology. McCarthy (1981) further develops the autosegmental model, and shows that the phonological segment must be decomposed into a *timing* (or skeletal) slot and a *melody*. The melody contains all of the distinctive features that characterize the segment, with certain features separated off onto special autosegmental tiers.

Employing autosegmental formalism, assimilation processes are represented as rules which create a multiple linking of segments to an autosegmental feature. For example, our rule of English Nasalization would appear as in (12), where the nasal autosegment linked to a nasal consonant associates with, or *spreads* onto a preceding vowel.

---

[4]Sagey (1988) argues convincingly that the Well-Formedness Condition is not itself a primitive constraint, but can be derived from the primitive notions of *precedence* and *overlap*. She demonstrates that with the correct definition of these primitives, a representation such as that in (11) encodes the contradiction that a segment both precedes and follows another segment. This violates that principle that there is always a discrete and unambiguous linear relationship between any two segments linked to the skeleton.

Introduction

12)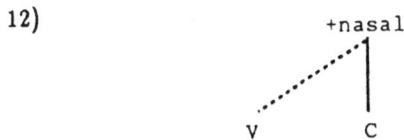

The representation of assimilation illustrated in (12) makes it clear why there is a relationship between the conditioning segment and the structural change of assimilation rules, as mentioned earlier. Namely, the conditioning segment provides the actual physical object—the assimilating feature—that effects the change. The rule of pseudo-English Nasalization given in (7) is given in (13), using the autosegmental formalism. The nasal feature is inserted into the representation and linked to the vowel. Comparing (12) with (13), it is obvious that (13) is the more complex rule, since it involves the insertion of a new feature not already present in the representation of the input to assimilation.

13)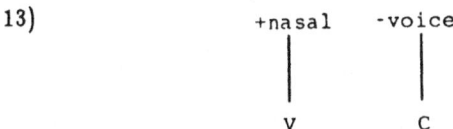

Recently, the spirit of Autosegmental Phonology has been more fully integrated in the proposals of Clements (1985), Halle (1986), and Sagey (1986) concerning the nature of the representation of a phonological segment. These proposals have in common the notion that *all* distinctive features are autosegments that are represented on distinct tiers or *planes* which connect together under a single *root node*.[5] The root node, together with all of the feature planes it dominates, characterizes the phonological segment and is linked to the core skeleton. The skeleton is comprised of timing units, devoid of any phonological or phonetic properties, represented by a sequence of x's.[6] A segment is taken to be the timing unit together with all of

---

[5]Both the terms *plane* and *tier* have been used to refer to a dimension of phonological representation which is distinct from the skeleton. For the remainder of this thesis, I adopt the term *plane*, in accordance with current usage.

[6]There are several competing proposals concerning the nature and even the existence of the skeleton. In early versions of Autosegmental Phonology, the skeleton was taken to be a sequence of C(onsonant) and V(owel) slots, specified for syllabicity. Levin (1983,1985) argues that skeletal slots are inherently unspecified, with the distinction between C and V a function of the position of the slot in

the distinctive features which are linked to it.

Clements, Halle, and Sagey argue further that all of the distinctive features are hierarchically ordered into a distinctive feature tree. The tree is dominated by the root node, and the terminal nodes are all articulatory features. The terminal nodes are further grouped together under various *class* nodes. The representation in (14) is the one proposed by Sagey (*op.cit.*), and is the model adopted in the analyses of this thesis. The class nodes are *laryngeal, supralaryngeal, soft palate, dorsal, coronal, labial*.[7]

14)

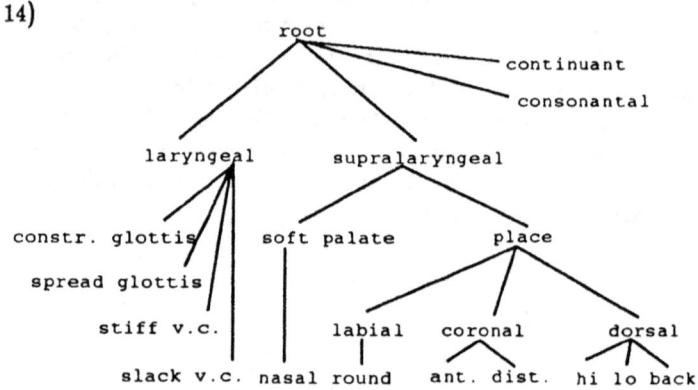

Note that in Sagey's model, not all of the features employed in the SPE model are terminal features. The SPE model did not make a

---

syllable structure. A more recent proposal is that the skeleton is not a part of phonological representation at all; root nodes directly incorporate into syllable structure, linking under nodes like σ (syllable) or μ (mora). See for example, McCarthy and Prince (1990, forthcoming) and Hayes (1989). I adopt here the x-slot model of Levin (1985), although this choice is not essential to the analyses that follow.

[7] Several aspects of the model in (14) are subject to dispute. For instance, Iverson (1989) argues against the existence of the Supralaryngeal node, claiming that Place links directly to the Root. McCarthy (1988) claims that major class features like [sonorant] and [consonantal] are part of the inherent specification of the root node. Debate continues as to the attachment site for [continuant], as well. The analyses presented in the following chapters do not bear directly on the attachment sites for [sonorant] and [consonantal], but the questions of how [continuant] fits into the feature tree and how it relates to the articulator nodes are relevant in the eventual analysis of several of the consonant symbolism systems presented in Chapter 3, in which consonant harmony involves the feature [continuant]. Although there is no clear consensus among phonologists, at the time of publication the model in (14) remains to a large degree the standard tree type of representation, and is adopted on this basis.

Introduction

typological distinction between features like [coronal] or [labial] and [back], [anterior], [round], etc. In Sagey's model, coronal and labial are class nodes, and [back], [anterior], and [round] are terminal features. Only the latter have "+" and "−" values. A segment will either bear a class node specification or not bear one, but there is no sense in which a segment can be "[−coronal]".

The way to view the representation in (14) is to imagine that in a sequence of root nodes attached to skeletal slots (X, C or V), the root nodes will be stacked exactly on top of one another, with the skeleton extending outwards from the page. Each terminal node links to skeletal positions (via intermediate class nodes) on its own plane, and there is a plane corresponding to every terminal node in the feature tree. Thus, the feature tree in (14) is most accurately considered as a tree of planes. Turning the diagram in (11) 90 degrees about the vertical axis, we obtain the picture in (15) (from Clements (1985)), which shows a sequence of three skeletal slots together with the feature trees that are linked to them.

15)

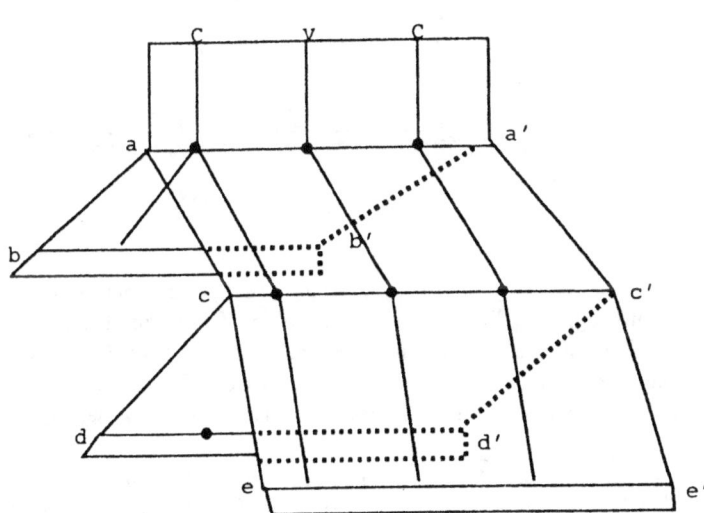

aa'=root tier, bb'=laryngeal tier, cc'=supralaryngeal tier, dd'=soft palate tier, ee'=place tier

The hierarchical representations in (14) and (15) group together all features which are actually seen to function together as a natural class in phonological rules across languages. The claim is that when several features are involved in an assimilation process, the features are not spreading individually, but rather the class node that dominates the features is the spreading node.[8] The following illustration shows the assimilation of a place node—dominating all place of articulation features—from a consonant onto an adjacent consonant.

16)

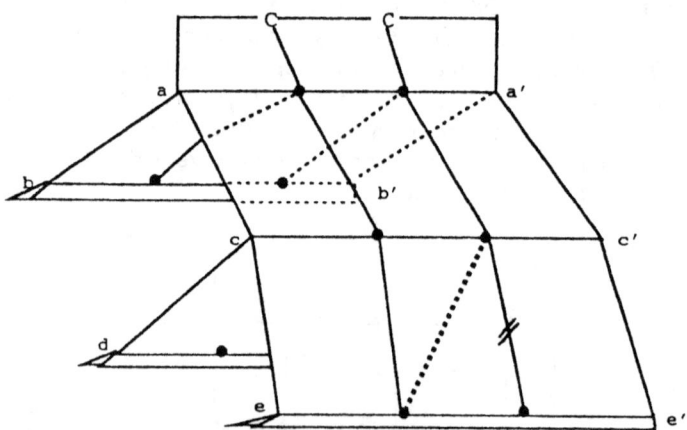

With representations like (15), any distinctive feature may act as an autosegment, linking to and delinking from skeletal positions independent of the linkings between other distinctive features and the skeleton. There is no longer a typological distinction between features which are involved in phonological spreading or delinking

---

[8]This claim may well have to be modified in light of the interesting vowel assimilation process in Barra Gaelic, discussed in Clements (1986) and Sagey (1987). Those data seem to indicate that total assimilation of vowel features involves the spreading of each vowel feature independently, and not the single spreading of the place node dominating the set of vowel features. If this finding is correct, it presents a serious challenge to the argument that the spreading of a set of features is evidence for grouping those features together under a single node in the feature tree. I will not address this issue further here, where it is assumed that there is sufficient evidence to support the feature groupings represented in the model in (14).

Introduction

rules, and features which are not. Thus, the term *autosegment* is no longer really appropriate—all features being autosegmental—and I will henceforth refer to this model of phonological representation as the *multi-dimensional* model.

The well-formedness condition (10) applies to the multi-dimensional model as it did to the less rich autosegmental model. An association between a node f_1 on the **F** plane and a parent node y cannot cross an existing association line linking f_2 on the **F** plane to y. We will see in Section 1.5 how the effects of the "no crossing association lines" convention result in preventing certain assimilation processes from occurring.

1.4 Underspecification

A second important theoretical innovation of recent years is the development of underspecification theory. In the SPE framework, phonological rules operate on feature matrices that are fully specified for each distinctive feature. However, it is a fact that in many cases, such full specification encodes a great deal of redundancy. For instance, the feature [voice] distinguishes between pairs of consonants like /p,b/, /t,d/, /k,g/, but in most languages [voice] does not serve similarly to distinguish among vowels or sonorants. Thus, [voice] is a redundant feature on vowels and sonorants in most languages.

Archangeli (1984, 1988) and Archangeli & Pulleyblank (in press), building on several earlier proposals, develop a theory in which redundant feature specifications are absent in underlying representations, and are filled in during the course of phonological derivation. They have further argued that for each distinctive feature present in underlying representation, only one value of that feature—"+" or "−"— is actually marked. The other value is inserted by a special type of redundancy rule, called a Complement Rule. The result is underlying representations which include only the minimal amount of feature specification needed to maintain phonemic distinctions. For example, a five vowel inventory /i, e, u, o, a/ could have the underspecified underlying form shown in (17).

17) Surface Representation   Underlying Representation

	i	e	a	o	u		i	e	a	o	u
high	+	−	−	−	+	high	+				+
back	−	−	+	+	+	back			+	+	+
low	−	−	+	−	−	low			+		
round	−	−	−	+	+	round				+	+

Redundancy Rules:
[ ] ⟶ [−high]
[ ] ⟶ [−back]
[ ] ⟶ [−low]
[ ] ⟶ [−round]

Sagey (1986) argues that in the unmarked case, unspecified class node features do not need to be filled in at the level of surface representation. For example, coronal consonants redundantly lack a dorsal specification in most languages. Therefore, it will not be necessary to posit a dorsal branch in the representation of coronals in every language. Referring to the tree structures of the multi-dimensional model, coronal consonants will have a coronal class node, possibly dominating some of the coronal terminal features, and will entirely lack a dorsal branch.

Since in many languages, vowels and consonants are specified for a disjunct set of terminal features, the feature trees for vowels and consonants will involve different terminal nodes—vowels will be specified for features dominated by the dorsal node, while consonants will be specified simply as dorsal, coronal, or labial. It will be a very rare case when in some language, all of the articulator class nodes (labial, coronal, dorsal, velar) are required in the specification of some segment.[9] So, combining Underspecification theory with the hierarchical feature trees, we arrive at underlying representations which encode only partial feature trees, as in the underlying form of the word /tip/ in some hypothetical language, given in (18):

---

[9] Sagey discusses several such cases in her treatment of complex, multiply-articulated segments.

18)

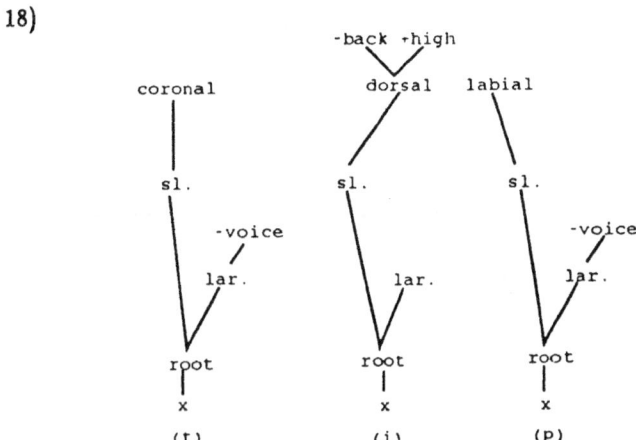

I adopt a version of Underspecification in this thesis which is slightly weaker than the version of Archangeli (1984), but consistent with Archangeli (1988), in conceding that in some cases both the "+" and "−" values of a particular feature may be present in underlying representation.[10] The role of Underspecification theory in explaining the skipping phenomena seen in many assimilation processes is discussed in the following section.

1.5 Harmony in Multi-Dimensional Phonology

Consonant and vowel harmonies are assimilation processes that typically affect more than one segment and can skip over segments that lie between a sequence of target segments, as described earlier. The question of how intervening segments are skipped receives an answer

---

[10]This conclusion is drawn on the basis of blocking phenomena in several languages. For example, in Bari, a regular rule of ATR harmony spreads the feature [+ATR] from certain marked vowels onto unmarked vowels (Cole & Trigo 1987). All vowels can potentially undergo general ATR harmony, except that in a substantial number of lexical roots, a low vowel /A/ fails to undergo harmony, and prevents harmony from propagating past it. These low vowels invariably surface as [−ATR]. The only way to capture these facts is to assume that in some lexical roots, the low vowel is underlyingly specified as [−ATR]. What is critical to this analysis is the fact that the blocking behavior of low vowels cannot be predicted on the basis of the phonological environment alone. These facts will perhaps be better understood in light of the material presented in Section 1.5. A similar argument for the necessity of binary specification in underlying representation is presented in Zsiga's (1989) treatment of [ATR] harmony in Igbo.

in the analysis of harmony employing multi-dimensional representations and Underspecification theory. Consider the rule of Turkish Back Harmony discussed above. Employing the formalism of the multi-dimensional model, the rule of Back Harmony indicates that a back feature from the final vowel of a stem spreads onto the dorsal node dominating each of the following suffixal vowels, as in (19).[11] A sample derivation of the form *yüz-ler-in* in (5) is given in (20).[12]

19) Turkish Back Harmony:

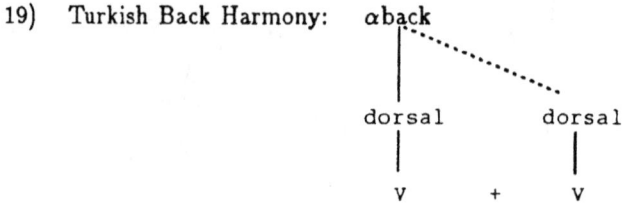

20)

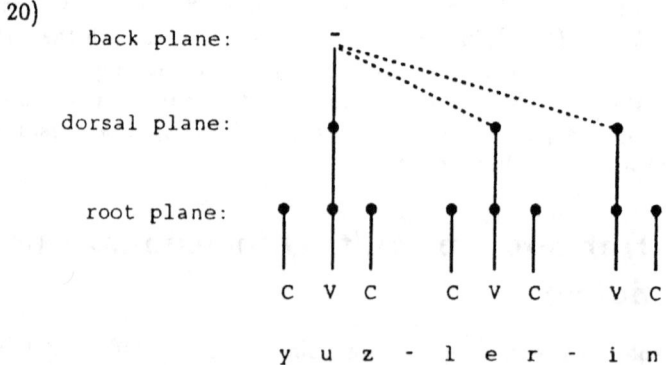

The transparency of consonants to back assimilation follows from the representation, as seen in (20). Since the consonants in this example do not bear a [back] specification (they are redundantly [+back]), there is nothing blocking the [−back] feature linked to the stem vowel

---

[11]The harmony rule spreads the feature [back] only onto dorsal segments that belong to a syllable nucleus. Thus, only vowels, and not consonants, are picked out as the targets of harmony. As a shorthand notation, I indicate this subclass of x-slots with a "V" on the skeleton. This is only a shorthand notation, though, and I am not advocating a theory which prespecifies the syllabicity of skeletal positions.

[12]In (20) I have only represented the parts of the feature tree that are relevant to the discussion of Back Harmony. The letters under the skeletal x-slots are meant only to indicate what features would be present in a more complete representation. These letters do not constitute part of the representation.

from spreading onto following suffix vowels. The Back Harmony rule specifies that [back] will link only to vowel positions; therefore, the transparency of consonants does not need to be explicitly stated in the rule at all. Constrast the simplicity of the rule in (19) with the same rule formulated in the SPE format, shown above in (8).

What would happen if some consonant lying between the trigger and target of harmony did bear a [back] specification? If Harmony were to spread over a consonant with an underlying back feature, the resulting structure would contain crossing association lines, which are prohibited. In fact, Turkish does make a distinction in some consonants between palatalized ([−back]) and non-palatised ([+back]) forms. The velars and /l/ have both realizations. When a palatal consonant, which is [−back], follows a [+back] vowel of a stem, the vowels to the right of the palatal consonant always surface as [−back]. In other words, palatal consonants serve to block Back Harmony. For example, the suffix vowels in (21) surface as [−back], even though the last stem vowel is [+back]. In both of these forms, the final stem consonant is palatalized when followed by the accusative singular suffix.

21)   *nom.sg.*   *acc.sg.*
      "perception"   idrak   idrāk-i
      "explosion"   infilak   infilāk-i

The explanation for this blocking phenomenon is that the well-formedness condition that prevents crossing association lines prohibits the application of Back Harmony in the forms in (21). The [−back] feature that surfaces on the suffix vowels can be considered to be the redundant value of backness, filled in by the redundancy rule: [ ] ⟶ [−back]. The ill-formed structure that would have resulted had Back Harmony applied is illustrated in (22).

Chapter 2

Blocking in Parasitic Harmony

In Chapter 1, we saw how harmony is analyzed in the multi-dimensional theory of phonology. We also saw examples of harmony systems in which the spreading of the harmonic feature [αF] is blocked by some segment which is specified as [βF]. This analysis of harmony provides a way of characterizing blocking segments in harmony systems: all and only those segments which are specified for the harmonic feature at the stage in the derivation where harmony applies will be able to block harmony. If harmony applies early in the derivation, before the redundancy rules have applied, then only segments which are underlyingly specified for the harmonic feature will block harmony.

Steriade (1987b) argues that phonological redundancy rules apply in two stages: *complement* rules fill in the redundant feature value of [F] on all segments which are distinct from some other segment on the basis of [F] alone. For example, the vowels /u/ and /o/ are distinguished only by the feature [high]. If [+high] is the underlying value, then /o/ will be assigned [−high] by the complement rule. All remaining segments, eg., /a/, will be specified as [−high] by a *default* rule, which is always ordered after the complement rule. With this analysis, harmony may apply before complement and default rules, in which case only segments which are underlyingly marked for the harmonic feature may block harmony, or harmony may apply after the complement rules, in which case all segments to which the complement rule has applied may additionally block harmony.

Whether harmony applies before or after redundancy rules, the class of segments which block harmony can be characterized by their specification for the harmonic feature. If we adopt a constrained version of Underspecification theory, in which the only redundancy rules which can be formulated are the complement and default rules, then we can predict for any harmony system what segments may potentially block harmony. In this chapter, I present data from two languages which pose a problem for the analysis of harmony sketched here. In each case, the segments that block harmony do not appear to bear a specification for the harmonic feature at the time harmony applies. I argue that these are *parasitic* harmony systems, in which harmonic spreading is dependent on both the trigger and target being multiply linked to some contextual feature. In parasitic harmony, an additional class of blocking segments is created by the presence of segments which do not bear the appropriate contextual feature.[1]

2.1 Parasitic Harmony

Many harmony systems share the property of allowing spreading of the harmonic feature **F** only when trigger and target are similarly specified $[\alpha G]$, for some contextual feature G. One well-known example of this type is Yokuts Round Harmony, illustrated in (1), which spreads [+round] from [αhigh] to [αhigh] vowels (Archangeli 1984, Kisseberth 1969, Newman 1941).

1) Yawelmani:

gloss	fut.pass.	pass.aor.	prec.ger.
'tangle'	xilnit	xilit	xil?as
'know about, recognize'	hudnut	hudut	hud?as
'take care of an infant'	gopnit	gopit	gop?os
'procure'	maxnit	maxit	max?as

Round Harmony does not apply when the trigger and target vowels are of dissimilar height, as in (2):

2) mo:xil?as   'grow old-prec.ger.'
   suhwa:hin   'make by means of supernatural powers'

It is possible to represent this condition as in (3), using the formalism of Autosegmental Phonology:

---

[1] The material in this chapter was previously published in Cole & Trigo (1988). I am indebted to Loren Trigo for discussion of these issues, and in particular, for the analysis of Maasai in Section 2.3.

3)

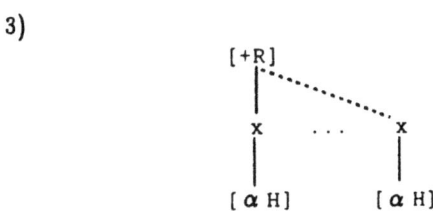

Yet, such a representation does not capture the significance of the fact that the contexts specified on both target and trigger must be identical. Equally plausible would be a harmony system which spread the harmonic feature only from [αF] triggers onto [−αF] targets, yet no such cases are known to exist.[2]

An alternate representation of the identity condition on Yokuts Round Harmony is obtained by allowing harmonic spreading of [+round] only when both target and trigger are linked to a single contextual feature [αhigh], as in (4). I will refer to this analysis as the Linked Structure Analysis.

4)

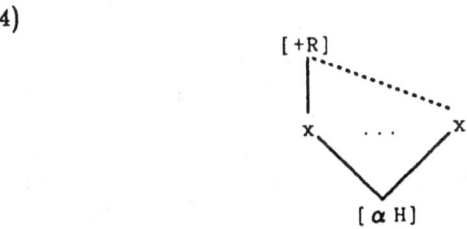

The representation of the harmony rule in (4) is simpler than (3), since it refers to fewer features. It also allows a clear expression of the identity condition. The Linked Structure Analysis makes the prediction that Round Harmony will be blocked whenever a segment which is specified as [−αhigh] at the time harmony applies intervenes between trigger and target. The presence of an intervening [−αhigh] segment will prevent the trigger and target from multiply linking to a single [αhigh] feature without creating crossing association lines. This situation is illustrated in (5), where the configuration in (i) cannot be

---

[2]In fact, there is only one example cited in the literature of a harmony rule which specifies a context on both target and trigger, yet where the contexts are not identical. This is the case of Sanskrit n-Retroflexion (*Nati*), which requires that the targets be [+nasal], while the triggers are [+cont, −ant, −dist]. See Whitney (1889), Schein and Steriade (1986).

interpreted as a possible environment for harmony to apply, as in (ii).

5)

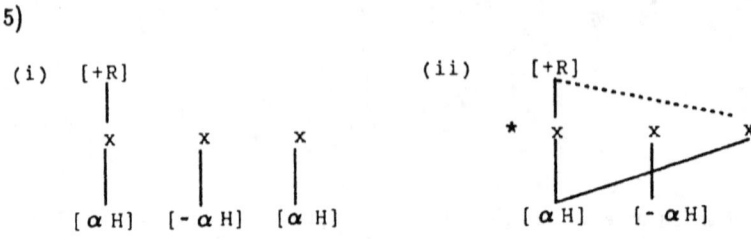

In fact in Yokuts, we can observe that [−αhigh] segments block harmony, and not [−round] segments.

The Linked Structure Analysis of harmony expresses the fact that in many languages harmonic spreading of [**F**] is dependent on prior association of a contextual feature [**G**]. Very clear examples of this sort are found in some of the Uralo-Altaic languages, where the application of one harmony process is dependent on the prior application of another harmony process (Steriade 1981, and references cited there). For example, in Kirghiz, Primary Round Harmony applies freely in words that have undergone harmonic spreading of [−back]. Words with [+back] vowels have not undergone Back Harmony (their [+back] specification is provided by redundancy rule), and consequently, do not exhibit uniform Round Harmony. Rather, words with [+back] vowels are subject to a Secondary Round Harmony rule which spreads [+round] onto vowels of similar height. Primary Round Harmony is thus seen to be *parasitic* on prior application of Back Harmony, which creates the multiply-linked contextual structure. The feature [+round] spreads across all segments linked to the same [−back] feature.

2.2 Menomini Height Harmony

Menomini vowel harmony is another example of dependency harmony, whose peculiar characteristics receive a straightforward explanation using the Linked Structure Analysis.[3] Menomini has a system of regressive height harmony which raises long /ē,ō/ when followed by one

---

[3]All Menomini data is obtained from Bloomfield (1962, 1975). For a more lengthy presentation of the facts relating to harmony, and other vowel alternations, see Cole (1986a).

of the high vowels /i,u/, in the same word.[4] For example, the long /ē,ō/ in the roots in (6i-iii) raise to /ī,ū/, respectively, when a suffix is added which contains /i/ or /u/:[5]

6) i- /kōnI-/ kūniak *'lumps of snow'* (MG p.96)
(c.f., kōn *'snow'* (MG p.96))

ii- /ātɛqnōhk-/ ātɛqnūhkuwɛw *'he tells him a sacred story'* (MG p.96)
(c.f., ātqnōhkɛw *'he tells a sacred story'* (MG p.96))

iii- /nēmU-/ nīmit *'when he dances'* (MG p.96)
(c.f., nēmow *'he dances'* (MG p.96))

The occurrence of the vowel /ɛ/ between the target and trigger of harmony will block harmony from applying, as seen in (6iv,v):

6) iv- kēwaskɛpīw *'he is drunk'* (MG p.96)
v- kēwɛ́tuaq *'when they go home'* (MG p.96)

In contrast, the vowel /a/ is transparent to harmony. In the form in (6vi), the root /o/ undergoes harmony triggered by the suffixal /i/; the intervening /a/ does not not block harmony, as /ɛ/ does in examples (6iv,v).[6]

6) vi- mōskamU- mūskamit *'if he emerges'* (ML)
(c.f., mōskamow *'he comes up from under water'* (ML))

Ignoring for a moment the behavior of transparent /a/ and opaque /ɛ/, we can say that Height Harmony is the regressive assimilation of a [+high] feature from a syllable head position to a long (branching) syllable head position. This rule can be formally stated as an autosegmental spreading rule, as in (7).

---

[4] The glides /y,w/ in onset and coda positions do not trigger harmony, although they derive from the same underlying segments—/I,U/—as the high vowels /i,u/. These facts can be explained by constraining the triggers to syllabic [+high] segments.

[5] The abbreviations MG and ML are used to indicate references in Bloomfield's *Menomini Language* (1962) and *Menomini Lexicon* (1975), respectively.

[6] In this example, Vowel Harmony is seen to apply after suffixation and subsequent loss of root final /U/. For a discussion of the coalescence rules that precede harmony, see Cole (1986a).

7) Height Harmony

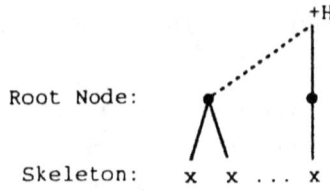

In this analysis, Height Harmony is a feature-filling rule which applies before the complement rule has supplied the feature [−high] to the mid vowels.

We will first address the problem of transparent /a/ in Menomini Height Harmony. Since /a/ is specified as [+low], assimilating [+high] to /a/ would result in the illicit feature combination [+high, +low]. I suggest that there is a filter that prohibits the combination of features [+high, +low], and that this filter acts as a constraint on derivations. In particular, this filter will prohibit Height Harmony from assimilating [+high] onto the vowel /a/.[7] However, while the filter prevents /a/ from undergoing harmony, it does nothing to stop the harmonic [+high] feature from spreading past /a/. The minimal statement of Height Harmony, together with the strategy of interpreting the filter as a constraint on derivations, results in a system where /a/ is transparent.

We turn now to the problem of opaque /ε/. In order to understand why it is that ε can block [+high] assimilation, we must first characterize the underlying vowel inventory of Menomini. Bloomfield recognizes six surface vowels, all with long and short variants, and two diphthongs: /i,e,ε,u,o,a/ and /ia,ua/.[8] The vowel /ε/ is a lax front vowel which is realized alternatively as æ~ ε ~ ɪ. The surface realization of this vowel depends on very idiosyncratic properties of Menomini syllables and words.[9] It appears that the vowel /ε/ can be

---

[7]For the use of filters in constraining derivations, see Kiparsky (1981) and McCarthy (1986).

[8]In this paper I am ignoring the interesting problem posed by the complementary distribution of the vowels u,o. In Cole (1986a), I argue that both vowels derive from underlying U, a [+high, +back] vowel, which is lowered in certain environments to o. Since U-Lowering must precede Height Harmony, the derived segment inventory at the time harmony takes place will include the vowel o. For clarity, we will abstract away from their underlying source, and treat u,o as distinct vowels.

[9]Short ε is realized as [ɪ] in the personal prefixes before hC. In all other words, [ε] is realized as [æ] before h or q, and as [ε] elsewhere. In rapid speech, ε, when not preceding h or q, is realized as [ɪ]. Long ε ranges over [ε],[æ] and even [a],

minimally distinguished from the other vowels solely on the basis of the feature [−tense], and perhaps [−back].[10] I argue that the height variation of the surface allophones of /ɛ/ derives from the fact that /ɛ/ bears no underlying specifications for the height features [high] and [low]. Thus, in underlying representation, /ɛ/ is specified only as [−tense]. But while this analysis offers the simplest explanation of the allophony of /ɛ/, it leaves us with the puzzling question of why a vowel that is specified only as [−tense] blocks the harmonic spread of [+high].

One solution would be to say that /ɛ/ directly blocks harmony by being specified as [−high] when harmony takes place, as in (8).

8)

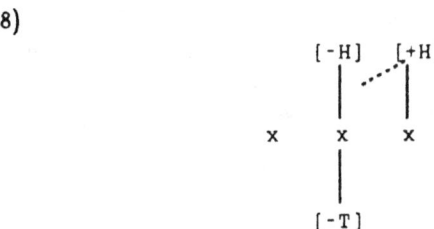

The [−high] feature on /ɛ/ is a redundant feature, and therefore should not be present in underlying representation. This means that in order to maintain that /ɛ/ blocks because of a [−high] specification, there must be a special redundancy rule that assigns [−high] to /ɛ/ before [−high] is assigned to the tense mid and low vowels. Allowing a language-particular redundancy rule of this sort weakens Underspecification theory, and results in a much weaker theory of harmony systems. If Menomini can employ a special redundancy rule to create a blocking segment, then other languages should be able to do the same thing. It should in principle be possible to specify almost any segment as opaque for a given harmony system, by the simple creation of a language-particular redundancy rule. Yet, the fact is that the choice of opaque segments for a given harmony system is not arbitrary. There seems to always be some relation between the opaque segment(s) and the triggers and targets of harmony—a relation which is not captured by allowing the unconstrained use of

---

although Bloomfield does not state the environments for these alternations.

[10] I do not present a complete analysis of the underlying underspecified vowel inventory here. In fact, it is possible to distinguish /ɛ/ solely on the basis of the feature [−tense], even though the low, back vowel /a/ is most likely also [−tense]. The [−tense] feature on /a/ is predictable, given the vowel inventory, on the basis of its [+low] feature.

language-particular redundancy rules.

There are facts about the phonology of Menomini which argue against specifying /ɛ/ as [−high] in underlying representation. We observe that the surface height of /ɛ/ is much more variable than the other vowels: high, mid and low variants of underlying /ɛ/ appear on the surface. Claiming that /ɛ/ is [−high] for harmony requires a more complicated statement of the rules that derive the surface forms of /ɛ/. Such rules would have to be formulated as feature-changing rules, instead of feature-filling or default rules.

The second way in which opaque segments are sometimes explained in autosegmental treatments of vowel harmony is by the introduction of filters which prohibit the harmonic feature from associating to and skipping over opaque segments (Kiparsky 1981). Thus, Menomini could invoke the filter in (9i) to prevent [+high] from linking to [−tense], and the filter in (9ii) would prohibit the harmonic spread of [+high] to skip over the opaque [−tense] segment.

9)

(i) -   +H
         |
    *   x
         |
         -T

(ii) -   +H
         /\
    *   x x x
         |
         -T

Leaving aside the plausability of filters of the sort in (9ii), we observe that there is no motivation for positing the filter (9i) in Menomini; [+high, −tense] segments *must* be derived in the phonology, since they appear in the surface vowel inventory.[11]

The opacity of /ɛ/ in Menomini Height Harmony can be easily

---

[11] As will be discussed in Chapter 4, filters of the type in (9ii) can be reinterpreted as locality conditions on harmony which prevent harmony from skipping any potential target. I am not arguing against filters and locality conditions here, rather I suggest that the filter analysis is not supported in Menomini. It would not be straightforward to subject Menomini Height Harmony to an analysis in terms of locality, as discussed in Section 4.6, since harmony must in any case be able to skip over all short mid vowels. In Section 4.6, I argue that locality can only be calculated at the well-defined prosodic levels of metrical structure, syllable structure and the skeleton. In this theory, there is no prosodic level that projects only branching nuclei, which are the targets of Menomini Height Harmony; therefore, it would not be possible to define a locality condition on harmony that would allow harmony to skip over short vowels. Even if it were possible to formulate such a locality constraint, that analysis would incorrectly predict that short /ɛ/ would also be skipped, and therefore transparent to harmony (cf, ex. (6iv)).

explained by employing the Linked Structure Analysis presented in the discussion of Yokuts, above. My proposal is that Height Harmony is dependent on structures which are already multiply linked to a single [+tense] feature. The Linked Structure Analysis directly relates the opacity of /ɛ/ to its [−tense] specification. The rule of Height Harmony is formulated in (10).[12]

10) Height Harmony

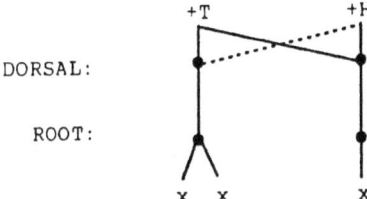

The formulation of Height Harmony in (10) explains the opacity of /ɛ/ in the following way. First, it is necessary to assume that there is a process within Menomini that conflates adjacent, identical [tense] specifications into a single, multiply-linked feature, as in (11):[13]

11) [tense] tier:

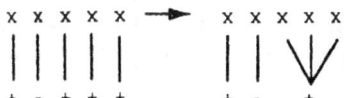

Let us assume that this process applies to all [tense] features before harmony applies. If [+high] assimilation occurs only when both trigger and target are linked to the same [+tense] feature, it follows both that /ɛ/ will not undergo harmony, and that it will block harmony. Blocking will occur because the [−tense] specification of /ɛ/, when it intervenes between the trigger and a potential target, will prohibit the trigger and target from becoming multiply linked to a single [+tense] specification, as illustrated in (12). Multiply linking

---

[12] Although in (10) it appears that the association lines linking [tense] and [high] cross, in true three-dimensional structures both of these features occupy independent planes. Also, I am assuming here that the feature [tense] links to the dorsal node. A different proposal is made in the following chapter (Section 4.3), where I suggest that [tense] is a feature dominated by a Tongue Root articulator.

[13] McCarthy (1986) argues that feature merging is a reflex of Plane Conflation. See discussion in Chapter 5.

the trigger and target to a single [+tense] feature creates a violation of the "no crossing association lines" principle.

12)

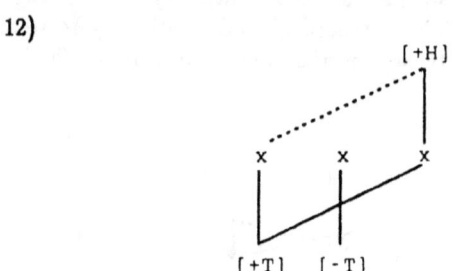

We have seen that the Linked Structure Analysis offers a simple explanation for the puzzling facts of Menomini, without invoking any *ad hoc* special rules or filters into the theory. Moreover, as is argued in Section 2.1, harmony rules which employ the Linked Structure context are well-motivated from general observations about the types of contextual information specified in those rules, as observed in known harmony systems.

2.3 Maasai [ATR] Harmony

The vowels in Maasai can be divided into two partially symmetric classes: a [+ATR] class and a [−ATR] class, as in (13).

13)   +ATR   −ATR
    i   u   I   U
    e   o   E   O
                 A

The vowels in roots and suffixes alternate between [−ATR] and [+ATR] by two rules of ATR Harmony—General Harmony and Diphthong-induced Harmony, described in the next two sections.

2.3.1 General Harmony

General Harmony has the effect of causing all non-low vowels in a word to surface as [+ATR] in the presence of a morpheme that contains an underlyingly [+ATR] vowel. If no vowel in a word has an underlying [+ATR] specification, then all vowels will surface as [−ATR]. We can say that [−ATR] is assigned by a default rule in Maasai. In the examples in (14i), a [+ATR] suffix vowel causes root vowels to surface as [+ATR], while in (14ii), a [+ATR] root vowel causes suffix vowels to surface as [+ATR]. (14iii) illustrates the default application of [−ATR] in words with no [+ATR] vowel.[14]

14) i- I-tOn-ie ⟶ i-ton-ie
2-sit-App.

A-IrobI-ju ⟶ A-irobi-ju
1-cold-Inc.

ii- E-dot-U ⟶ e-dot-u
3-pull-MT

E-nor-IshO ⟶ e-nor-isho
3-hunt-intran.

iii- E-jIn-U
3-enter-MT

A-I-sUf-IshO
1-II-wash-intran.

As illustrated in (14i), and in the forms in (15) below, the low vowel /A/ blocks General Harmony.

15) i- O-lE-m-AA-nin
MS-Rel-Neg-1-hear
(cf, o-le-m-e-nin from O-lE-m-E-nin)

ii- E-nUk-Ar-ie-kI ⟶ E-nUk-Ar-ie-ki
3-bury-MA-APP-Pass

iii- I-gurAn-U ⟶ i-gurAn-U
II-play-MT

Since /A/ is not minimally distinguished from any other underlying vowel by the feature [ATR], it will receive its [−ATR] value by the

---

[14]The sources for these forms are Levergood (1984) and Tucker & Mpaayei (1955).

default rule, in the constrained theory of underspecification sketched earlier. The default rule will assign [−ATR] to all unspecified vowels at the same time. Since we observe that the mid and high vowels undergo General Harmony, and that no vowel other than /A/ blocks General Harmony, we conclude that General Harmony must apply before the default rule assigning the value [−ATR] applies. But this means that /A/ will not be assigned [−ATR] when harmony applies. How then do we account for the blocking effects of /A/?

One explanation of the opacity of /A/ would be to say that /A/ is (redundantly) specified as [−ATR] in the underlying inventory. Under this account, the [−ATR] feature linked to /A/ will prevent [+ATR] from spreading past it, as in the forms in (15). This solution is somewhat ad-hoc, since it does not really explain why it is /A/ that blocks, and not some other vowel. It would be equally plausible to stipulate that /E/ is underlyingly [−ATR], in which case it would be the blocking vowel. Cole & Trigo (1987) present further evidence against this analysis from the rule of Raising. Raising has the effect of changing all occurrences of /A/ in a suffix to /O/ after a [+ATR] root vowel. The derived /O/ can subsequently undergo General Harmony, surfacing as [+ATR] /o/. If /A/ were underlyingly [−ATR], then it would have to lose this specification as a side-effect of Raising. Adding this complication to the Raising rule is unnecessary if we assume that /A/ is underlyingly unspecified for [ATR]. Raising is exemplified in the following example.

16) kI-tA-bol-A-kI-t-A ⟶ ki-tA-bol-o-ki-to
    2-Past-open-Ep-Dat-Pl-Past

Another explanation for the opacity of /A/ would be to say that there is a filter in Maasai,

17)

which prevents the low vowel /A/ from acquiring the feature [+ATR], and further, that General Harmony is a local process which cannot skip over any vowels that do not undergo Harmony. This is the type of explanation that is offered for the blocking segment in the Warlpiri Labial Harmonies in Chapter 4 (see Sections 4.4 and 4.6). The problem with this analysis is that in certain environments /A/ actually does assimilate [+ATR], surfacing as [ə]. Tucker describes a local [+ATR] assimilation process in Maasai that spreads the feature [+ATR] from lexically specified [+ATR] glides onto the immediately preceding and following vowels, irrespective of the height of the preceding vowel. Consider the following examples:

18) i- A-I-rOwA ⟶ A-I-rowə
       Inf-II-hot

   ii- A-I-wAn ⟶ A-i-wən
       Inf-II-evade

   iii- Ol-owAru ⟶ ol-ow əru
        MS-beast

We can see from the form in (18i) that this local assimilation rule follows General Harmony, since the derived root vowel /o/ does not cause the preceding prefix to surface as [+ATR] /i-/. If we were to adopt the filter analysis, we would have to say that the filter in (17) is somehow deactivated before local [ATR] assimilation takes place.

A third alternative to explaining the opacity of /A/ is to say that General Harmony is parasitic on structures linked to the feature [−low]. This accounts for the fact that all high and mid vowels undergo harmony, and that the vowel /A/ is the only blocker. Parasitic General Harmony is formulated in (19). A sample derivation of (15(ii)) is given in (20).

19) Parasitic General Harmony (bidirectional)

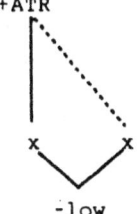

20)

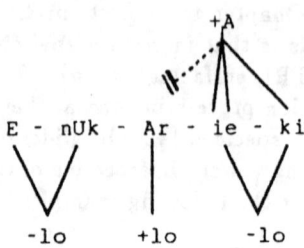

E - nUk - Ar - ie - ki

    -lo   +lo   -lo

While the analysis of General Harmony as parasitic on a linked [−low] configuration does explain the opacity of /A/, it is not the only explanation. An analysis invoking the filter in (17) and a locality condition on harmony is also plausible, if we allow filters to apply only to some levels of derivation. A better argument for parasitic harmony is presented in the following discussion of Diphthong-induced Harmony.

2.3.2 Diphthong-induced Harmony

Another source of [+ATR] vowels in Maasai is the rule of Diphthong-induced Harmony. We saw in the preceding section that certain lexically specified glides in onset position trigger [+ATR] harmony. In contrast, all glides that are the first member of the diphthongs /yA/ and /wA/ trigger [+ATR] harmony on preceeding high vowels, as in (21).

21) i-   I-tU-pUnU-t-U-A ⟶ i-tu-punu-t-w-A
          2-Past-come-Pl-MA-Past

    ii-   kI-tI-bIrI-A ⟶ ki-ti-biry-A
          1P-Past-come-Pl-MA-Past

    iii- ImArIrI-A ⟶ ImAriry-A
          look up to-Past

Mid vowels do not undergo Diphthong-induced Harmony; rather, they block this harmony process, as shown in (22).

22) i-   A-I-nOr-U-A ⟶ A-I-nOr-w-A
         1-II-look-MT-Past

    ii- k-I-nOr-U-tU-A ⟶ k-I-nOr-u-t-w-A
         1p-II-look-Pl-MT-Past

    iii- En-k-ItOrE-A ⟶ In-k-ItOry-A
         FS-II-command-Nom.

    iv- Il-nOjInE-AA ⟶ Il-nOjiny-AA
         MP-hyena-Pl

Dipthong-induced Harmony must follow General Harmony, since otherwise the blocking effects of the mid vowels would never be realized. The reverse ordering would result in the following ill-formed derivation of the word in (22ii).

23)   k-I-nOr-U-t-U-A
        k-I-nOr-u-t-w-A   Diphthong-induced Harmony
     * k-i-nor-u-t-w-A   General Harmony

I propose that the blocking behavior of mid vowels in Diphthong-induced Harmony is explained by stipulating that Diphthong-induced Harmony is parasitic on structures linked to a [+high] contextual feature, as in (24).

24) Parasitic Diphthong-induced Harmony:

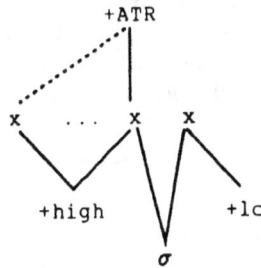

If we allow the mid vowels to undergo the complement rule specifying them as [−high] before harmony applies, then we can account for their blocking behavior. Their presence in between a glide and a high vowel target prevents the glide and the high vowel from being linked to the same [+high] feature, as in (25).

25)

One might suggest that mid vowels block Diphthong-induced Harmony by virtue of being specified [−ATR] at the time harmony applies. If this were the case, then the derivation of (22iv) could proceed as in (26).

26)

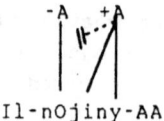

The problem with this analysis is that it requires a special redundancy rule that will specify the mid vowels as [−ATR] before the high vowels. The complement rule for [ATR] will specify [−ATR] on mid and high vowels at the same time (since these are the vowels for which the feature [ATR] is minimally distinctive in underlying representation). Therefore, this analysis would require introducing a special redundancy rule into Maasai, an undesirable result for Underspecification Theory.

Of course, it would be possible to allow Diphthong-induced Harmony to apply after both high and mid vowels are specified as [−ATR]. In this case, harmony would have to be a feature-changing rule that transforms [−ATR] high vowels into [+ATR] high vowels. Under this analysis, we would still need some way of explaining why mid vowels do not undergo harmony, and the linked structure analysis in (24) seems the best explanation.

2.4 Conclusion

Menomini and Maasai illustrate that not all blocking phenomena can be explained by referring to specifications of the harmonic feature alone. In these two cases, the class of blocking segments is characterized by referring to some contextual feature: the blocking segments form the complement of the class of segments that trigger and undergo harmony with respect to the contextual feature. In Menomini Height Harmony, the [+tense] vowels comprise the triggers and undergoers, while the [−tense] vowel blocks. In Maasai ATR Harmony, the [+high] vowels are triggers and undergoers, while the [−high] vowels block. What is important is that the unusual blocking phenomena in both of these languages is explainable by referring only to properties of the representations to which harmony applies. By adopting the multi-dimensional theory of phonological representation, together with the theory of underspecification, we can explain both these cases of blocking and the cases mentioned in Chapter 1 without the introduction of powerful filters or diacritic devices.

Chapter 3

Consonant Symbolism

Some of the most unusual and interesting agreement phenomena in phonology are seen in the consonant symbolism systems of the northwest Native American languages. In many of these languages, diminutive, augmentative, and other semantically related morphological categories cause a shift in a subset of the consonants that appear in a word.[1] For example, in the Salish language Coeur d'Alene, diminutive forms will exhibit uniformly glottalized sonorant consonants, as in (1) (Reichard 1938). The (b) words are the diminutive forms of the (a) words. In non-diminutive forms, sonorant consonants may or may not be glottalized underlyingly.

1) i. a- mar-marím-EntEm-ilc
      'they were treated one by one'
   b- m'-m'ar'-m'ar'ím-En'tem'-il'c
      'they littleones were treated one by one'

   ii a- yār-yār-p   'wagon, they roll'
      b- y'-y'ār'-y'ār'-p   'cart'

In some of these languages, like Coeur d'Alene, the agreement phenomenon is quite straightforward; the class of segments affected

---

[1] In all of the languages exhibiting consonant symbolism, the diminutive forms trigger the consonant shifts. Some of the languages show additional shifts for augmentative and other semantically related morphological categories, such as repeated action. Since the diminutive shift is common to all of the systems, I will refer to the diminutive morphology as the conditioning environment for consonant symbolism throughout this chapter.

form a natural class, easily definable using distinctive features, and the structural change that these segments undergo is also easily definable. However, there are several consonant symbolism systems which are much more idiosyncratic and seem to involve several narrowly defined changes affecting distinct subclasses of consonants. Perhaps the most complicated among these is seen in Wishram, where diminutive forms cause the following consonant alternations:[2]

2) i- $\begin{bmatrix} C \\ +\text{voice} \\ -\text{sonorant} \end{bmatrix} \longrightarrow [-\text{voice}]$ (ex. b $\longrightarrow$ p)

ii- $\underset{[-\text{voice}]}{C} \longrightarrow [+\text{constricted glottis}]$ (ex. p $\longrightarrow$ p')

iii- $\underset{[+\text{low}]}{C} \longrightarrow [-\text{low}]$ (ex. q $\longrightarrow$ k)

iv- $\underset{[-\text{anterior}]}{C} \longrightarrow [+\text{anterior}]$ (ex. č $\longrightarrow$ c)

3) i. a- inigəlč'im "I struck him with it"
   b- i-mi-čq'ičx "you are short and broad"

ii. a- inik'əlc'im "I hit a child with something small"
    b- i-mi-ck'ick "you are short"

The phonological changes observed in diminutive, augmentative and related forms always signal the semantic category, but the semantic category is not always identified by an overt morpheme. Of the 21 languages described in Nichols (1971), 9 regularly show an overt affix whenever the diminutive form is used; 5 show an overt affix in most cases, but the diminutive form can be expressed by the consonant symbolism alone; and 7 show fairly productive consonant symbolism without any overt affix marking the semantic category. It would thus appear that the consonant symbolism is more central to

---

[2]All of the languages examined in this section are discussed in Nichols' (1971) article, "Diminutive Consonant Symbolism in Western North America". In many cases, I have examined the sources listed in her references, at times coming to rather different conclusions about the nature of the system in question. However, unless explicitly noted, all data is taken from that article. I thank John McCarthy for directing my attention to this material.

the morphological form than the presence of a particular affix.

In this chapter, I argue that the diminutive consonant symbolism systems described by Nichols are cases of consonant harmony; the consonant alternations resulting from phonological assimilation processes. Section 3.1 presents three arguments in favor of treating consonant symbolism as a phonological process. Section 3.2 discusses three possible counter arguments to the phonological assimilation analysis. I argue that a non-phonological analysis of this phenomena fails to explain the pattern of alternations observed, and forces the adoption of a rule formalism that is excessively powerful.

3.1 Consonant Symbolism as Assimilation

Nichols (1971) compiled the following list of all the consonant alternations found in the 21 diminutive consonant symbolism systems she reviewed:[3]

4) I. voiced stop ⟶ voiceless stop
stop ⟶ glottalized stop
sonorant ⟶ glottalized sonorant

II. θ ⟶ č
w ⟶ b
s ⟶ c/ś/š
š ⟶ ś/s
č ⟶ c/t
ṣ/ṛ ⟶ s/r
t ⟶ č
λ ⟶ c
x ⟶ š
k/q/q̇ ⟶ k'/k'/k
k' ⟶ k
k ⟶ q

---

[3]Several of the languages reviewed by Nichols do not have productive consonant alternations, but show only a handful of forms which reflect a vestigial consonant symbolism. These languages are not represented in the list in (4).

The 21 languages with productive consonant symbolism included in Nichols survey are Luiseño, Yurok, Wiyot, Karok, Yana, Diegueno, Cocopa, Whishram, Sahaptin, Nez Perce, Kalispel, Coeur d'Alene, Tillamook, Twana, Squamish, Thompson, Quinault, Clallam-Lkungen, Hupa, Nootka, and Dakota.

4) III. l ⟶ r/n
       r ⟶ n/δ
       ɬ ⟶ l
       n ⟶ l

The first set of alternations involve a change in the laryngeal features of a stop consonant. The second set involve a change in the continuancy of a consononant and/or a shift in anteriority or height. The third set involves a shift among coronal sonorants involving either continuance and/or anteriority. The languages reviewed by Nichols show anywhere from one to four of the alternations listed in (4), and there is a great variety in the actual combinations of consonant alternations that occur in individual languages.

It is clear that in the languages that exhibit consonant symbolism, the effects of the dimunitive morphology include a phonological change in the consonants involved in the symbolism. There are many ways in which we might choose to treat these consonants alternations formally. Perhaps the least interesting account is the one which simply lists all of the consonants alternations seen in a given language as a side-effect of the morphology. This list would encode a series of mapping functions of the type $C_{input} \to C_{output}$, where the context for this mapping function is provided by the dimunitive morphology. Let's refer to this as the morphological analysis. We'll examine the details of the morphological analysis in Section 3.2.

Another possible analysis is one which likens the consonant alternations seen in the consonant symbolism systems to harmony processes in other languages. This analysis would maintain that the alternations arise due to a phonological assimilation process (or processes), triggered by the presence of the diminutive morpheme. I'll refer to this as the phonological assimilation anaylsis.

In this section I present three facts about the alternations involved in consonant symbolism which support the phonological assimilation analysis.

First, all the alternations observed in (4) involve a distinctive feature(s) which is seen to participate in phonological assimilations in other languages. Not all distinctive features are equal in this respect. Some features commonly occur in assimilation processes, such as [nasal], [continuant], [anterior], [back], etc. Other features such as [consonantal] [sonorant], and [syllabic] are not known to assimilate in any language. Phonological processes other than assimilation certainly do make reference to, or cause a change in non-assimilatory features. For, instance, any phonological rule which effects the alternation $i \sim y$ or $u \sim w$ causes a change in the feature [syllabic]. The non-participation of certain features in assimilation processes crosslinguistically is not currently explained in the theoretical framework adopted in this thesis; however, I assume that it is not an accidental gap in the typology of assimilation that certain manner features never assimilate. At the very least, we might assume that universal grammar encodes a constraint which prohibits features like [syllabic], [sonorant] and [consonantal] from undergoing spreading. The fact that none of the consonant symbolism systems reviewed by Nichols involve alternations of non-assimilatory features is explained under the phonological assimilation analysis, insofar as universal grammar can be said to constrain the class of assimilating features.

The second point to make about the alternations in (4) is that all of them can in principle be characterized by an assimilation process. This need not be the case. Notice that many of the alternations involve an affricate as either input or output. An alternation which could not be explained as assimilation would be a shift from an affricate to a stop at the same place of articulation. This process would involve the deletion of a [+continuant] feature—a process fundamentally distinct from assimilation.[4] The absence of alternations which could not result from assimilation represents a rather striking gap in the data, but one that is explained if we assume that all of the consonant alternations must be achieved by an assimilation process. If the alternations were not in principle limited to assimilation, then it would be a surprising coincidence if none involved the deletion of features, given the wide range of alternations recorded.[5]

Another interesting observation about the data shown in (4) is that there is no single language in which the continuants /s,š/ undergo some shift, but not the affricates /c,č/.[6] In Wishram, both the plain

---

[4]Other alternations may involve the deletion of an underlying feature, but if the deletion is part of a feature changing rule ([+continuant] ⟶ [−continuant]), then it is really a replacement—a process which can be represented as assimilation.

[5]The careful reader will have noticed that there is one alternation in (4) in which an affricate becomes a stop. This is the alternation č ⟶ t, found in Cocopa. However, it is clear that the loss of the [+continuant] feature is secondary to the shift in anteriority. Cocopa does not have the alveolar affricate /c/, and thus when the palatal affricate gets fronted, it must undergo some change in order to conform to the phonemic inventory of the language. Cocopa chooses a simplification from affricate to stop. Such secondary shifts are not uncommon in the consonant symbolism systems examined here. In general, it seems that the output of consonant shift must always be an existing phoneme in the language (with the sole exception being Nootka (Nichols p.845)).

[6]Wiyot is an apparent counterexample to this claim, since the plain continuants /s,š/ show a different pattern of alternation than the affricates and plain stops.

continuant /š/ and the affricates /č,č'/ undergo a shift to [+anterior] /c,c',s/. In Hupa, the [−anterior] affricates /dž,č/ become [+anterior] /dz,c/ (but note the absence of [−anterior] stops in this language). In Nootka, the continuants and affricates /c,s,č,š/ all become the palatal continuant /š/. In Cocopa, the [−anterior] affricate /č/ becomes [+anterior] /t/ (see ft. 5), but the [−anterior] continuant /š/ is not affected.

These facts are also explained if we assume that the alternations in question arise due to assimilation. An assimilation rule that picks out /s,š/ as the targets must mention the feature [+continuant] (in a language that also has non-continuant /t/—which all the languages in question have.) However, having targeted [+continuant] segments, the rule would also apply to the affricates, since they too bear the feature [+continuant].[7] The formalism of the multi-dimensional theory adopted here does not provide a mechanism for referring to the absence of a feature in the statement of a phonological rule. Therefore, it would not be possible for a rule to apply only to plain continuants, and not to affricates, on the basis that the plain continuants lack a [−continuant] feature. If we were to assume the morphological anlaysis, in which the consonant alternations are merely listed as a side-effect of a morphological process, then there would be nothing to rule out a system in which only the plain continuants, and not the affricates, are involved in the consonant symbolism.

I should call attention here to a language which, according to Nichols' description, appears to encode an alternation that could not be the product of assimilation. Nichols, following Jacobs (1931), reports that the diminutive consonant alternations in Sahaptin are as follows:

5) x̣/q/q'/qw ⟶ x/k/k'/kw
    č   ⟶ c
    n   ⟶ l
    s   ⟶ š
    š   ⟶ s

No single assimilation rule could account for [−anterior] /š,č/ becoming [+anterior] /s,c/ and [+anterior] /s/ becoming [−anterior] /š/. This looks like the product of a function that maps [αanterior] onto

---

These facts are analyzed in detail in the next chapter, Section 4.3.

[7]I am assuming the autosegmental analysis of an affricate as a contour segment—a single timing unit linked to both a [+continuant] and a [−continuant] feature.

[−αanterior] for the continuants. However, the recorded alternations are somewhat suspicious, since the [+anterior] affricate does not undergo any change at all. In fact, upon reviewing the data in Jacobs (*op.cit.*), I have found that there are no examples with both /s/ and /š/ in the same word in which we might see the simultaneous application of the [anterior] shift. Second, there are many suffixes in which the consonants /s/ and /š/ alternate in an environment that does not include diminutive morphology, and several suffixes in which /s/ and /c/ alternate, again without a diminutive reading. These data suggest that there may be more going on in the consonant alternations in (5) than can be attributed solely to the diminutive consonant symbolism system. Unfortunately, the grammar is not explicit on any of these points, and the forms needed to unravel the interaction of the rules involved are simply not attested. We can therefore not yet accept Sahaptin as a real counterexample to the proposal that all alternations in the diminutive consonant symolism systems arise due to phonological assimilation processes.

There is a third argument that can be made in support of the phonological assimilation analysis of consonant symbolism. Whenever an overt suffix containing specified segments is present, in all cases but one it bears the feature that is involved in the consonant alternations. Consider the following facts:

1. In Wiyot, there are two diminutive suffixes, /-ac/ and /-ač/ and one augmentative suffix, /-ačk/, which condition consonant alternations. All three suffixes cause [−continuant] coronals /t,d,l/ to become [+continuant] /c,č,dz,dž,r/. The two suffixes containing [−anterior] affricates condition the [−anterior] alternations, while the suffix containing the [+anterior] affricate conditions the [+anterior] alternations.

2. In Karok, the suffixes are /-ič/, /-ač/, /-iš/, all of which cause the [+anterior] coronal continuants /θ,r/ to become [−anterior] /č,n/.

3. In Cocopa, the [−continuant] prefix /n-/ causes a [+continuant] /č/ to surface as [−continuant] /t/.

4. In Luiseño, the suffix /-mal/, which contains the [+anterior] segment /l/, causes [−anterior] /ṣ, r/ to surface as [+anterior] /s, δ/; whereas the suffix /-may/ causes /l/ to surface as palatal /ḻ/.

All the other systems mentioned by Nichols that involve overt affixes use reduplicating affixes which bear no inherent segmental features.[8] The only system that regularly involves an overt affix not containing a segment which somehow relates to the phonological change in consonants is Yana, in which the two suffixes /-p'a/ and /-c'eegi/ trigger a shift from /l/ to /n/.

This near perfect correspondence between the segmental nature of the affix and the phonological change it conditions very strongly suggests an assimilation analysis. If the consonant alternations were not dependent on the feature content of the diminutive affix, then we should expect to see more systems in which, for example, a suffix containing a [−anterior] segment triggers a shift to [+anterior] in stem consonants.

To summarize, I have presented three arguments for treating consonant symbolism as a phonological assimilation processes. First, only features which are seen to be involved in assimilatory processes crosslinguistically are involved in the consonant alternations. Second, no alternations are observed which *cannot* be explained as resulting from assimilation. Third, when an overt affix is present to indicate the diminutive morphology, in almost all cases it bears the feature(s) involved in the consonant alternations. We turn now to consider some arguments which might be posed against the assimilation analysis.

3.2 The Morphological Analysis

There are several reasons why the consonant alternations involved in diminutive symbolism, listed in (4), do not seem quite like ordinary phonological assimilations. First, as already noted, in many languages, the consonant alternations occur regardless of the presence of an overt phonological trigger. Second, the actual phonological change cannot be attributed to a single assimilation process in languages like Wishram (discussed on above), where it is clear that several processes comprise the diminutive consonant symbolism system. Thirdly, and perhaps most significant, is the exceptionless nature of the alternations in all of the languages examined. In this respect, the diminutive consonant symbolism systems differ from harmony systems in other languages. Harmonic alternations that arise due to assimilation are frequently blocked from applying in certain phono-

---

[8]I am following the analysis of reduplication proposed in Marantz (1982) and Levin (1983).

logical environments.[9]. In all the diminutive symbolism cases, the consonant alternation permeates the entire word, regardless of the identity of segments intervening between the consonants undergoing the change. I will discuss the first two issues here. The third issue, dealing with the exceptionless nature of the consonant alternations, is treated in Chapter 4.

3.2.1 Floating features as assimilation triggers

The fact that there is not always an overt trigger for the consonant alternation is not in itself reason to disregard the possibility that such processes are indeed phonological assimilations. There are many well-documented cases of phonological rules being triggered by elements not explicitly represented in the segments actually present in a word. The autosegmental model was in fact heralded for providing a formalism which could naturally represent such phenomena. In the autosegmental formalism, the objects representing distinctive features are independent of the skeletal slots that distinguish the actual number of segments in a word; therefore, it is entirely possible to have a distinctive feature active in the derivation of a word even if that feature is not associated to any segment. Such unassociated features are termed *floating* features, and are repesented as in (6), where the floating feature is circled.

6)

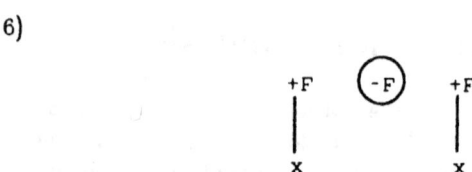

Floating features have been invoked in many different ways in phonological analyses. For example, Pulleyblank (1986) uses floating tones to condition downstep in his analysis of Tiv. Levergood (1984) and Clements (1981) use floating features to account for cases in Maasai and Akan, respectively, where [+ATR] harmony is triggered by a root whose only vowel is [−ATR] /A/. Many other examples can be adduced.

If consonant symbolism is viewed as a phonological assimilation process, then in all instances where there is no overt trigger, we are

---

[9]Recall the discussion of blocking phenomena in Turkish vowel harmony in Section 1.5

forced to say that a floating feature is present in the derivation and serves to trigger harmony. In languages where there is an optional affix denoting the semantic category *diminutive*, the assimilation analysis would posit two allomorphs of this affix. One would contain the segments that actually surface when the affix surfaces, and the other would minimally contain only the floating feature required to trigger harmony.

3.2.2 The complexity argument

The second problem noted above for the phonological assimilation analysis relates to the complexity of the phonological alternations comprising the consonant symbolism system in languages like Wishram (see (3) above). The objection is that no single assimilation process could account for the range of alternations in the more complex cases. This is not really an argument against the assimilation analysis, since there is nothing preventing more than one assimilation being triggered by a single morpheme. Examples can be found in regular harmony systems where more than one feature spreads harmonically. Consider the Uralo-Altaic languages, many of which display both Back and Round Harmony (Steriade 1981). In fact, in many of these languages, the Back and Round Harmonies show different conditions on spreading, and must necessarily be analyzed as involving two distinct phonological rules.

We cannot avoid the fact that the phonological assimilation analysis would be complex for languages in which the consonant alternations do not fall neatly into one class, like Wishram. Recall that in Wishram there are four consonant shifts, involving the features [voice], [constricted glottis], [low], and [anterior]. The phonological analysis would have to posit four distinct floating features associated with the diminutive morpheme (which adds no new segments to the word), and four distinct association rules to link each floating feature to the appropriate subset of consonants affected by the morphology.

Let's consider for a moment what formal mechanism other than a phonolgical assimilation process could cause the consonant alternations in (4). As mentioned in the previous section, the assimilation analysis can be contrasted with the morphological analysis, in which the consonant alternations are simply seen as a side-effect of the morphological process, and do not derive from any particular phonological property of the diminutive morpheme. Adopting the morphological analysis, the consonant alternations will be listed as a series of mapping functions, as in (7):

7) $C_{input} \longrightarrow C_{output} / [\ldots \underline{\quad} \ldots]_{diminutive}$

For Wishram, there will be four separate rules of the type in (7), corresponding to the four distinct components of the system. Note that this way of analyzing the consonant alternations does not in any way reduce the complexity of the system. Therefore, the morphological and phonological analyses of consonant symbolism will be equally complex for languages like Wishram.

3.2.3 Restricting the power of phonological rules

We can conclude that neither the lack of overt triggers, nor the complexity inherent in some of the consonant symbolism systems is reason alone to reject the phonological analysis. On the other hand, I argue that there are principled reasons to reject the morphological analysis. First, it is clear that the morphological analysis cannot explain why the consonant alternations listed in (4) are constrained in exactly the way that phonological assimilation processes would be constrained, as discussed in Section 3.1. Were we to assume that the alternations in (4) resulted from many individual mapping rules of the sort in (7), then it would simply be an accident that there are no rules involving non-assimilatory features, or rules that could not be treated as assimilations, such as rules that just delete structure.

There is a second, more serious problem with the morphological analysis that has to do with the rule format in (7) which is required to state the context for the consonant alternations. This kind of phonological rule is very powerful, because it allows a phonological alternation to be dependent on the presence of a morphological boundary which can be arbitrarily far from the segment undergoing the phonological change. It could in principle encode any kind of structural change affecting any subset of segments.

Let's look carefully at what the rule in (7) expresses. This rule says that any consonant belonging to a certain phonological class undergoes a structural change whenever it is contained in a word of a certain morphological category. This type of rule differs significantly from other known phonological rules which are morphologically governed in that the morphological context for the rule may be arbitrarily far from the target. Consider the English rule of Shortening, described in Chomsky & Halle (1968). Shortening accounts for the alternation in the final stem vowel in the pairs *satire* ~ *satiric* and *volcano* ~ *volcanic*. Shortening applies to a stem final long vowel only before a few suffixes like /-ic/, /-id/. The English Shortening rule is more typical of morphologically governed rules, in that the segment undergoing the rule is generally either adjacent to the conditioning morpheme, or in a syllable that is adjacent to it. Lieber (1981, pp. 202-3) recognizes this special property of morphologically governed phonological processes and suggests that such processes are always governed by a locality constraint.[10]

If we were to license phonological rules like (7), allowing the context for a phonological rule to be arbitrarily far from the target of the rule, then we would open the door to all sorts of phonological processes which are simply not attested. For example, using a rule format as in (7), we could formulate a hypothetical rule of epenthesis which had the effect of globally inserting a vowel in consonant clusters only in plural noun forms, as in (8):

8) $\emptyset \longrightarrow V \ / \ [\ldots C \_\_ C \ldots]_{noun,plural}$

Another funny rule which could be formulated in this way is a harmony rule which operates only in a subclass of the lexicon. Consider the rule of Sibilant Harmony in Navajo, informally stated in (9). This is a feature-changing harmony rule which causes all sibilants in a word to surface as /s/ if the rightmost sibilant is /s/, and as /š/ if the rightmost sibilant is /š/.

9) i- $s \longrightarrow š \ / \ \_\_ + \ldots š$

  ii- $š \longrightarrow s \ / \ \_\_ + \ldots s$

By adopting a morphological environment like the one in (7), we could easily formulate a rule of pseudo-Sibilant Harmony in which the harmony takes place only in verb forms, or only in adjectives. However, there is no harmony system known to me which is restricted to applying only in a particular morphological category.[11]

Insofar as rules of this type are unattested, there must be some principled grounds for their exclusion. One such explanation is available if we adopt a locality constraint on the accessibility of morpho-

---

[10] Lieber does not actually formalize any such constraint, nor is she able to motivate a locality constraint. She adds to her theory the stipulation that string dependent morphological rules always be local. I discuss how such a constraint might be motivated by constraints on morpho-phonological processing in Chapter 5.

[11] I am excluding here cases where the trigger is limited to a certain morpheme or class of morphemes. For discussion of such cases, see Chapter 4.

logical structure in phonological rules. Informally stated, this constraint will allow morphological structure to condition a rule only if the trigger or target of the rule is adjacent to the relevant morpheme boundary.[12] Note that we must define adjacency in such a way that a vowel in an initial or final syllable will still be considered adjacent to the word boundary even if the peripheral segment on the skeleton is a tautomorphemic consonant. I propose that adjacency always be calculated at some level of prosodic structure—the prosodic levels being the skeleton, syllable structure, and perhaps metrical structure.[13]

If we assume an adjacency condition on the accessibility of morphological structure, then we can no longer entertain the morphological analysis of consonant symbolism discussed above. This analysis requires rules like (7) to provide the morphological environment for the consonant alternations, yet (7) violates the adjacency condition proposed here.[14] The adjacency condition does not prevent us from adopting the phonological assimilation analysis of these consonant alternations. Since the assimilating feature is in all cases contained within the initial syllable of the diminutive affix, a special assimilation rule can be formulated that spreads that feature onto a designated class of consonants, as in (10).

---

[12]This constraint will be reformulated in Chapter 5. In particular, the constraint on adjacency will be reinterpreted as a constraint requiring that the contextual morpheme c-command the constituent which contains the target of the rule in the hierarchical morphological structure.

[13]Steriade (1987a) makes a similar proposal, namely that all phonological processes are local—where locality is prosodically defined.

[14]Note that the rule in (7) does not violate another well-motivated constraint on the accessibility of morphological information that is internal to stems. Williams (1981) formulates the Atom Condition in (i) to limit morphological affixation such that it can only be sensitive to properties apparent on the external brackets of the stem. Morphological information can percolate to the external brackets from the head of the structure.

(i) *The Atom Condition* (Williams 1981:253)
    A restriction on the attachment of an affix to Y can only refer to features realized on Y.

If we assume that the diminutive labeling can percolate to the outermost brackets, then the morphological information encoded in (7) will be accessible under the Atom Condition. Inasmuch as we need to exclude (7) as a possible phonological rule, we need a stronger constraint than the Atom Condition on the accessibility of morphological structure.

10)

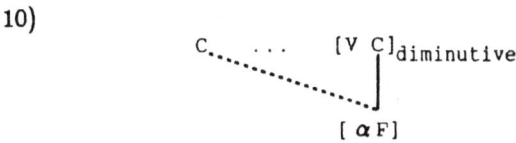

I postpone formulating the locality condition until Chapter 5, where additional data is discussed which bears on this issue. The adjacency condition on the accessibility of morphological information may well follow from a more general adjacency condition on phonological rules. We saw in Section 1.5 that a harmony rule is always blocked when the target and the trigger of harmony are not adjacent on the plane of the harmonic feature. Whenever a segment specified for the harmonic feature intervenes between the trigger and target of harmony, harmonic spreading would result in an ill-formed structure with crossing association lines. Blocking phenomena is illustrated in Turkish, where a palatalized consonant blocks the harmonic spread of [+back], as in the example from Section 1.5, repeated below. In (11) the vowel /a/ and the suffixal vowel /i/ are not adjacent on the back plane.

11) (=1.22)

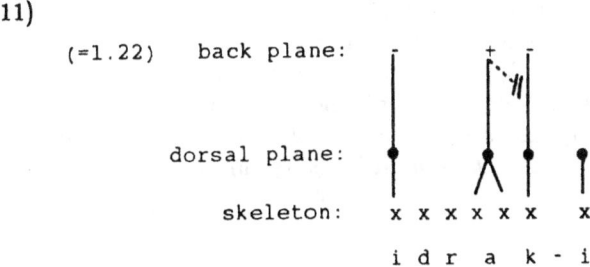

It is not immediately clear how the adjacency constraint I am proposing relates to the constraint which is responsible for blocking phenomena in harmony, as illustrated in (11). As mentioned in Chapter 1 footnote 4, Sagey (1988) demonstrates that the adjacency condition realized by the "No crossing lines constraint" is not primitive, but rather derives from the primitive notions of precedence and association (*overlap* in Sagey's terminology). However, the adjacency condition on morphologically governed rules is not similarly reduceable, since there are no overlap and precedence relations being created as there are in the assimilation process. An adjacency condition limiting the assimilation in (11) would be a constraint on a *process*, while the adjacency condition I am proposing to eliminate rules like (7) from the theory is a condition on *visibility* that does not involve creating a structural relationship between the two elements subject to adjacency. It remains an open question at this time whether the two notions of adjacency can be derived from one general cognitive constraint. For the purposes of the analysis here, I will assume that grammatical theory explicitly encodes a constraint limiting the accessibility of morphological information in phonological rules by requiring adjacency between the contextual morpheme boundary and the trigger or target of the rule.

To summarize the findings of this chapter, I have argued that the patterns observed in the consonant alternations that comprise consonant symbolism are explained if we assume that consonant symbolism is a phonological assimilation process. Moreover, I have argued against a non-assimilation analysis of this data on the grounds that it necessitates a type of phonological rule which is excessively powerful. The rule required to account for the consonant alternations in the non-assimilation analysis must allow a morpheme boundary to condition a phonological change in a segment arbitrarily far from the morpheme boundary. This rule violates a locality condition on the accessibility of morphological structure in phonological rules that I argue is necessary to rule out unattested rule types.

In Chapter 4, we return to examine the consonant symbolism of Coeur d'Alene and Wiyot in greater detail. As mentioned above, in treating these systems as phonological assimilation processes, we must explain why they differ from most other long-distance assimilation processes in failing to exhibit blocking phenomena in predicted environments.

Chapter 4

Morphologically Governed Harmony

In Chapter 3, I presented several arguments for analyzing consonant symbolism as phonological assimilation. These assimilations belong to the class of morphologically governed assimilation processes. In this chapter, we will see that morphologically governed assimilation differs from non-morphologically governed assimilation in the type of blocking phenomena that occurs. The special properties of morphologically governed assimilation are seen to follow from the form of the phonological representation such processes operate on. The analysis employed here makes essential use of a proposal made by McCarthy (1981, 1983a, 1983b, 1986, 1988) that morphemes occupy their own phonological planes, and morphological affixation results in the introduction of a new plane in the phonological representation of a word. The details of McCarthy's *Morpheme Plane Hypothesis* are reviewed in Section 4.1. Following this, four cases of morphologically governed harmony processes are analyzed.

4.1 The Morpheme Plane Hypothesis

4.1.1 Semitic morphology

In his work on the morphology and phonology of Semitic languages, McCarthy observes that the traditional notion of a morpheme and its formal representation does not extend to Semitic. In the traditional analysis, stemming largely form work on Indo-European languages, morphemes are viewed as strings of phonemes which are either free (in the case of free-standing roots) or bound (in the case of affixes), and which combine with one another by means of string concatenation in the formation of words. However, in Semitic the picture is much more complicated.

Semitic verb and noun paradigms exhibit a complex set of alternations which affect the internal structure of a stem. Semantically related words differ in their syllable structure and in the quality and quantity of vowels. Consider the verb paradigm in (1), from McCarthy (1981:116).

1)
   a. kataba   "he wrote"
   b. kattaba   "he caused to write"
   c. kaataba   "he corresponded"
   d. takaatabuu   "they kept up a correspondence"
   e. ?iktataba   "he wrote, copied"
   f. kitaabun   "book (nom.)"
   g. kuttaabun   "Koran school (nom.)"
   h. kitaabatun   "act of writing (nom.)"
   i. maktabun   "office (nom.)"

McCarthy notes that "there is a clear sense in which the forms in (1) are morphologically related to one another although they do not share isolable strings of segments in concatenated morphemes" (1981:116). What these forms have in common is the discontinuous sequence of consonants /ktb/. This sequence of consonants is associated with the semantic field "write".

In languages with concatenative morphology, the morphological analysis of a word is given by isolating distinct morphemes inside brackets or by representing morpheme boundaries with symbols like "−" or "+", as in (2).

2)   un + happy + ness
          [[un [happy]] ness]

The root morpheme in paradigms like (1) consists of a series of discontinuous consonants. By the traditional representation, morpheme boundaries would be placed between every consonant and vowel in Semitic forms like (1a), as in (3). The expression of the consonants /ktb/ as a morphemic unit is still unachieved.

3)   k+a+t+t+a+b+a

Following Harris' (1941) treatment of the morphology of Biblical Hebrew, McCarthy recognizes a distinction between two types of morphemes. *Roots* consist of an ordered set of consonants or vowels, as in the analysis of the root /ktb/, above. *Patterns* provide the syllabic information that specifies how the consonants and vowels of the root morphemes are realized. Both types of morphemes contribute specific semantic information to the word.

McCarthy provides a novel interpretation of the root and pattern distinction, employing the formalism of Autosegmental Phonology. Since purely segmental material is in many cases separable from syllabic material, McCarthy proposes that the root morphemes consist solely of segments which are not associated to any skeletal slots. In the formalism of the multi-dimensional model assumed here, roots are composed of segments, which represent only the *quality*—not the *quantity*—of the segments that characterize them. Patterns consist of skeletal configurations to which the root segments associate. For example, in the word *kattab* "to write", the verb root is characterized by the consonants /ktb/, the vowel /a/ indicates the perfective active tense, and the skeletal pattern CVCCVC indicates the causative aspect of the word.

The segments from two or more root-type morphemes are interspersed in the surface representation of a word, therefore, it is not possible to provide an isolated representation of each root-type morpheme if we assume an autosegmental representation as in (4).[1]

```
4)   C   V   C   C   V   C
     |   |   |   |   |   |
     k   a   t   t   a   b
```

To solve this problem, McCarthy proposes that each root-type morpheme occupies an independent plane in the phonological representation of a word, as in (5). Towards the end of the derivation, these separate planes are conflated, to provide the uni-planar representation in (4).

---

[1] I am following McCarthy's form in representing skeletal slots with C's and V's. McCarthy's analysis antedates Levin's (1983) article, in which she argues that skeletal slots are not prespecified for syllabicity. In all cases being considered here, the CV notation can be directly translated into the bare "x" slot notation.

5)

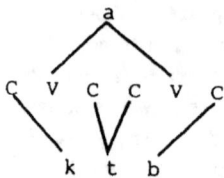

4.1.2 Morpheme planes and anti-gemination

McCarthy (1986) proposes to extend the morpheme plane analysis to cover cases of concatenative morphology as well as the non-concatenative Semitic type of morphology. His arguments have to do with the application of syncope in several languages. Basically, McCarthy notes that in some languages, like the Ethiopian language Afar, a distinction is made between tauto-morphemic and hetero-morphemic geminates, and he attributes this distinction to the planar representations involved.

As described by McCarthy, following Bliese (1981), Afar exhibits a syncope process in which an unstressed peninitial vowel in a two-sided open syllable is deleted, as in (6):

6) darágu   darg-í   *"watered milk"*
   digib-t-é digb-é   *"she/I married"*

Syncope does not apply if consonants on both side of the peninitial vowel are identical, and belong to the same morpheme, as in (7i). However, if the peninitial vowel is flanked by identical consonants that belong to separate morphemes, then syncope is permitted, resulting in a geminate consonant, as in (7ii).

7) i-   sababá   *"reason"*
        xarar-é   *"he burned"*

   ii- as-is-é-y-yo → asséyyo *"I will cause to spend the day"*
        xas-is-é-y-yo → xasséyyo *"I will cause him to motion"*

McCarthy explains the difference between (7i) and (7ii) by appealing to the notion that morphemes occupy distinct planes of phonological representation. He argues that there is a universal constraint, the Obligatory Contour Principle, that prohibits two adjacent identical segments from occurring on the same morpheme plane. The application of syncope in (7i) would yield the structure in (8i) which violates this constraint; therefore, syncope is blocked from applying. In the forms in (7ii) the identical consonants on either side of the peninitial vowel reside on separate morpheme planes. Syncope, applying after the suffix /-is/ is attached, yields the structure in (8ii), which does not violate the constraint.

8)

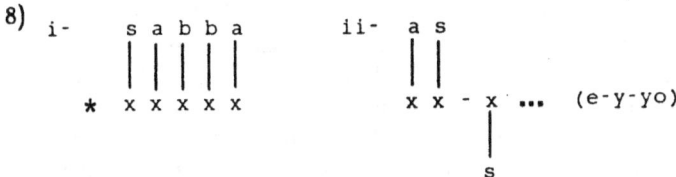

As mentioned above, the multi-planar representations derived by affixation are linearized later in the derivation by a process of *Plane Conflation*.[2] In order for McCarthy's analysis of Afar syncope to succeed, it is crucial that syncope apply before Plane Conflation. McCarthy contrasts the pattern of syncope in Afar with syncope in other languages like Yup'ik Eskimo, where syncope is blocked whenever the vowel in the deletion site is flanked by identical consonants, regardless of whether the consonants are heteromorphemic or tautomorphemic.[3] McCarthy claims that Yup'ik differs minimally from Afar in ordering syncope after Plane Conflation. He argues that special morphological conditions on syncope in Afar support ordering this rule early, in the lexical phonology. In contrast, Yup'ik syncope is a very general rule, "demonstrably very close to the last rule in the phonological derivation [...] in all respects indifferent to morphological information"(McCarthy 1986:244). McCarthy suggests that these are the characteristic properties of rules applying after Plane Conflation.[4]

---

[2] More often referred to as *Tier Conflation*, with the same meaning. *Plane* seems the more appropriate term, given the actual geometry of these representations. Recall that each morpheme plane is in reality a three-dimensional space which is occupied by the family of intersecting planes that comprise the distinctive feature trees for each segment contained on the plane (see the diagrams in Chapter 1, (1.14) and (1.15).

[3] McCarthy cites the following sources for Yup'ik: Reed et al.(1977), Woodbury (1982), and Myaoka (1971).

[4] Halle & Vergnaud (1987), in their analysis of stress and cyclicity, propose that only cyclic morphemes (those that trigger cyclic phonological rules) are represented on distinct morpheme planes. Non-cyclic morphemes are represented on the existing plane of the stem to which they are attached. It follows that all roots must be cyclic/planar. With this distinction, one could argue that affixes in Yupik are uniformly non-cyclic and hence non-planar. None of the languages examined

In his (1989) article, McCarthy makes an important revision to the Morpheme Plane Hypothesis of his earlier work. He considers two versions of the Morpheme Plane Hypothesis: the Strong MPH, in which morphemes are equated with planes; and the Weak MPH in which a morpheme always implies a plane, but which allows the possibility of planes which do not correspond to distinct morphemes. He argues that the Strong MPH is falsified by languages like Yawelmani (Archangeli 1983,1984), which warrants V/C segregation as in Semitic, although there is no sense in which the vowels and consonants form distinct morphemes. McCarthy also argues that the Weak MPH has no status as an independent principle of linguistic theory. He states that "the effects of the WMPH follow from the observation that planar segregation means nothing more than the lack of inherent linear order relations and from elementary considerations of linear order among separate morphemes in nonconcatenative morphological systems." (p. 87) In other words, McCarthy is stating that two segments or morphemes will reside on separate planes if and only if they are not linearly ordered with respect to one another. Thus, multi-planar representations will always reflect either templatic morphology (Semitic, Yawelmani), or the presence of a morphemic floating feature.

McCarthy refers to the analysis of Coeur d'Alene presented in section 4.2, to illustrate an example in which a new morpheme plane is invoked by the presence of a floating glottal feature that marks the Diminutive morphology. His interpretation of the MPH works for Coeur d'Alene, as we will see below, since the glottal feature that must reside on a separate plane is not underlying linked to any segment. Properly speaking, the floating feature does not precede or follow any segment on the stem. However, in addition to Coeur d'Alene, multi-planar representations are invoked in the following sections to account for the properties of morphologically governed harmony in several other languages, and it is not the case that the harmony feature is floating in all of these examples. Thus, I am using multi-planar representations in a few cases when they are explicitly not allowed under McCarthy's (1989) analysis. I do not attempt to reconcile my use of the MPH in this chapter with McCarthy's subsequent reinterpretation of the MPH, choosing instead to leave this topic for future research.[5]

---

here provide independent evidence for correlating morpheme planes with cyclicity, nor for identifying non-cyclic (non-planar) morphemes, although there is likewise no counterevidence to this proposal.

[5]I may note here that McCarthy's reinterpretation of what licenses a multi-

Morpheme Planes and Assimilation

The Morpheme Plane Hypothesis makes very strong predictions about the possible applications of assimilation rules. If phonological rules can be ordered before Plane Conflation, then we should expect to find some language in which an assimilation rule operates on the pre-conflation, multi-planar representation. How would such an assimilation rule differ from a post-conflation assimilation? Recall from Section 1.5 that a harmony process is always blocked whenever it encounters a segment that does not undergo harmony, but which bears a specification for the harmonic feature. This was the explanation given for the blocking behavior of palatal consonants in Turkish Back Harmony. In order for this account of blocking to work, it is essential that the segment blocking harmony and the segment triggering harmony are both specified on the same phonological plane, as in the representation given in example (1.22), repeated here:

9)

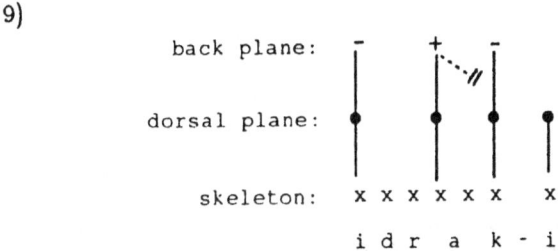

Now consider what happens in a language where harmony is ordered before Plane Conflation. A segment specified for the harmonic feature that intervenes between trigger and target will block only if it is tauto-morphemic with the trigger. In this case, the intervening segment will be represented on the same morpheme plane as the harmony trigger, as in (10).

---

planar representation is not without difficulty. For instance, to accomodate the Coeur d'Alene example, he allows a floating feature to define a new plane if it is not linearly ordered with respect to the rest of the representation. Yet, as I argue in Chapter 6 with respect to the tonal phonology of Tiv, it is necessary to derive an ordering between floating features on affixes and stem segments at the time Plane Conflation occurs. So it is not entirely correct that floating features on an affix are not ordered with respect to stem segments.

10)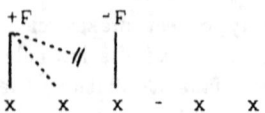

If, however, the intervening segment belongs to a different morpheme than the trigger, it will be represented on a different morpheme plane, as in (11a). An interesting question to consider is what happens if [+F] tries to spread rightward onto the adjacent morpheme before the two planes are conflated? If spreading in a bi-planar representation as in (11) is possible, then it predicts that the segment specified as [−F] will not block spreading. Spreading across morpheme planes is illustrated in (11b).

11)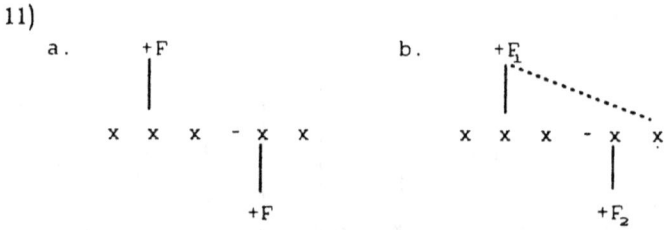

Note that in (11b) the feature [+F] spreads from the trigger on one morpheme plane to a target which is specified on another morpheme plane. It is important to realize that the plane containing the trigger is not bounded by the segments of that morpheme. When an affix is added to a stem, a new morpheme plane is introduced, and this new plane extends over the entire word. In a sense, the addition of a new plane just increases the planar dimensionality of the word by one. Thus, there are no boundaries or edges on a plane other than the boundaries determined by the entire word or phrase.

A potential problem for cross-plane spreading, as in (11b), is that the spreading feature has no root node to dock onto on the spreading plane. By hypothesis, the segment to which [+F] is spreading has a root node specified on a separate plane. I propose that spreading can occur in such configurations, but that an appropriate node structure is created as the docking site for the spreading feature. This proposal entails that a segment that acquires a feature under cross-plane spreading as in (11b) may actually bear two (partial) feature trees on two distinct planes. The operation of Plane Conflation must then be viewed as an operation which merges the two partial trees.

In the remaining sections of this chapter, we will observe four instances of the type of assimilation illustrated in (11). I argue that this type of assimilation is characteristic of morphologically governed harmony processes, a fact which follows from the analysis of the representation of morpheme planes that I adopt.

4.2 Harmony in Coeur d'Alene

Coeur d'Alene exhibits two harmony systems which have very different blocking effects. The Glottal Harmony system is described by Reichard (1938). It characterizes the diminutive consonant symbolism, as briefly mentioned in Chapter 3. Glottal Harmony glottalizes sonorant consonants, and is not blocked by segments that are underlyingly glottalized. The second harmony system is Faucal Harmony, discussed by Reichard (1938) in her grammar of Coeur d'Alene, and later in an insightful article by Sloat (1972). Two Faucal Harmony rules cause vowels to lower, lax and/or back in the context of lax vowels and "faucal" consonants.[6] The faucal consonants block the harmony that is triggered by lax vowels. I argue below that the harmonic feature underlying these shifts is [tongue root]. We will see that an analysis of harmony that incorporates the Morpheme Plane Hypothesis accounts in a principled manner for the different blocking behavior of segments in the two harmony systems.

4.2.1 Glottal Harmony

In Coeur d'Alene, all words with diminutive or repeated action meaning show a glottalization of sonorant consonants. The segment inventory reveals an underlying contrast between glottalized and non-glottalized obstruents and sonorants, as shown in (12):[7]

---

[6]The faucal consonants are the uvular and pharyngeal consonants and /r/. The inclusion of /r/ in this class is somewhat puzzling; Ewa Czaykowska-Higgins (p.c.) informs me that Columbian, a related language, shows a faucal (retracted) contrast for /l,s,c/, although not for /r/. This might be interpreted as a secondary pharyngeal articulation.

[7]"Cw" represents a labialized consonant, to be interpreted as a single, multiply-articulated segment. "L" represents the voiceless lateral fricative. It does not pattern with the sonorants in that it does not undergo Glottal Harmony. Note Reichard's use of /c/ and /tc/ in place of the more standard /š/, /tš/. There seems also to be a contrast between glottalized and non-glottalized vowels in this language. Reichard (1938:529) transcribes four vowel qualities: $V, V^v, V'^v, V'V$.

12)	lab.	cor.	pal.	vel.	uvul.	phar.
+voice	b	d	dj	gw		
−voice	p	t	ts	tc	kw	q qw
+con.glot.	p'	t'	ts'	tc'	kw'	q' qw'
+cont.		s	L	c	xw	X Xw
+nasal	m	n				
+con.glot.	m'	n'				
−nasal	w	r	l	y		R Rw
+con.glot.	w'	r'	l'	y'		R' Rw'

Glottalization of sonorants always accompanies the reduplication of the initial stem consonant that indicates the diminutive and repeated action forms, as illustrated in (13).[8] In some words, there is no reduplicative affix, and the sonorant glottalization alone signifies the semantic category, as in (13i). In the following examples, the (a) forms are "neutral" stems from which the diminutive and repeated action (b) forms are derived by reduplication and/or sonorant glottalization.[9]

The first is a short vowel; the second is described as a long vowel where the second component is whispered as an "echo"; the third vowel is described as a vowel followed by a whispered repetition of that vowel with an intervening glottal stop, analyzed by Reichard as a glottal stop released "in the vowel position"; the fourth vowel is found in certain reduplication processes, and is described as a vowel followed by a glottal stop and another full vowel. It is beyond the scope of this investigation to verify and account for the differences between these vowel forms.

[8] Coeur d'Alene makes great use of reduplication, not all of which expresses diminutive or repeated action morphology. Other forms of reduplication do not involve sonorant glottalization.

[9] In some of the examples in (13), an epenthetic E is inserted between the reduplicated consonant and the stem consonant.

13)

i	a-	mar-marím-EntEm-ilc	'they were treated one by one'
	b-	m'-m'ar'-m'ar'ím-En'tem'-il'c	'they little ones were treated one by one'
ii	a-	yär-yär-p	'wagon, they roll'
	b-	y'-y'är'-y'är'-p	'cart'
iii	a-	cāl-ulumxw	chop ground
	b-	cE-cEl'-úl'um'xw-n'	'hoe, something which gives the ground little chops'
iv	a-	ts'āl	'plural objects stand or project'
	b-	t-ts'E-ts'El'-ts'El'-ítct	'twigs'
v	a-	p'ān-äLniw'	'long objects lie alongside'
	b-	hin-p'E-p'En'-p'En'-aLn'íw'	'shafts, little long objects lie in alongside' [10]
vi	a-	yāp'-yEp'-ic	'rocker'
	b-	y'āp'-y'Ep'-m'En'-tsut	'he rocked, used himself to sway repeatedly

In Chapter 3, I argued extensively that the alternations of diminutive consonant symbolism should be analyzed as phonological assimilations. In the case of Coeur d'Alene, this means attributing the harmonic feature to the reduplicative affix, for those forms that bear an overt affix. Following Marantz (1982) and Levin (1983), we will say that reduplicative affixes consist of bare skeletal positions onto which the stem melody is copied. There is no single skeletal position within the reduplicative affix to which the glottal feature could be prelinked. The glottal feature will link only to a sonorant segment, and thus the form of the stem melody will determine whether any sonorant will link to the skeletal slot of the reduplicative affix. Therefore, we will say that the glottal feature that triggers Glottal Harmony is a floating 'morphemic' feature associated with the diminutive and repeated action affixes, represented as in (14i). For those forms that do not show an overt diminutive or repeated action affix, we will postulate an allomorph of the reduplicative affix that contains only the harmonic feature, and no skeletal slots, as in (14ii).

---

[10] The /n/ in the prefix /hin-/ does not undergo glottal harmony. This fact is consistent with the failure of prefix segments to undergo other prosodic and segmental processes that affect stem and suffix segments.

14)

i. $\left[\begin{array}{c} [\text{+constricted glottis}] \\ x \end{array}\right]$ *diminutive/repeated action*

ii. $\left[\begin{array}{c} [\text{+constricted glottis}] \\ \end{array}\right]$ *diminutive/repeated action*

If the glottal feature originates in the affix, then it must link to sonorants within the word by the special association rule (15), which I assume applies in a left-to-right fashion.[11]

15) [+constricted glottis]
⋮
x
|
[+sonorant]

Observe that, having linked to the leftmost sonorant in the word, the glottal feature must continue spreading past segments that are underlyingly glottalized, as in the (b) forms in examples (13iv,v,vi).[12] In the discussion of harmony in Section 1.5, we assumed a model in which there is one plane for each distinctive feature in the phonological representation of a word. For any given distinctive feature **F**, all segments in a word that are specified for **F** will be specified on the single **F** plane. Adopting this type of representation for Coeur d'Alene causes the (b) forms in (13iv,v,vi) to present a perplexing problem for a theory of harmony processes. In order for the harmonic feature to spread onto all sonorants in a word, it would have to cross the association line of underlyingly glottal segments, as in the following derivation of (13iv.b). [13]

---

[11] It would make no difference if the rule were to associate the glottal feature first to the rightmost sonorant in the word. I am assuming left-to-right linking as the unmarked option (see Goldsmith (1976) and McCarthy (1981)).

[12] Also problematic are the many forms in which the harmonic feature must spread past the glottal feature of glottalized vowels (see ft. 5)

[13] The floating harmonic feature is circled in this example.

16)

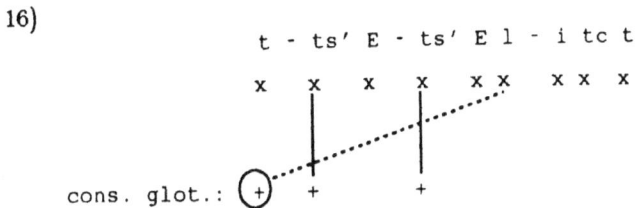

Given this representation, and the explanation for blocking phenomena presented in Section 1.5, we predict that harmonic spreading will not be able to propagate past the underlyingly glottal segments in Coeur d'Alene. Yet the forms in (13) clearly show that harmony does propagate beyond glottal segments.

One possible solution to the association problem illustrated in (16) would be to arbitrarily allow the glottal feature of underlying glottal segments to reside on a plane which is distinct from the plane of the harmonic glottal feature, as in (17).

17)

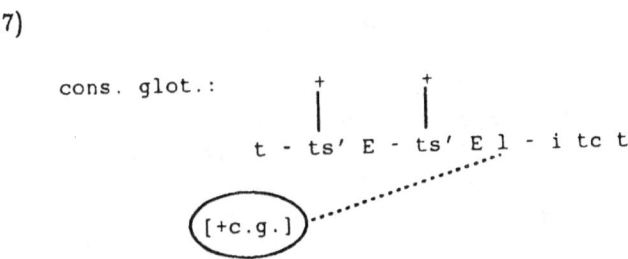

Vago (1985) and Lieber (1987) suggest similar analyses for the treatment of transparent segments in harmony systems. Although the solution I will propose below for Glottal Harmony relies on multiplanar phonological representations, my analysis differs from those of Vago and Lieber in providing an explanation for *why* some segments are specified for a harmonic feature on a different plane than other segments. The analyses of Vago and Lieber make it a property of individual grammars to determine which segments will be harmonically active (specified for the harmonic feature on the harmonic plane), and which segments will be harmonically inert (specified for the harmonic feature on a different plane). Thus, these analyses make the implicit claim that it is not possible to predict, for a given harmony system, which segments will undergo harmony and which segments will be transparent or opaque. As discussed in Cole & Trigo (1987), there appears to be a non-arbitrary relationship between the class of segments that undergo harmony and the class of transparent or opaque segments in every known harmony system, suggesting that there are constraints on harmony systems that are not expressed in the multi-level theories of Vago and Lieber.

The multi-level analyses cited allow the introduction of a new feature plane whenever there is an assimilation process in the language that must "skip over" segments specified for the assimilating feature. Thus, these analyses involve a very unconstrained theory of phonological representation, in which there is no principled bound on the number of planes used to represent a single distinctive feature. A theory which allows the introduction of new distinctive feature planes just to account for the behavior of harmony processes is a much more powerful theory than one which treats harmonic feature specifications the same as non-harmonic feature specifications by assigning both to a single plane in the representation of a morpheme.

I am inclined to reject any multi-level analysis that allows for the unconstrained introduction of new feature planes in the analysis of harmony systems, but assuming only uni-level representations for Coeur d'Alene Glottal Harmony makes the association problem illustrated in (16) seem intractable. However, a theory which incorporates the Morpheme Plane Hypothesis allows multi-planar representations in one special circumstance, namely, under morpheme concatenation. The process of morphological affixation will introduce a new plane of phonological representation.[14] Thus, the multi-planar representation that results from assuming the Morpheme Plane Hypothesis allows the same feature to be represented on two distinct planes for two segments, providing that the two segments in question belong to different morphemes.

With this in mind, it is a revealing observation that Glottal Harmony in Coeur d'Alene is morphologically governed, and not a general harmony process that is conditioned by the appearance of a glottal feature at any arbitrary place in a word. Being introduced under morphological affixation, the glottal feature triggering Glottal Harmony will always be on a separate plane from the glottal specifications of any other segment in the stem, at least before the operation of Plane Conflation. If we assume that morphologically governed phonological

---

[14]More accurately, what is added is a new *family of planes* which consists of one plane corresponding to each node in the distinctive feature tree that comprises a phonological segment, and additional planes for the metrical representations of stress and syllable structure associated with these segments.

Morphologically Governed Harmony

processes must apply before Plane Conflation (an assumption which is discussed further in Chapter 5), then the Morpheme Plane theory of phonology actually makes the prediction that morphologically governed harmony processes will not display the same blocking effects found in general (non-morphologically governed) harmony processes. Thus, a solution to Coeur d'Alene Glottal Harmony that employs morpheme planes not only allows for the mechanics of association to operate simply and straightforwardly, but it also relates the fact that underlyingly glottal segments do not block harmony to the fact that the harmony process is morphologically governed. A derivation of the form in (13iii-b) employing morpheme tiers is given in (18):[15]

18)

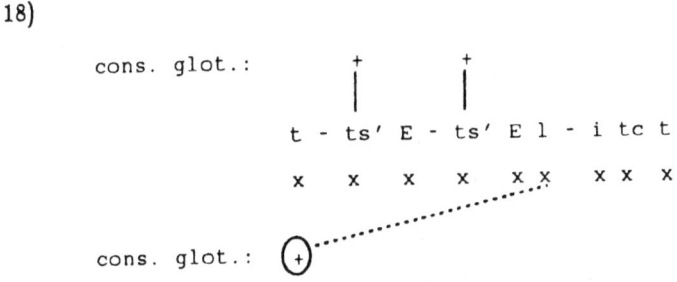

It will be instructive at this point to consider what a solution to the association problem in Glottal Harmony would look like if we did not incorporate morpheme planes into the analysis. Since it is a fact that in a uni-planar repesentation, association spreads beyond an underlyingly glottal segment, there would need to be some mechanism which allows the spreading feature to merge with the glottal feature of the glottal segment. Such a Merger Rule would have the effect of collapsing adjacent, identical feature specifications in the course of the spreading rule of harmony, as illustrated in (19):

---

[15] I have employed a shorthand notation in (18), whereby I use letters to represent combinations of feature specifications on distinct planes. The letters can be thought of as representing the root node dominating the features comprising each segment. I have separated the [constricted glottis] features to make it clear that these specifications do not interact in any way with the plane on which the floating morphemic [constricted glottis] feature is located.

19)

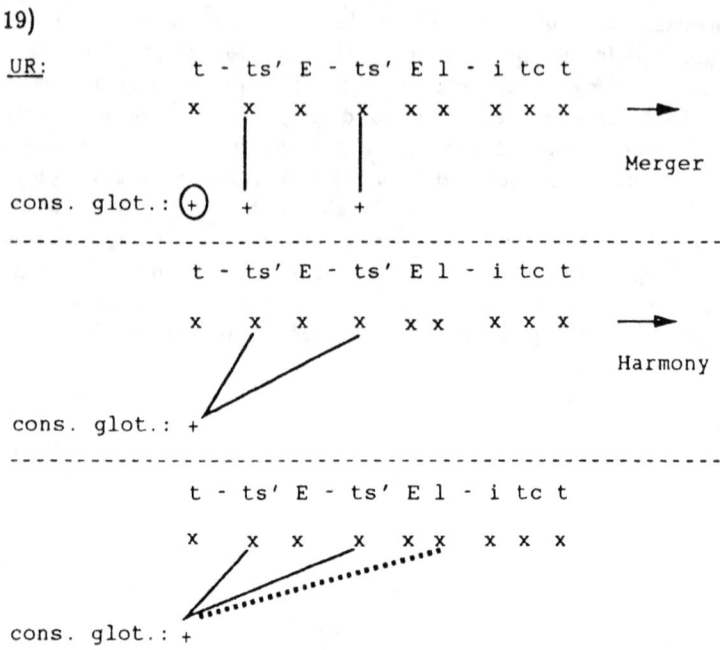

The Merger Rule could collapse only adjacent feature specifications that were identical, and thus only segments specified for the same value as the harmonic feature could become transparent to harmony under this analysis. Any segment which was [−constricted glottis] at the time Glottal Harmony applies would still block harmony.

Adopting the Merger solution within the uni-planar analysis is tantamount to saying that it is not predictable for any given language whether segments specified for the harmonic feature will block harmony, or whether Merger will apply to unite the harmonic and blocking feature values. From this we would have to conclude that there is nothing about the nature of the harmonic feature and the underlying segment inventory that will predict the application of Merger. Consider for example the process of Round Harmony in Khalkha Mongolian. In that system, round vowels block harmonic spreading of [+round]. The words in (20) illustrate the Round Harmony process in Khalkha. The roundness of an initial non-high vowel spreads to other non-high vowels in the words in (20i), and is blocked by a high round vowel /u,ü/ in (20ii). Any non-high vowel occurring after /u,ü/ will surface with the default value [−round]. Further, the high unrounded vowel /i/ is transparent to harmony—it neither undergoes nor blocks harmonic spreading of [+round], as in (20iii).[16]

20) i- erctee 'twisted' (B:252)
      ōrg-ōgd-ōx 'to be raised' (S:5)
      sons-ogd-ox to be heard (S:52)

    ii- dörbüülen 'today' (B:205)
        ogtorguidax 'situated in the sky' (B:112)

    iii- bōliigōx 'to cause to bow' (B:198)
         orgilox 'to billow' (B:219)

This harmony system can be analyzed as a feature filling rule spreading [+round] from non-high vowels to non-high vowels. Feature-filling harmony applies before the redundancy rules fill in the unmarked value of the harmonic feature. Thus, all vowels undergoing harmony are unspecified for [round] at the time harmony takes place. While non-high round vowels derive their roundness from the initial non-high vowel, the high round vowels are necessarily [+round] underlyingly. Therefore, the blocking effects of the high round vowels can be attributed to their underlying [+round] feature blocking the harmonic spread of [+round]—but only if there is no Merger rule applying that would unite the [+round] value of an initial non-high vowel with the underlying [+round] value of a high vowel. If Merger were to apply, no blocking would result, as illustrated in (21):

21)

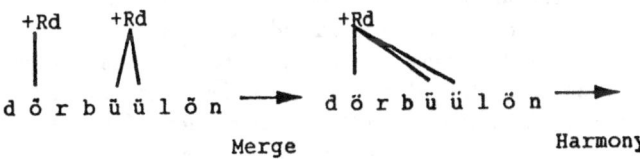

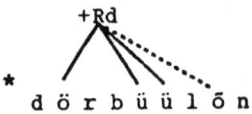

---

[16]The page numbers following each example refer to the pages on which these examples are found in Steriade (S) (1981) and Bosson (B) (1964).

Thus, within a uniplanar theory, the anlaysis of Coeur d'Alene requires Merger, while the analysis of Mongolian precludes Merger. The result is that the presence of Merger in the grammar of a language is unpredictable, and we would be forced to stipulate for every harmony system whether or not Merger precedes harmony. Adopting the Morpheme Plane Hypothesis allows us to make a principled distinction between the presence of blocking segments in Turkish and Khalkha and the absence of blocking segments in Coeur d'Alene Glottal Harmony. The morheme plane analysis allows us to make the prediction that all morphologically governed harmonies will behave like Coeur d'Alene Glottal Harmony. Thus, the morpheme plane analysis goes farther in actually explaining the phenomena than the stipulatory Merger analysis.

We can consider the plausibility of another alternative solution to Glottal Harmony. It might be argued that the glottalization of sonorants effected by Glottal Harmony is typologically distinct from the glottal feature on obstruents, or the glottal feature affecting vowel articulations. It is true that there is a great perceptual difference between the acoustic effects of glottalization on sonorants and glottalization on obstruents. However, it is also true that both types of glottalization involve stricture of the glottis. Given the theory of phonological representations that we are assuming, in which distinctive features are defined and organized on the basis of the articulations involved in their implementation, any segment involving glottal stricture will at some point in its derivation involve the feature [+constricted glottis]. One could claim that sonorant glottalization of Glottal Harmony does not involve the feature [+constricted glottis], but under the theory adopted here, those sonorants would necessarily become specified as [+constricted glottis] at some later stage in the derivation. Claiming that Glottal Harmony spreads some feature other than [+constricted glottis] forces the adoption of a highly abstract analysis of sonorant glottalization. Some feature other than [+constricted glottis] will distinguish glottalized from non-glottalized sonorants, although it will remain true that at a later stage in the derivation, the feature [+constricted glottis] will also redundantly effect this distinction.

4.2.2 Faucal Harmony

The Faucal Harmony system in Coeur d'Alene consists of two harmony rules: a regressive harmony triggered by pharyngeal and uvular ("faucal") consonants, and a progressive harmony triggered by

Morphologically Governed Harmony

the lax vowels /a,o/.[17] Both rules are completely general—they will apply anytime their respective environments are found, regardless of the morphological structure of the word. We will examine these two rules in turn.

Regressive Faucal Harmony

Regressive Harmony causes all non-lax vowels to alternate in the presence of a faucal consonant following the vowel anywhere in the word. The faucal consonants are /q, q', qw, qw', X, Xw, R, R', Rw, Rw', r, r'/ (refer to the phoneme chart in (12), page 62). The vowel phonemes are provisionally listed in (22).[18]

22)

	i	ä	u	o	a
High	+	−	+	−	−
Back	−	−	+	+	+
Low	−	+	−	−	+
Tense	+	+	+	−	−

The vowel alternations of Regressive Harmony are given in (23) (where "Q" stands for any faucal consonant), with examples following in (24).

23) Regressive Harmony: i ⟶ a
    i ⟶ ä / __ ...Q
    u ⟶ o
    ä ⟶ a

---

[17] We will conclude below that regressive harmony is triggered both by faucal consonants, and the lax vowels /a,o/. Almost all of the data examined here that have a lax vowel in position to trigger regressive harmony have a faucal consonant that could also be triggering. However, there is one example, shown in (36vi), where it can be argued that a lax vowel triggers regressive harmony, since there is no potential faucal consonant trigger.

[18] But see the discussion below for a fuller specification of underlying vowels. In particular, I introduce two vowels into underlying representations that do not actually surface: /I/ and /ɛ/. Also, the vowel schwa, represented here as E, appears in surface forms, but is most likely not phonemic. In the discussion that follows, I argue for interpreting the tense/lax distinction in terms of the feature [advanced (tongue root)].

24) i-   ako-stq   "he answered back"   (cf, ākwn)
     ii- tsāc-alqw   "he is tall"   (cf, tsic)
     iii- t-poxw-qEnts   "he blew on her head"   (cf, puxw)
     iv- tc-lop-qEnts   "she dried his hair"   (cf, lup)

The two alternations for the vowel /i/ suggest that at some point there was a high back unrounded /I/ vowel in the language that eventually merged with /i/. I will assume that /I/ is the underlying vowel in the $i \sim a$ alternation in (23).

Among the vowels that are the output of Regressive Harmony, /a/ and /o/ are lax; therefore all the alternations involve laxing except the alternation $i \longrightarrow \bar{a}$. In addition, all the alternations involve lowering, except $\bar{a} \longrightarrow a$. I argue below that the harmonic feature involved in all the alternations is [tongue root].

We must somehow make a distinction between the velar, uvular and pharyngeal consonants in this language, since only the latter two classes trigger faucal harmony. One possibility would be to analyze all these consonants as involving the Dorsal articulator, and invoke the features [low] and [high] to distinguish three levels of height: velars would be [+high, −low], uvulars would be [−high, −low], and pharyngeals would be [−high, +low]. Adopting this analysis, Faucal Harmony would be the assimilation of [−high] from the uvulars and pharyngeals onto vowels. Assimilating [−high] would account for the lowering observed in the alternations in (23), but additional rules would have to be added to get the laxing effects. The problem with this analysis is that the high vowels do not block harmony, as seen in the following form:

25) ni'-ip'-i'qs-En $\longrightarrow$ ni'-ap'-i'qs-En   "handkerchief"

In this example, Regressive Harmony is triggered by the suffixal /q/, and causes a shift in the underlying vowel /i/ in the root /ip'/.[19] The [+high] suffixal vowel /i/ intervenes between target and trigger, but does not block harmony. The transparency of /i/ would be totally unexplained if [−high] were the harmonic feature.[20]

---

[19] Harmony does not affect the vowel /i/ in the suffix, suggesting that Regressive Harmony applies only in derived environments (see (34) below). The prefix /ni'-/ is outside of the domain for harmony, as well as several other rules of Coeur d'Alene phonology.

[20] I am assuming that [+high] is the underlyingly marked value. Even if we were to argue that [−high] is underlyingly marked on vowels, the analysis for harmony would be problematic. If [−high] were the marked value, then the high vowel /i/ could be said to be unspecified for height when harmony takes place, and

I suggest that the feature that distinguishes uvulars and pharyngeals from velars, and the feature involved in Faucal Harmony, is [tongue root]. [tongue root] is introduced as a new articulator node into the feature hierarchy of Sagey's (1986) model.[21] The tongue root articulator will be involved in both uvular and pharyngeal articulations, grouping these two segments together as a natural class. The tongue root is also responsible for laxing in vowels, and it can be said to dominate the feature [+/− advanced], as in (26),

26)
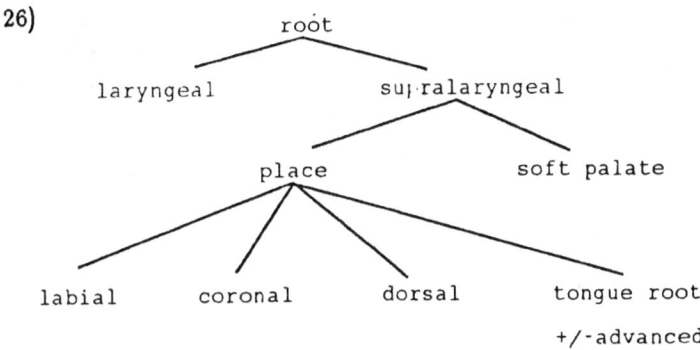

Following a suggestion by D. Steriade, I represent the velars, uvulars, and pharyngeal consonants as in (27):

27)
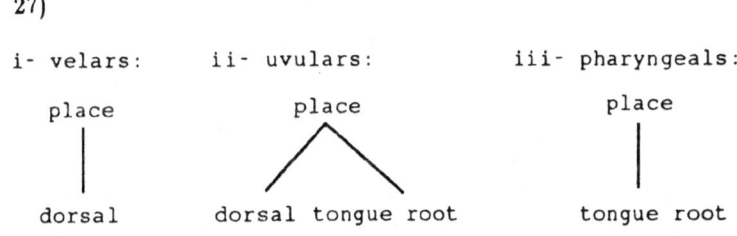

---

therefore transparent to [−high] harmony. However, Regressive Harmony must also skip over the low vowel /a/, as seen in forms like (24ii), where the harmony trigger is preceded by /a/ in the same suffix. If [−high] were the marked value, then /a/ would be specified [−high] when harmony applies, and should therefore block harmony. Assuming either value of [high] to be the harmonic feature in Regressive Harmony predicts that some class of vowels will block harmony, when in fact no vowels are seen to block.

[21] Steriade (1986a) comes to a similar conclusion in her discussion of Javanese tense/lax alternations, and McCarthy (1988) provides several arguments for a Guttural node dominating uvular, pharyngeals and in some cases laryngeals.

Steriade (p.c.) observes that uvulars and velars function as a natural class in some languages; for example, they both condition Spirantization in Tigrinya (Schein (1981) and Schein and Steriade (1986)), and they behave as homorganic consonants with respect to an articulator dissimilation rule in Pomo, an American Indian language (Oswalt 1971). By saying that uvulars are specified for a velar articulation, as well as the tongue root articulation, we can define a natural class which includes velars and uvulars, but excludes pharyngeals.

Adopting the representations in (27), Regressive Harmony can be analyzed as the spread of the [tongue root] articulator node from consonants onto vowels. We need only add a rule of interpretation that adds the feature [−advanced] to any vowel that bears a tongue root articulation. These rules are formulated below:

28)

29)

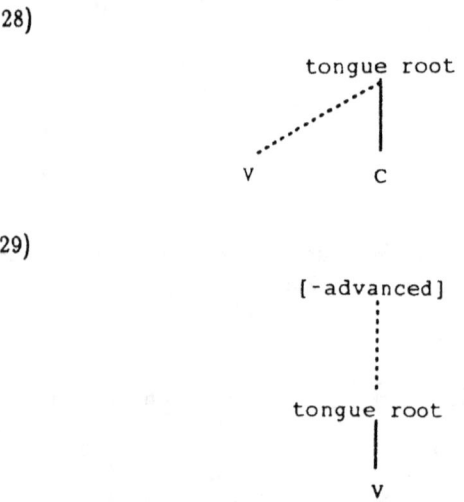

Further support for the analysis of Faucal Harmony as the assimilation of the Tongue Root node comes from the fact that in the related Salish language Squamish, described by Kuipers (1967), uvular and pharyngeal consonants are said to regularly cause adjacent vowels to surface as lax. In Squamish, this laxing is not accompanied by lowering.

To complete the picture, we need to explain how the surface vowel forms indicated in (23) are derived from an assimilation of [tongue root], and subsequent realization of the feature [−advanced] on underlying vowels. Let's consider the output of rules (28) and (29) as they apply to the underlying forms of the vowels /i, ā, I, u/:[22]

30) i ⟶ [+high, −back, −advanced]
    ā ⟶ [−back, +low, −advanced]
    I ⟶ [+high, −round, −advanced]
    u ⟶ [+high, +round, −advanced]

Notice that in all cases, the resulting feature combination produces a vowel which is not present in either the underlying or surface vowel inventories of the language. Rather than allow these non-phonemic vowels to surface, the grammar makes some change in each of the feature combinations in (30) which results in a phonemic vowel.[23] We can see from (23) that a derived [+high, −advanced] vowel lowers, and the front low vowel [ā] becomes back when it acquires [−advanced]. At present there is not a clear understanding of the nature or role of the kind of "clean-up" rules necessary to derive the correct output in these examples.[24] The rules in (31) are a partial set of clean-up rules:

31) i-   [+high] ⟶ ∅ / [__, −advanced]
    ii- [−back] ⟶ [+back] / [__, +low, −advanced]

The first rule will affect all of the high vowels—/i,I,u/—and deletes their [+high] specification, reflecting the absence of [+high, +advanced] vowels in this language. The unmarked value [−high] will then be supplied by redundancy rule. (31i) will derive the mid lax vowels [ɛ, ɔ, ʌ]. The non-round vowels undergo further lowering, and the round vowel actually becomes [+advanced]. The lowering of the non-round vowels reflects the absence of mid non-round vowels in the vowel inventory. For underlying [I], the lowering is straightforward, producing [−advanced] [a]. For underlying [i] it is somewhat strange that the lowering results in [+advanced] [ā]. It seems that for both underlying [i] and [u] the combination [+high,−advanced] results in the surface as [−high, +advanced]. We cannot consider this the result of a single rule, however, since underlying [I] does retain its [−advanced] feature. The second clean-up rule (31ii) causes underlying [ā] to become [+back] when it acquires the feature [−advanced].[25]

---

[22] I am assuming that only the values [+high], [−back], [+low], and [−advanced] are marked in the underspecified vowel inventory.

[23] The same kind of regularization or phonemicization is seen in the consonant symbolism systems discussed in Chapter 3.

[24] But see Calabrese (1987) for an inventory of types of clean-up strategies.

[25] The problem of clean-up rules in these examples is perplexing and presents in my opinion a serious challenge to the feature system adopted in this thesis. The

There is additional support for the two-step derivation $i \rightarrow \epsilon \rightarrow \bar{a}$. There is reason to believe that /ɛ/ actually occurs as an underlying vowel in Coeur d'Alene. Certain roots with surface /ā/ exceptionally trigger Progressive Faucal Harmony (35) (discussed below), which is otherwise only triggered by the *lax* vowels /a,o/. I argue that these exceptional triggers actually contain the lax vowel /ɛ/, which is neutralized to /ā/ in surface representation by application of (31iii). This analysis allows us to say that all and only the lax vowels trigger Progressive Harmony. Examples of roots with surface /ā/ that trigger harmony are provided in (32).

32) i- tcin-LEp'-LEp'-äp'-ātct *"my hand became welted"*
(root: /Läp'/ *"mark, make welt"*, /-itct/ *"hand"*)

ii- Xäm-än-tsót-En *"he went to live with his in-laws"*
(/-tsut/ *reflexive*)

iii- hin-LEl-LEl-änä'-äntEm *"he was ear-sprinkled"*
(root: /Läl/, /-inä/ *"ear"*)

Adopting the analysis presented above for the alternations in (23) and (32), we can now revise the underlying vowel inventory to include /ɛ/ and /I/, as follows:

33)

	i	ɛ	ä	u	I	o	a
High	+	–	–	+	+	–	–
Back	–	–	–	+	+	+	+
Low	–	–	+	–	–	–	+
Tense	+	–	+	+	+	–	–
Round	–	–	–	+	–	+	–

Finally, we note here that Regressive Harmony skips over all labial, coronal, and velar consonants, as seen in the examples in (24). This is to be expected if harmony is a process of Tongue Root node assim-

---

Regressive Harmony rule may be viewed as causing a lowering of one step, which preserves backness and roundness for the high vowels. One-step lowering rules are notoriously difficult to express in the binary feature inventory of SPE. See Hyman (1988) for an underspecification approach to a similar lowering problem in Esimbi, and Clements (1989) for an interesting proposal for a hierarchically organized vowel height feature. An analysis of the Coeur d'Alene data using unary features in a type of dependency phonology approach is presented in van der Hulst (1988).

ilation. It is also subject to the Derived Environment Condition, as evidenced by the existence of a number of disharmonic roots and one disharmonic suffix that contain a faucal consonant following vowels which have not undergone harmony. The following examples were obtained from Reichard (1939):[26]

34)
Disharmonic Roots: yirkw', ts'uq'un, q'i'qixwā?, sitqaps, yanuq', xāliqwā'ā, l'āliqw'ilc, sxwulotqEn, sxuxwom'qEn', āququl'i't
Disharmonic Suffix: -i'qs

Progressive Faucal Harmony

The second faucal harmony process is a Progressive Harmony that is triggered by the vowels /a,o/ in a root, and causes a stressed suffixal vowel /í,Í,ú/ to surface as ā́,á,ó /, respectively.

35) Progressive Harmony:

$$\begin{matrix} i \rightarrow \ddot{a} \\ I \rightarrow a \\ u \rightarrow o \end{matrix} \Big/ \; \left\{ \begin{matrix} a \\ o \end{matrix} \right\} \cdots \underset{[+\text{stress}]}{\overline{}}$$

Aside from the non-participation of the vowel /ā/, Progressive Harmony causes the same alternations as Regressive Harmony. This suggests that the segments triggering both harmony processes share a feature specification. I suggested for Regressive Harmony that the harmonic feature is the Tongue Root node, realized as [−advanced] on vowels, anticipating the analysis of Progressive Harmony. I propose here that the alternations seen in Progressive Harmony are also caused by the assimilation of the Tongue Root node, which causes the [−advanced] feature from the lax vowels to appear on a stressed high vowel. The vowels /a/ and /o/ are the only two lax vowels, apart

---

[26]Some of these roots are clearly compositional, but Reichard listed them as unanalyzable stems in her stem list. Of course, the fact that harmony is not applying across the supposed morpheme boundaries supports the hypothesis that these forms have been lexicalized, since the same suffixes regularly induce harmony elsewhere throughout the grammar.

from non-phonemic /E/, in the surface inventory.[27] Describing Faucal Harmony as a Tongue Root harmony that causes a vocalic shift to [−advanced] gives an explanation for why /a/ and /o/ function as a class in triggering Progressive Harmony, and also for why the faucal consonants cause the same vowel alternations in Regressive Harmony. The faucal consonants and lax vowels share in common a specification on the Tongue Root node that is not shared by any other consonant or vowel segment. Progressive harmony is exemplified by the forms in (36).[28]

36) i-   pas-átc-stmEn   "I will play a trick on him" (cf, -itc)
    ii-   tci'ts-po's-tsán   "I am joking" (cf, -tsin)
    iii- p'at'-áswal   "trout" (cf, -isgwal)
    iv-   tsán-p'at'-cán-En   "cement" (cf, -cin)
    v-   t'ap-stcánt   "he shot" (cf, -stcint)
    vi-   hin-p'at'-p'at'-os-Entsót'   "he dreamed" (cf, -us, -Entsut)

There is a class of roots which are exceptions to Progressive Harmony. Although they contain a lax vowel, they fail to trigger harmony. All such roots contain a faucal consonant in the root-final consonant cluster, following the lax vowel. Consider the following forms, all of which contain a suffix with a stressed high vowel that does not undergo Progressive Harmony:

---

[27] Although recall from the discussion in the preceding section that /ɛ/ occurs as an additional underlying lax vowel, and also triggers Progressive Harmony.

[28] The form in (36vi) is interesting because the vowel in the suffix /-us/ also undergoes harmony, although it does not bear surface stress. It appears between the low vowel trigger and the stressed vowel target. There are two possible explanations for this fact. One possibility is that Progressive Harmony is ordered before Regressive Harmony, and the stressed vowel becomes a trigger for Regressive Harmony. There is otherwise only extremely limited evidence that low vowels also count as triggers for Regressive Harmony. The second possibility is that the two underlying /u/ vowels in the suffixes are linked to the same feature matrix, and thus, when one undergoes harmonic lowering, so also does the other. The problem with this analysis is that the multiply-linked vowel counts as a geminate structure, and should be subject to some sort of condition on geminate blockage (see Hayes (1986), Schein and Steriade (1986)), whereby neither member of the geminate pair may undergo a phonological rule if only one member meets the structural description of the rule.

37)
i-	a-n-car-íc-iL	*"upstream"*
ii-	kw'aR-aR-p-El-íy'ā'	*"coasting"*
iii-	t-Xolqw'-ātcs-En-tsút	*"I wound string around my hand"*
iv-	t'E-t'aX-íl'-kwā'	*"small rapid"*
v-	sE-sar-ítcn'	*"squirrel or chipmunk"*

Both the lax vowels and the faucal consonants are specified by the Tongue Root articulator, as proposed above. Therefore, the blocking behavior of the faucal consonants in (3) is exactly what is predicted by this analysis. The Tongue Root node dominating the [−advanced] feature of the lax vowels can't associate past the Tongue Root node of the faucal consonant to affect the stressed suffixal vowel. The derivation of (37v) is illustrated below ("A" stands for the feature [advanced], and "T.R." stands for Tongue Root.):

38)

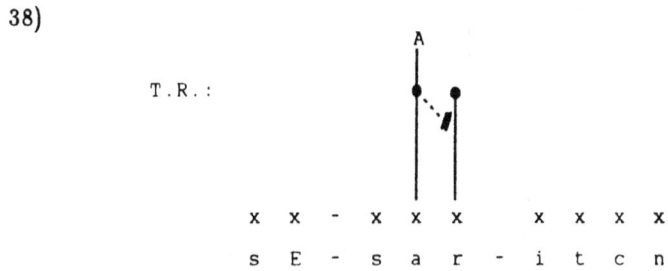

The faucal consonants block Progressive Harmony in the examples in (37) because their Tongue Root specification lies on the same Tongue Root plane as the Tongue Root specification of the lax root vowel. It is in this regard that Glottal Harmony differs from Progressive Faucal Harmony. The floating glottal feature triggering Glottal Harmony is introduced on a phonological plane which bears no other glottal specifications—hence, no blocking segments are encountered. The Tongue Root node triggering Progressive Faucal Harmony is specified on a plane on which other tauto-morphemic Tongue Root segments are also specified—these tauto-morphemic Tongue Root segments block harmony.

In all of the examples in (37), the blocking faucal consonant belongs to the same morpheme as the lax vowel trigger of harmony. Under any version of a theory incorporating morpheme planes, these two Tongue Root features will be on the same plane. The remaining data to be examined concerning blocking segments in Progressive

Harmony are forms in which a faucal consonant intervenes between the trigger and target of harmony, but where the faucal consonant does not belong to the same morpheme as the trigger vowel. There are two cases to consider. First, the faucal consonant could be the initial consonant of a suffix containing a high stressed vowel, as in the suffix /-qin/ "*head*". When such suffixes follow roots with lax vowels, and in words where no additional faucal consonant intervenes between the harmony trigger and the suffix in question, our analysis predicts that the suffix-initial faucal consonant will not block harmony if harmony is ordered before Plane Conflation. A hypothetical form is given in (39):

39)

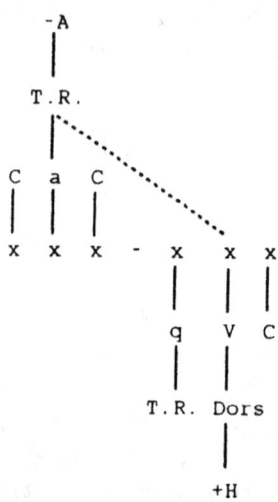

No blocking occurs in (39) because the faucal consonant is not represented on the same phonological plane as the segment that triggers Progressive Harmony. Unfortunately, no such forms have been found in any of the sources available to me. [29]

The second type of word, which I have also not encountered, is one in which the faucal consonant belongs to a suffix that intervenes between the lax root vowel and the suffix containing the high stressed vowel. The faucal consonant will block in this case only if Plane Conflation has aligned the root plane with the plane of the inner suffix

---

[29] I acknowledge the help of Ivy Doak in searching her corpus for harmony forms.

before harmony takes place. This conflation would result in placing the Tongue Root nodes of the faucal consonant and the root vowel on the same plane. A hypothetical example appears in (40):

40)

```
                    -A
                    |
T.R.:        •----------•
             |    ⫽     |
        C    a    C  -  q    V    C
        |    |    |     |    |    |
        x    x    x  -  x    x    x  -  x    x    x
                                         |    |    |
                                         C    V    C
                                              |
dors:                                         •
                                             +H
```

The discovery of forms like those in (39) and (40) would help us to determine the proper ordering of Progressive Harmony with respect to Plane Conflation in Coeur d'Alene.[30]

---

[30] For the reader interested in confirming the findings of this section, we note here the existence of two low-level rules in Coeur d'Alene which produce output that on the surface violate the rule of Progressive Harmony. First, there is a general laxing of vowels in stressless positions, and this rule has the same output as harmony for the high vowels: /i/ alternates with /ä/ and /u/ alternates with /o/. Thus, it can appear as though a high unstressed vowel is undergoing Progressive Harmony when it follows a root with a lax vowel, when what is actually observed is the effects of this rule of laxing, as in the form /t'am-älgwäs-tsän-Em/ from underlying /t'am-ilgwäs-tsin-Em/.

Second, there is a local assimilation rule that laxes and lowers vowels immediately following faucal consonants. When the vowel to the right of a faucal consonant is /I/ or /ä/, this local rule creates /a/. However, this /a/ will not trigger Progressive Harmony, as seen in the form /tEl'-tEl'q-aL-ts'ä-úl/ from underlying /tEl'-tEl'q-il-ts'ä-úl/. The suffix /-il/ first undergoes stressless laxing, and then becomes [−advanced] in the context of the leftward faucal consonant (recall that the realization of [−advanced] on /ä/ always results in the back vowel /a/). This local Pharyngeal assimilation rule also accounts for the fact that roots that surface with Qa(C) frequently do not trigger Progressive Harmony, as in /Xas-Xas-ílgwas/, which Reichard cites as containing the root /xäs/.

To summarize, we have seen in Coeur d'Alene two different harmony systems—one in which [αF] segments block [αF] harmony, and one in which they do not. The difference between these two harmony systems is explained by adopting the Morpheme Plane Hypothesis. In Progressive Faucal Harmony, segments specified for the harmonic feature that occur on the same morpheme plane as the harmony trigger intervene between trigger and target. These segments block harmony. In contrast, the triggering feature for Glottal Harmony is contained on a morpheme plane which contains no other glottal specifications; hence no blocking occurs. In Section 4.4, we will see that a similar explanation accounts for the different blocking phenomena observed in the two rounding harmony rules of Warlpiri.

4.3 Wiyot Anterior/Continuant Harmony

Wiyot, an Algic language spoken in north coastal California, is another one of the languages with diminutive (and augmentative) consonant symbolism mentioned in Chapter 3. Wiyot has one of the more complicated consonant symbolism systems seen among the northwest Native American languages. The complexity of the system seems at first to provide arguments against an assimilation analysis of consonant symbolism. In particular, one part of the system displays both a shift from [+anterior] to [−anterior], and from [−anterior] to [+anterior]. Such a pattern of alternation cannot be accounted for by a single [anterior] assimilation rule. In this section I examine the complexities of the Wiyot system, and demonstrate that certain aspects of the alternations attributed to the diminutive symbolism arise from other phonological processes attested in the language. I provide an assimilation analysis for the phenomena that remains in the scope of diminutive and augmentative consonant symbolism.

The sound symbolism of Wiyot is discussed in the grammars of Reichard (1925) and Teeter (1964).[31]

---

[31] These two sources use very different transcriptions. Most of my examples and analysis are based on Reichard's data—which is more detailed and plentiful than Teeter's—and I assume her transcription, largely to help anyone who wishes to verify the data cited in my examples (although Teeter's phonemic transcription is formally preferable to Reichard's pre-phonemic transcription). When citing forms from Teeter's grammar, I modify his examples to conform with Reichard's transcription, at least with respect to the consonants. The vowel correspondences between the two systems are less transparent. The following correspondences between the two transcription systems have been established by Gensler (1986), and are assumed here:

The consonant inventory of Wiyot is shown below. The use of /c/ instead of more standard /š/ conforms to Reichard's transcription, and should be noted throughout this section. The symbol /r/ represents an apico-alveolar tap consonant, as in Japanese, and /ṛ/ represents the retroflex liquid, like the English /r/.

41)

lab.	cor.	pal.	lat.	vel.		glot.
p	t	ts	tc	k	kw	ʔ
b	d	dz	dj	g	gw	
	s	c	L			h
m	n					
v	r	y		w		
	ṛ		l			

Wiyot makes a distinction between three semantic categories in noun and verb forms: *neutral, diminutive,* and *augmentative*. The diminutive forms are expressed by the consonant alternations in (42), and the optional presence of a diminutive suffix /-ats/.[32]

42) t ⟶ ts
  d ⟶ dz(/ts)
  tc ⟶ ts
  (dj ⟶ dz/ts)
  s ⟶ c
  l ⟶ ṛ

Reichard consistently transcribes a shift from /d/ to /ts/ in diminutive forms. Apparently, she did not recognize a voiced fricative /dz/ in the language. Teeter consistently transcribes an alternation be-

	Teeter	Reichard		T.	R.
Consonants:	p,t,k,kw	b,d,g,gw	Vowels:	i	i,ɪ,e
	ph,th,kh,kwh	p,t,k,kw		u	u,o
	š	c		o	a
	čh,č	tc, dj		a	a
	c,ch	ts, (ts)			
	b,d,g	v,r,γ			
	l	L			
	r	ṛ			

[32] The consonant alternations involve only coronal consonants. The coronal consonants /n, ṛ/ are not mentioned in (42) and do not undergo any change when occuring in words with the diminutive suffix. The non-alternating coronals /n, ṛ/ may occur with alternating coronals in the same diminutive forms.

tween /t/ and /c/, and between /th/ and /ch/ (using his orthography, see footnote 27), which indicates that he did recognize what Reichard would have transcribed as /dz/. I will assume that voicing/aspiration distinctions are maintained in the alternations in (42), and I have regularized Reichard's transcription to this effect in the examples of this section. The alternation $dj \longrightarrow dz$ is not attested, but is predicted on analogy with $tc \longrightarrow ts$.

There are three factors that can be isolated in the alternations in (42). First, there is a shift to [+continuant] seen in the alternations $t \longrightarrow ts$ and $l \longrightarrow r̯$. Second, there is a shift to [+anterior] seen in the alternations $tc \longrightarrow ts$, $dj \longrightarrow dz$. Third, there is a shift to [−anterior] seen in the alternations $s \longrightarrow c$ and $l \longrightarrow r̯$. We can attribute the first two of these shifts to the presence of the affricate /ts/ in the suffix. I adopt an autosegmental representation of the affricate as a contour segment, as in (43).

43)

```
         .                       .
         .                       .
         .                       .
       laryngeal           supralaryngeal
            \               /
             \             /
              \           /
               root
              /   \
             /     \
      [-continuant]   [-continuant]
```

The affricate /ts/ bears the features [+continuant] and [+anterior], and can be said to trigger the assimilation of these two features onto all segments but /s/. In cases where the alternations in (42) appear without any overt diminutive suffix, we will attribute the alternations to the presence of an allomorph of /-ats/ that bears only the floating features [+continuant] [+anterior], but adds no new segments to the stem. What remains puzzling is the shift $s \longrightarrow c$. Why should a suffix characterized by the feature [+anterior] trigger a shift to [−anterior] in the fricative /s/? We'll return to this question after examining the data from the rest of the paradigm. Examples of the alternations in (42) are seen in (44) (unless otherwise indicated, all examples are from Reichard, pp.30-1):

44) i-   cwat ⟶ cwats-a:ts "small bow"
     ii- delol ⟶ dzirur-a:ts "small storage basket"
     iii- hudjwodj ⟶ hutswots-a:ts "small basket" (Teeter p.22)
     iv- we:liL ⟶ we:ril-a:ts "little foot"
     v-   bas ⟶ bac-a:ts "small plate"

In addition to the alternations in (42), Wiyot displays a second series of consonant alternations that are triggered by the augmentative suffix /-atck/ and by the allomorph /-atc/ of the diminutive suffix.

45) t   ⟶ tc
     d   ⟶ dj
     ts   ⟶ tc
     (dz ⟶ dj)
     s   ⟶ c
     l   ⟶ r̯

The alternation $dz \longrightarrow dj$ is not attested, but predicted on analogy with $ts \longrightarrow tc$.

The alternations in (45), like those in (42), involve the features [continuant] and [anterior]. The non-continuants /t,d,l/ gain a [+continuant] feature. All coronal segments gain [−anterior]. Both [+continuant] and [−anterior] can be said to originate in the affricate /tc/ of the diminutive and augmentative suffixes. Examples are seen in (46) (from Reichard pp.30-1):

46) i-   pLatk ⟶ pLatcwitc-a:tc "small rock"
     ii- delol ⟶ djirur-a:tc "small storage basket"
     iii- waiyits ⟶ wātc-a:tc "puppy"
     iv- salavasal ⟶ caravac-a:tc "little niece"

There are two questions to be addressed in the analysis of this system: i) What is the relation between [continuant] and [anterior] such that they should function together in the assimilations of (42) and (45)? ii) How is the alternation $s \longrightarrow c$ triggerred by the suffix /-ats/? We'll address the second question first.

There is no principled explanation for why a [+anterior] /ts/ causes /s/ to surface as [c]. I suggest that this alternation is not properly a part of the consonant harmony system. On the observation that all examples illustrating the $s \sim c$ alternation show /s/ in root-final position, I formulate a special rule of sibilant disimilation in (47). The rule is formulated to apply to both diminutive allomorphs, /-ats/ and the segmentless version, alike.

47) S-Dissimilation:

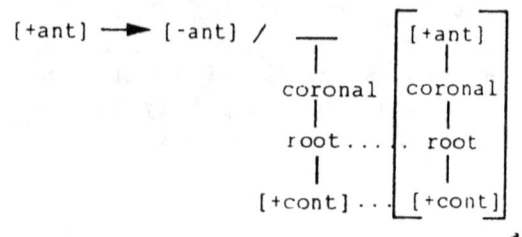

S-Dissimilation applies only if /s/ is the final coronal in the stem preceding the diminutive suffix. If another coronal were to occur between /s/ and the diminutive suffix, then /s/ would not be adjacent to the trigger of dissimilation on the coronal plane, and should therefore not be able to undergo the phonological change. I stress that the data in this regard is extremely limited. However, given the adjacency condition on morphologically governed rules discussed in Chapter 3, it would not be possible to formulate a morphologically governed dissimilation rule that affected a /s/ appearing anywhere in a stem.

There is some additional support for factoring the $s \sim c$ alternation out of the consonant harmony system. We note that an underlying /c/ is not affected by the presence of the diminutive suffix. If /c/ were a potential target, we would predict $c \longrightarrow s$ on analogy with $tc \longrightarrow ts$. In order to exclude /c/ from the set of targets for the harmony process, I formulate the harmony rule to include only [−continuant] segments in the set of targets. (The rule is formulated below in (52).) Under this analysis, we are forced to appeal to a separate rule for the $s \longrightarrow c$ alternation in (42).

Underlying /s/ is realized as [c] before the augmentative suffix as well, as shown in (45). I claim that in this case as well as in the Diminutive forms, the harmony rule that characterizes the Diminutive and Augmentative forms is not responsible for the $s \longrightarrow c$ alternation. The phonological process responsible for the $s \longrightarrow c$ alternation in (45) is a general Anterior Harmony mentioned briefly by both Teeter and Reichard. They claim that the [anterior] and [continuant] features of the first stem coronal assimilate onto all following coronals in a word, except in words containing the diminutive and augmentative suffixes. The [continuant] and [anterior] features of these suffixes always dominate the values of stem segments. While I have not been able to substantiate such a general harmony process—indeed, I found more counterexamples than examples—it does seem to be true that whenever a stem contains the [−anterior] fricative /c/, it will cause /s/ and /l/ in the same word to become /c/ and /r̩/, respectively. These shifts occur in words which do not bear any diminutive or augmentative connotation, as shown in the forms in (48) (from Reichard pp.34-5).

48)

i-	dicγaγ-ac	(-as *2sg.obj.*)	*"I love you"*
ii-	dicγa-wer̩-at	(-wel *1sg.obj.*)	*"you love me"*
iii-	dagw-atgac-ar̩a-wer̩-iL	(-ala *do of one's own volition*, -wel *1sg.obj.*)	*"he gave me a tap on the head"*
iv-	pe:c-a:d-ir̩	(-il *1sg.passive*)	*"I have a blister"*

It is clear from the forms in (48) that the plain [−continuant] stops do not participate in this harmony process. I am not able to ascertain whether or not the affricates undergo a shift to [−anterior] in the presence of the [−anterior] continuant /c/.

In addition to the forms in (48), a survey of the stems in Reichard's stem list shows no stems containing a [+anterior] /s/ in the context of a [−anterior] consonant, and only a few instances of [+anterior] /l/ in the context of a [−anterior] consonant. There are, however, more plentiful examples of stems containing [+anterior] stops in the context of [−anterior] consonants. These data suggest a process of [−anterior] harmony that affects /s, l/. It is entirely consistent with the above observations on the distribution of /s/ and /l/ to formulate a bidirectional rule of General Anterior Harmony that spreads [−anterior] from /c/ onto /s,l/ that occur anywhere in the same word, as in (49).

49) General Anterior Harmony:

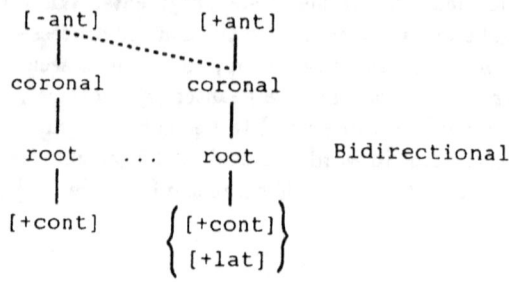

General Anterior Harmony can account for the alternations in (48) as well as the $s \longrightarrow c$ alternation of (45) (ex. in (46iv)). Note that as (49) is formulated, it will target *any* [+cont, +ant] segment, including the affricate /ts/. Again, the data are not attested to verify the behavior of the affricate here. (49) would have to be revised if the affricates in fact do not pattern with the plain fricative with respect to Anterior Harmony.[33]

To summarize, at this point we have characterized Diminutive and Augmentative Harmony as the set of consonant alternations in (42) and (45), excluding $s \longrightarrow c$ in both cases. Diminutive and Augmentative Harmony target only [−continuant] segments, and involve a change in the features [continuant] and [anterior]. Two distinct rules are responsible for the $s \longrightarrow c$ alternation: (1) General Anterior Harmony, and (2) a very limited rule of S-Dissimilation. The latter rule, as formulated in (47), is really an arbitrary addition to the more general Augmentative/Diminutive Harmony, but I see no principled treatment of this problem at this time.

We turn now to the formulation of the Diminutive and Augmentative Harmony rule. The least interesting hypothesis is that the [+continuant] and [αanterior] features from the diminutive and augmentative suffixes spread individually onto coronal non-continuants. Such a rule would be formulated as in (50):[34]

---

[33]It is not immediately clear how such a rule could be reformulated. The assimilation has to mention the feature [+continuant] to exclude the plain stops from the class of targets, but any rule targeting [+continuant] segments ought to apply to affricates as well.

[34]I have represented the affricate as bearing both the features [+continuant] and [−continuant]. I am assuming that these features are unordered in the phonological representation, and that the linear realization of these features is determined in the phonetic component, by language specific rules (see Sagey (1986) on the implications of this analysis for the interpretation of complex segments crosslinguistically). I have ordered [+cont] before [−cont] in (9) simply to make the

50) Diminutive/Augmentative Harmony:

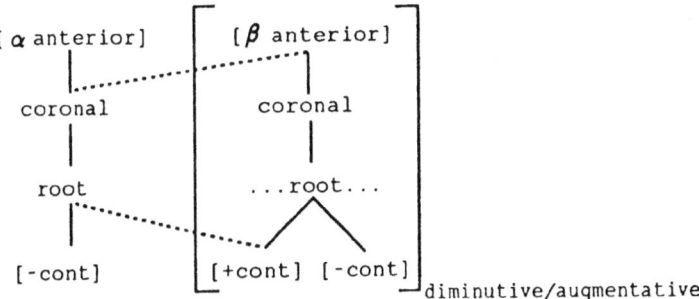

The problem with this analysis is that there is no way of relating the two spreading features. One of the motivations behind adopting the hierarchial representation of distinctive features is that it provides a way to group together those features which are actually seen to function together in phonological rules (Clements (1985), Sagey (1986)). Features which assimilate together are placed together under a single node; for example, in total vowel assimilation, all the features dominated by the dorsal node assimilate. When an assimilation rule involves more than one feature, it is analyzed as spreading the first node which dominates all the features involved. If this were the case in Wiyot, then we would have to say that the root node is the assimilating node, since that is the only node that dominates both [anterior] and [continuant].[35] Of course, it could not possibly be the case that the root node spreads in this harmony system, since many root nodes may intervene between the target and trigger of harmony, and these intervening root nodes would block harmony. How, then, can we reconcile the assimilation in (50) with the idea that multiple-feature assimilation is always caused by spreading a single class node?

One possible solution would be to claim that the feature [continuant] actually links directly to the articulator on which it is realized. That analysis necessitates a weakening of the assumption that every feature has a unique mother node in the feature tree. A slight twist on that analysis would be to say that [continuant] links directly to the Root, as in Sagey's model, but then somehow percolates down to the

---

association of [+cont] easier to represent.

[35] Referring to the diagram (1.14) in Chapter 1, it is seen that the root node dominates all other nodes, and is the only node that dominates the manner feature [continuant].

articulator node on which it is realized. This is the approach chosen below for the formulation of the Diminutive/Augmentative Harmony. I adopt Sagey's representation, as in (51), in which the linking (or percolation) of the [continuant] feature is indicated by an arrow from [continuant] pointing to the articulator node on which it's realized.

51)

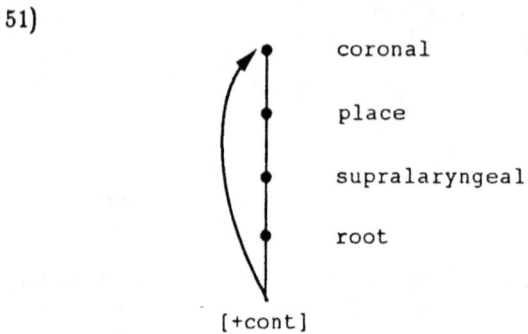

My proposal is that (i) Sagey's linking mechanism actually allows percolation of the linking relation down to any feature dominated by the articulator node; (ii) once linked, the manner feature is represented on the articulator/feature node; (iii) when an articulator/feature node assimilates, it takes with it the specification of any linked manner features; (iv) the only time manner features are explicitly linked to an articulator node is when the relation between manner features and articulator nodes is not one-to-one; (v) in an affricate structure, only the marked feature value of the pair of manner features need be explicitly linked. Combining these five assumptions, we can derive the representation of diminutive/augmentative harmony in Wiyot given in (52).

52) Diminutive/Augmentative Harmony (revised):

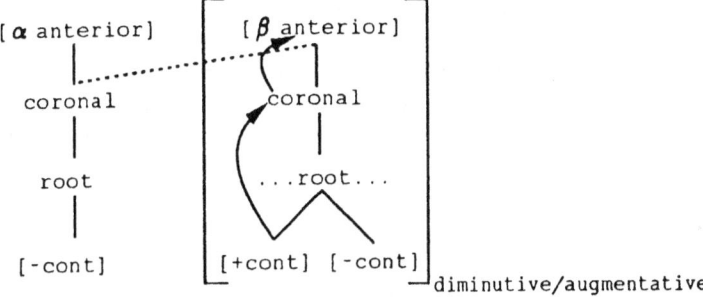

Assumption (i) is required to get the manner feature realized on the node that spreads in Wiyot—which is not the articulator node. Assumptions (ii) and (iii) are needed to account for the parasitic spreading of the continuant feature. Assumption (iv) is needed to explain why in the normal case, articulator nodes and the feature nodes they dominate can spread without spreading their manner features. Assumption (v) accounts for the fact that only the [+continuant] feature associated with the affricate trigger spreads, and not both continuant features.

The formulation of assimilation proposed in (52) formally relates the two features involved in Wiyot diminutive/augmentative harmony, but it is not essential to the analysis of this system proposed here. It is interesting to note, however, that assuming either (50) or (52), we observe the same lack of blocking phenomena in Wiyot that we saw in Coeur d'Alene Glottal Harmony. I have argued that the feature [anterior] spreads onto non-continuants in Wiyot. The forms in (53) indicate that this spreading takes place even across coronal continuants (underlined in the examples), which will also bear a specification for [anterior] (examples from Reichard pp.30-3, unless otherwise noted).[36]

53) i-   salavaṣal ⟶ caṛavac-aːtc "little niece"
    ii- laɣatwaṣwaL ⟶ ṛaɣatswacwaL "kindling wood"
    iii- dalad-atɣas-alaɣ ⟶ tsaṛats-atsɣac-aṛaɣ
         "very small owl with flat head"

The derivations in (53) are illustrated in (54). The floating harmonic

---

[36]Notice that the forms in (53i,ii) also show the effects of General Anterior Harmony, spreading [−anterior] from /ṛ/ onto /s/, deriving /c/.

feature is circled. In each case, the assimilation of the [anterior] feature must cross the association line linking the feature [+anterior] to /s/. These derivations all violate the constraint against crossing association lines, although the forms actually surface as though this association was well-formed. I am assuming that the alternations in (53ii,iii) are triggered by the segmentless allomorph of the diminutive suffix which contains only the floating features [+continuant,+anterior].

54)

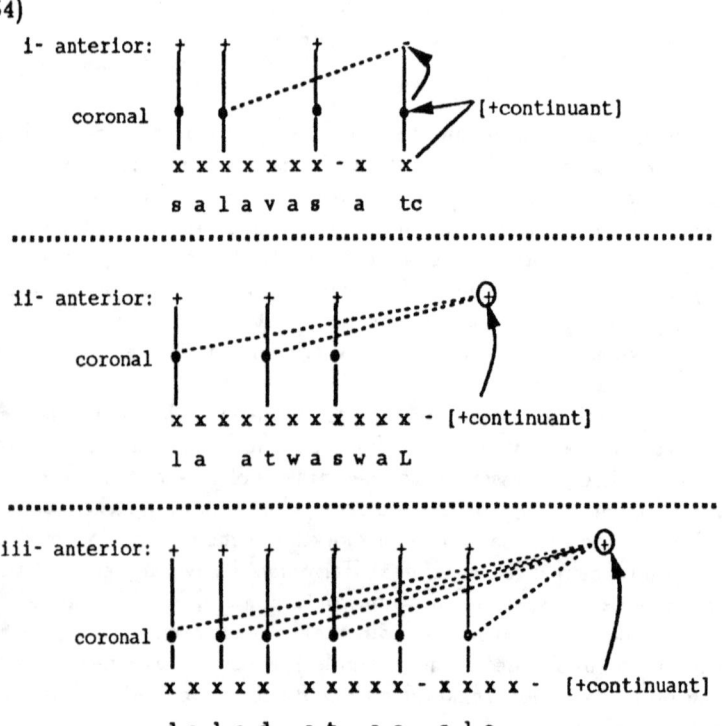

The crossing association lines will result whether we order diminutive/augmentative harmony before or after rule (49), the anterior harmony rule effecting the $s \sim c$ alternation. This is because diminutive/augmentative harmony involves both values of the feature [anterior], and therefore can be assumed to take place after the redundancy rule filling in the unmarked value for [anterior] has taken place. This means that both [−anterior] and [+anterior] will be specified on all coronals when diminutive/augmentative harmony takes place, and therefore, both /s/ and /c/ will bear a [anterior] specification.[37]

If we assume that [continuant] spreads independently of [anterior], as in (50), then many examples of harmony spreading over non-coronal [+continuant] segments can also be adduced. We will solve the crossing association lines problem illustrated in (54) as we did in Coeur d'Alene, by invoking the Morpheme Plane Hypothesis. Since the diminutive and augmentative [anterior]/[continuant] harmony in Wiyot is morphologically governed, it will operate on representations involving two morpheme planes—one for the stem, and one for the diminutive/augmentative suffix. The [αanterior] segments that intervene between the target and trigger of harmony in (53d) will not be specified on the [anterior] plane on which harmonic spreading takes place, as in (55).

55)

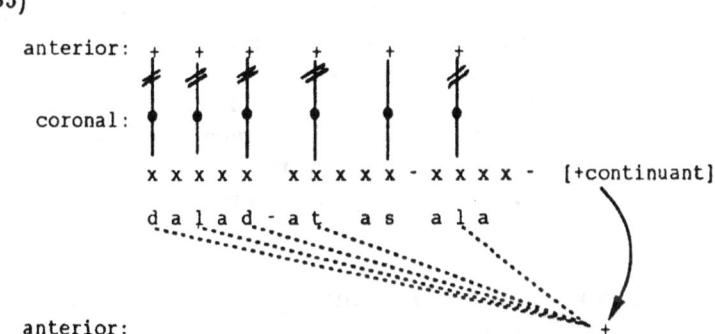

To summarize, we have seen that the complex alternations seen in words with diminutive/augmentative connotation arise due to a rule of S-Dissimilation (47) and two independent harmony processes. General Anterior Harmony (49) causes a shift from /s,l/ to /c,r/ in any word that contains a [−anterior] segment. Diminutive/Augmentative Harmony (52) spreads the feature [αanterior], and parasitically [+continuant], onto non-continuant coronals. Further, Diminutive/Augmentative Harmony was observed to have the lack of blocking effects seen in morphologically governed harmonies. The explanation for this lies in the fact that harmony operates on the multi-planar representations created by affixation, assuming the Morpheme Plane Hypothesis. As a final comment on the Wiyot system, I note that this case presents a counterexample to the revised Morpheme Plane Hypothesis argued

---

[37]See the discussion of underspecification in Section 1.4.

for in McCarthy (1989). The analysis of Wiyot presented here relies on a separate morpheme plane for the Diminutive and Augmentative morphemes, both when the allomorph consists of a single floating feature tree, and when the allomorph contains segments linked to skeletal positions. McCarthy allows morpheme planes only when the morpheme consists of segments which are not linked to prosodically licensed (skeletal) positions.

4.4 Warlpiri Labial Harmony

Warlpiri is another example of a language with a morphologically induced harmony process. Like Coeur d'Alene, Warlpiri also has a second, non-morphologically governed harmony process. These two harmonies differ with respect to the type of segments which block each process.[38] Unlike Coeur d'Alene, both harmony processes in Warlpiri involve an alternation between the same two vowels: /i/~/u/. The fact that the two harmony processes seem to involve the same feature makes it even more puzzling that there is a difference between the two in the class of segments that block harmony. The Morpheme Plane Hypothesis once more draws the appropriate formal distinctions between the two harmony processes and accounts for the differences observed.

4.4.1 Progressive Harmony

Progressive Labial Harmony operates both morpheme-internally and across morphemes. It can be analyzed as the harmonic spreading of the Labial node dominating the [-round] feature of the vowel /i/. This harmony is blocked by labial consonants and the vowel /a/.

Morpheme internally, the effects of harmony are seen in the distribution constraints on vowels. Warlpiri has three underlying vowels: /a,i,u/. What is noticeable about the distribution of vowels in roots is that the sequence /i...u/ occurs morpheme-internally only when a labial consonant or /a/ intervenes, as in the roots in (56):

56) pipipuka "bereaved father"
    miyalu   "stomach"

Across morpheme boundaries, the effects of Progressive Labial Harmony are seen in vowel alternations in all nominal suffixes, verbal

---

[38]The data in this section are from Nash (1980) and the Warlpiri-English Dictionary (Hale, et al, in prep.).

enclitics, and verbal suffixes that contain high vowels. These suffixes surface with the vowel /i/ after roots whose final vowel is /i/, and with /u/ after roots whose final vowel is /a/ or /u/, as seen in (57):

57) i- maliki-kirli-rli-lki-ji-li
       dog- Prop-Erg-then-me-they

   ii- kurdu-kurlu-rlu-lku-ju-lu
        child-

   iii- minija-kurlu-rlu-lku-ju-lu
        cat-

   iv- ya-nu-juku   *"went-still"*

   v-   wanti-mi-jiki   *"fall-still"*

   vi- wanti-ja-juku   *"fell-still"*

   viii- paji-ki   *"cut-Fut."*

   ix- paka-ku   *"strike-Fut."*

The blocking effect of /a/ is seen in (57iii,vi) above, where suffixes which follow a root containing /i/ surface with /u/ vowels when an /a/ intervenes between the /i/ and high suffixal vowels. The blocking effects of labial consonants can be seen across morpheme boundaries in the examples in (58i-iii), where a suffix with an initial labial consonant surfaces with a following non-alternating /u/, even after roots whose final vowel is /i/.

58) i-   ngamirni-puraji   *"your mother's brother"*

    ii- milpirri-puru   *"cloud-during"*

    iii- ngali-wurru   *"you and I are the ones"*

Both the constraints on vowel distribution morpheme-internally and the alternations in suffix vowels can be accounted for by the same rule of Progressive Labial Harmony. This rule will spread the [−round] value of /i/ onto a high vowel, unless a labial consonant or /a/ intervenes. The blocking behavior of the labial consonants is explained by specifying the spreading node to be the class node Labial, instead of the terminal node [round], as shown in (59):

59)

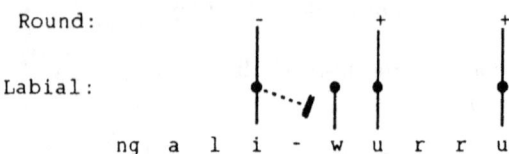

This harmony system is somewhat remarkable in having what is generally assumed to be the unmarked value for roundness—[−round]—be the only harmonically active value. We can account for this fact in one of two ways: 1) We could specify the marked underlying value of [round] to be [−round], and allow harmony to be a feature-filling rule. The vowels in the suffixes that undergo harmony would be unspecified for roundness, surfacing as [−round] as the result of harmony, or surfacing as [+round] by redundancy rule when no harmony takes place. 2) We could maintain that [+round] is the underlying value for [round]—perhaps universally—and allow harmony to be feature-changing, operating on vowels fully specified for the feature [round]. In this case, harmony would apply after the redundancy rules filling in [−round] have applied. We adopt the second solution here.[39]

If harmony is a feature-changing rule triggered by [−round] vowels, then the underlying form of the vowels in suffixes that alternate must be [+round], since that is the surface value of the vowels when no harmony takes place. A difficult question arises as to the underlying representation of root vowels if we adopt the analysis of harmony as a feature-changing rule. All vowels that surface as /u/ or /a/ will be marked [+round] or [+low], respectively, in underlying representation, since there is no other mechanism by which they could receive these values (the default values are [−round] and [−low]). Likewise, the leftmost vowel that surfaces as /i/ in a root must be underlyingly unspecified for [round], receiving the value [−round] by application of the redundancy rule, since there is no other way that this vowel could receive the feature [−round] and come to function as a trigger for harmony. The problem arises as to the underlying form of vowels

---

[39]The existence of feature-changing harmony systems has been demonstrated in Poser (1982) and McCarthy (1984).

that follow the leftmost /i/ in a root and that themselves surface as /i/. We can assume that such vowels are underlyingly unspecified for [round]. In this case, they will also receive the value [−round] by redundancy rule, thereby correctly surfacing as /i/.

Of course, any /i/ following an initial /i/ could also be underlyingly [+round]—harmony would apply in every case to remove the [+round] feature. However, since there would never be any evidence for this underlying representation, I assume that all these non-initial /i/'s are unspecified for [round].

Finally, the opacity of /a/ can be accounted for in the following way. First, we note that [round] is not distinctive outside of the set of high vowels. The low vowel in Warlpiri, as in most languages, is redundantly [-round]. Let us assume that there is a universal markedness filter that assigns a high markedness value to a language in which both the features [round] and [low] are present in the underlying representation of a segment. This filter will prohibit the co-occurence of [round] and [low] on a single segment in most languages, and can be "turned off" only at considerable expense in a grammar. More generally, it is possible to state this prohibition in terms of the labial node, as in (60). The filter in (6) is to be interpreted as a statement about the markedness of underlying segment inventories, but I argue that it also has a more direct function in the phonology in preventing any derivation in which a segment is specified both for a labial articulation ([round]) and the feature [+low].[40]

60)

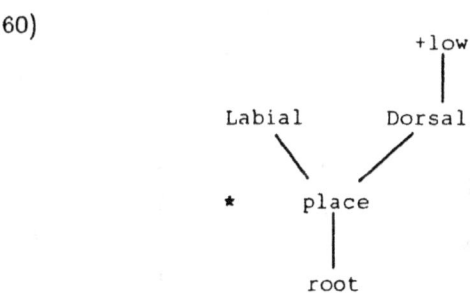

The filter in (51), acting as a constraint on derivations, would not in itself derive the opacity of /a/. It would merely prevent /a/ from undergoing harmonic assimilation of the spreading Labial node. In order for /a/ to block harmony, we need to make an additional stipulation about the mode of application of harmony. Specifically, I argue

---

[40] Similar suggestions have been made by McCarthy (1984) and Kiparsky (1981).

specifying that Progressive Labial Harmony is strictly local. By local, I mean that harmony cannot skip over any potential target which, for some independent reason, fails to undergo harmony. In this view, harmony creates a chain-like structure, in which the harmonic feature spreads iteratively from one segment to another. Whenever a link in the chain can not be completed, the entire chain breaks off.[41] A brief discussion on the use of locality conditions on harmony rules is found in Section 4.6, where I argue that since locality is a parameter which must in any case be specified on a phonological rule, invoking locality in this account of blocking phenomena does not involve adding any new machinery to the theory. The rule of Progressive Harmony is stated in (61), and a sample derivation illustrating the opacity of /a/ is seen in (62):

61) Progressive Harmony:

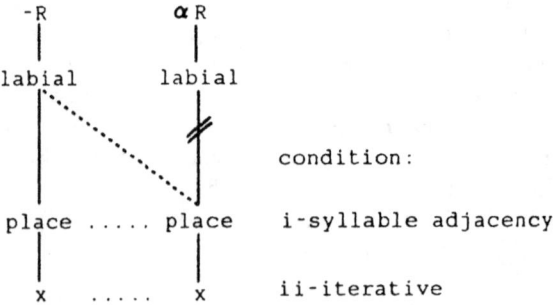

62)

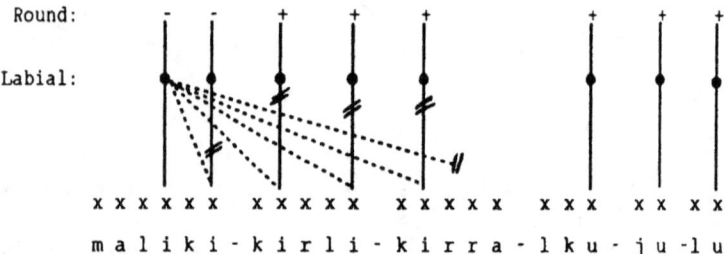

---

[41]For a similar conception of the locality of harmony processes, see Archangeli and Pulleyblank (to appear).

Morphologically Governed Harmony

This analysis is not the only means of capturing the opacity of the blocking segments. In particular, Nash (1980) suggests a different analysis of the opacity of /a/ which we should consider here. He claims that that harmony propagates across [+high] vowels by virtue of being parasitic on structures multiply linked to a unique [+high] feature. He suggests that harmony is a feature-changing rule which spreads the [−labial] node from a high vowel onto a high vowel which is linked to the same [+high] feature. Harmonic spreading applies after a merging rule has collapsed adjacent identical values for the feature [high], as in the following example:

63)

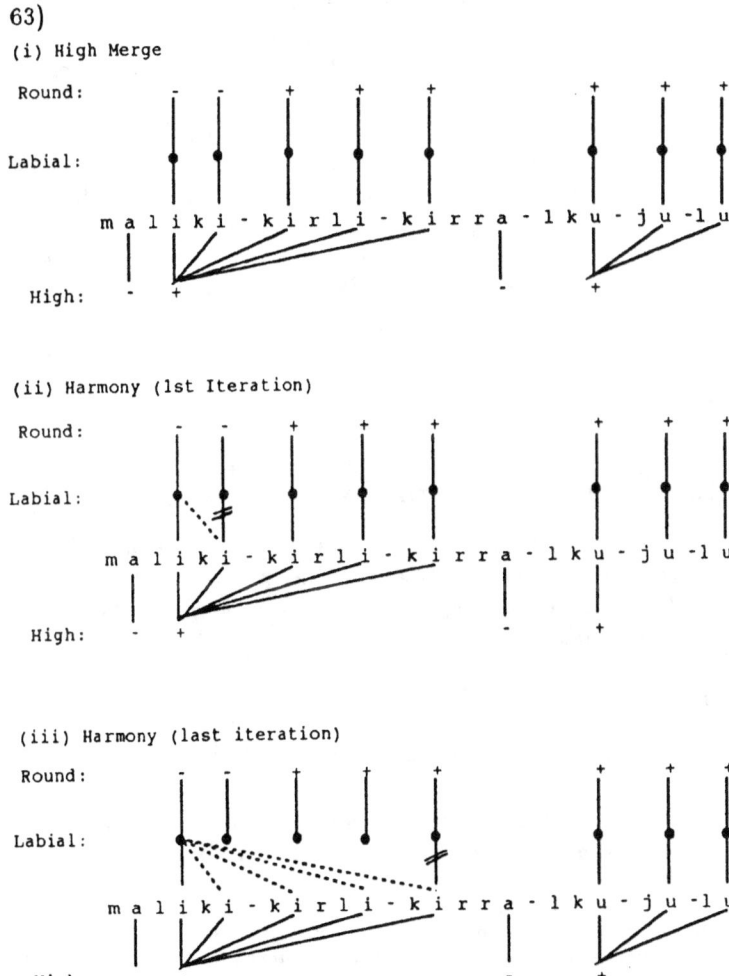

The blocking effect of /a/ results from its specification as [−high], which prohibits the merger rule from associating high vowels on either side of /a/ to the same [+high] feature.

Although the formal mechanism of Nash' analysis of parasitic harmony is well-motivated (see discussion in Chapter 2), his analysis of the opacity of /a/ does not extend to the regressive labial harmony process in Warlpiri, in which /a/ is also opaque, given the analysis of regressive harmony proposed below.[42] The two harmony systems effect inverse alternations: $i \rightarrow u$ and $u \rightarrow i$. I argue below that they involve an assimilation of opposite values of the same feature. Given this, a solution which provides the same explanation for the opacity of /a/ in the two systems is preferable to one which can not.

Finally, we note here that in order for our explanation of the blocking effects of the labial consonants to succeed, it is necessary that the rule apply at a stage in the derivation where all morphemes are represented on the same plane. This is necessary since the labial consonant that blocks Progressive Harmony may belong to a different morpheme than the triggering vowel. I know of no counter-evidence to ordering harmony very late in the derivation, after Plane Conflation, and after all morphological affixation has taken place. In fact, since the rule applies within morphemes in a feature-changing manner, it must be a non-cyclic rule, or else it would violate the Strict Cycle Condition. This fact also suggests that it is ordered late in the derivation, after all cyclic rules.

4.4.2 Regressive Harmony

In addition to Progressive Harmony, Warlpiri has a system of Regressive Harmony in which the presence of the Past suffix containing the vowel /u/ cause a preceding /i/ vowel to become /u/. Observe the following examples:

64) i) pangu-rnu   *"dig-Past"*   (cf, pangi-ka)

   ii) kuju-rnu   *"throw-Past"* (cf, kiji-ka)

The labial consonants do not block Regressive Harmony, as seen in (65i,ii), although the vowel /a/ does, as in (65iii).

---

[42] In Nash's account, the opacity of /a/ in both systems is explained by making both harmony processes parasitic on structures linked for [+high]. We argue against this solution below.

65) i) yurrpu-rnu   "insert-Past"   (cf, yirppi-rni -NPast)

   ii) kupu-rnu   "winnow-Past"   (cf, kipi-rni -NPast)

   iii) yirra-rnu   "put-Past"

Regressive Harmony is clearly morphologically governed, since not all suffixes with underlying /u/ trigger the rule. Indeed, as was seen in the last section, all the suffixes that undergo the Progressive Harmony rule are represented underlyingly with /u/ vowels, and obviously do not trigger Regressive Harmony.

Once again, we can take advantage of the multi-planar representations licensed by the Morpheme Plane Hypothesis in explaining the fact that labial consonants do not block Regressive Harmony. Regressive Harmony, like Progressive Harmony, will involve the assimilation of a Labial node, this time from the [+round] segment /u/ onto /i/. Further, Regressive Harmony will be ordered before Plane Conflation, so the harmonic Labial node will lie on the plane created by the Past suffix, which is distinct from the plane of the stem to which it attaches, as in (66). Therefore, Labial specifications of segments belonging to the stem will not interfere with harmonic spreading. Consider the following derivation of the form in (65i):

66)

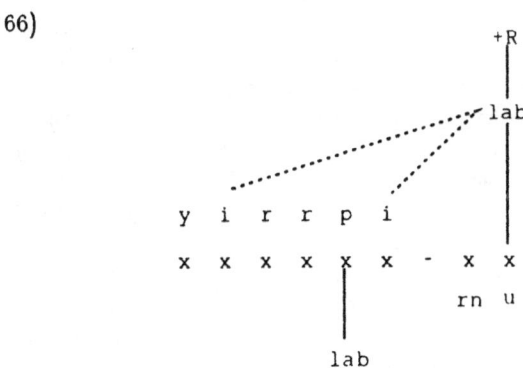

The proposed analysis of Regressive Harmony relates the transparency of the labial consonants to the fact that this harmony process is morphologically governed. It also predicts that there could not be a language of pseudo-Warlpiri which has two harmony processes identical to Warlpiri, but in which the labial consonants block the morphologically governed harmony and not the general harmony process.

Let us consider for a moment an alternative analysis of the transparency of labial segments in Regressive Harmony. A simple explanation would be to say that the assimlating feature node in this case is [+round], and not the Labial node. Since the labial consonants presumably bear no specification for roundness, they would not be expected to interfere in the operation of a rule of [+round] assimilation. Let us refer to this analysis as the Round Harmony analysis, and contrast it with the analysis of Labial Harmony proposed here.

The Round Harmony analysis seems less satisfactory on two grounds. First, it hides the relation that both harmony rules cause the same alternation between the vowels /i/ and /u/. This relation is more clearly expressed in the Labial Harmony analysis, which assigns the same assimilating feature to both rules. Second, the Round Harmony analysis does not relate the non-blocking of labial consonants in Regressive Harmony to the fact that Regressive Harmony is morphologically governed. The Round Harmony analysis could just as easily describe a system where labial consonants blocked in Regressive Harmony, but not in Progressive Harmony. The Labial Harmony analysis proposed here makes a much stronger prediction: only in the morphologically governed harmony process will labial consonants be transparent. Thus, the Labial Harmony offers an explanation for what the Round Harmony analysis must stipulate.

We turn now to the problem of the opacity of /a/ in Regressive Harmony. Since the feature specifications of /a/ will always lie on a different plane than the plane on which harmonic spreading takes place, /a/ can not block harmony by virtue of being specified [−round] at the time harmony takes place. It is also not possible to adopt Nash' solution to the opacity of /a/ discussed above. Recall that in that analysis, the opacity of /a/ is attributed to its [−high] feature. Harmony can only propogate across segments whose [+high] features have merged into one, and since the occurrence of /a/ between two [+high] segments will block such merging, /a/ will block harmony. This solution is not available to us because the [high] feature of the vowel triggering harmony will never be on the same plane as the [high] feature of the target vowel. Since we are assuming the independence of phonological planes, the two [+high] features will never be able to merge into one. A linked structure condition on harmony is stateable only if all segments are represented on the same phonological plane.

These facts motivate the explanation of the opacity of /a/ based on a locality condition on harmony, as proposed in the previous section. The vowel /a/ will be prevented from undergoing harmony due to the filter in (60), and a locality condition on the spreading rule will stop harmony from spreading past /a/.

4.5 Mixtec Nasal Harmony

Like the three languages discussed in the preceding section, Mixtec has a morphologically governed harmony process. Due to the details of the system, Mixtec does not provide direct evidence for the Morpheme Plane Hypothesis. However, it is interesting to look at because, like Warlpiri, this morphologically governed harmony process is blocked by segments occurring in a different morpheme than the harmony trigger. I will show how blocking can be accounted for in the Mixtec harmony, assuming the Morpheme Plane Hypothesis.[43]

In the preceding sections, I have presented three instances of morphologically governed harmony, where I argue that the reason segments specified for the harmonic feature do not block harmony is that they are specified on a different morpheme plane than the harmony trigger. In the case of the morphologically governed rule of Warlpiri Regressive Labial Harmony, we saw that harmony is blocked by the vowel /a/. This blocking was analyzed as the interaction of a filter prohibiting the vowel /a/ from undergoing harmony, and a locality condition preventing harmony from skipping over the non-undergoer /a/. Thus, the theory which incorporates the Morpheme Plane Hypothesis predicts that in morphologically governed harmony systems, blocking segments will not be characterized as those that are specified for the harmonic feature, but may be characterized as those segments which, for independent reasons, are not able to undergo harmony. In Mixtec, we will see that there is another way in which morphologically governed harmonies may be blocked, but which still accords the morpheme plane analysis of these systems.

Mixtec has a Nasal Harmony rule that is conditioned by the 2nd person familiar suffix. The presence of this suffix causes vowels in a stem to become nasalized. The phonological effects of this morpheme are seen only in the nasalization of stem vowels; it contains no full

---

[43] Piggot (1989) proposes a very different analysis of Mixtec which does not allow morpheme planes. His anlaysis is formulated under a very different set of assumptions about phonological representations and rules. For example, he derives surface prenasalized stops by the insertion of a floating Root node which links to a [−continuant] segment, creating a contour segment. Under the assumptions adopted here, a floating root node could never associate to anything but the immediately adjacent segment without violating the constraint on crossing association lines. A full comparison of the two approaches is beyond the scope of this discussion.

segments of its own. We will analyze this suffix as consisting only of the floating feature [+nasal], represented linearly by the symbol "N" in the examples in (67).[44]

67) i- [[kužu] N]$_{2f,subj}$ ⟶ kũžũ *'you are dilligent'*

    ii- [[kI?vi] N]$_{2f,subj}$ ⟶ kĩ?vĩ *'you will be drunk'*

Nasality is underlyingly distinctive for vowels except /o/, as indicated in the underlying vowel inventory in (68i). The absence of underlying /õ/ can be considered an accidental gap, since derived [õ] does occur. The underlying consonant inventory is given in (68ii). Note that the distinction between voiced and voiceless stop consonants is also indicated by nasality: the voiced stops always surface with prenasalization.

68) i- Vowels:

	front	central	back
high	i ĩ	I Ĩ	u ũ
mid			o
low	æ æ̃		a ã

68) ii- Consonants:

	lab.	cor.	pal.	vel.
stop	p	t		k	kw
	mb	nd		ng	ngw
affricate| c	č			
fricative|		ž		
		s	š		
	v	θ	θy		
sonorant		l r			
nasal	m	n	ny		

Of interest is the fact that Nasal Harmony is blocked by a voiceless consonant contained in the stem, as shown in (69).

---

[44]The data on Mixtec comes from an article written by Eunice Pike (1975) and from the fieldwork of Priscilla Small. All of the data presented in this section have been taken from the recent analysis of Trigo (1987), whose conclusions are largely consistent with those drawn here.

69)

   i-   [[koto-ndææ] N]$_{2f\,subj}$ ⟶ kotõ-ndǽæ̃   'you will examine'

   ii-   [[ka?ta] N]$_{2f\,subj}$ ⟶ ka?tã   'you will sing'

Voiced consonants, both the prenasalized stops and the continuants, do not block harmony. This is illustrated by the forms in (67i) and (69i), as well as the following examples:

70)   i-   [[ki-θĩĩ] N]$_{2f\,subj}$ ⟶ kĩ-θĩĩ "you will get angry"

        ii- [ku-vĩndĩ] N]$_{2f\,subj}$ ⟶ kũ-vĩndĩ "you will get warm"

Neither nasal consonants nor underlyingly nasal vowels block harmony. The transparency of nasal vowels is illustrated in (70i,ii) above. Transparent nasal consonants are seen below.

71)   [[kama] N]$_{2f\,subj}$ ⟶ kãmã   'you will hurry'
        [[kunu] N]$_{2f\,subj}$ ⟶ kũnũ   'you will run'
        [[ki-θĩĩ] N]$_{2f\,subj}$ ⟶ kĩ-θĩĩ   'you will get angry'

The transparency of the nasal consonants and vowels is predicted by the morpheme plane analysis. Nasal Harmony is triggered by the floating nasal feature of the second person familiar suffix, therefore we can argue that harmony applies at the stage in the derivation when this suffix occupies a morpheme plane which is distinct from the stem plane. The problem lies in the explanation of the blocking behavior of voiceless consonants.

I suggest an analysis of Mixtec Nasal Harmony similar to the analysis of Menomini Height Harmony in Chapter 2. Nasal Harmony can be analyzed as a parasitic harmony, spreading the feature [+nasal] onto vowels that are linked to a unique [+voice] feature. The first step is to associate the floating [+nasal] feature onto the rightmost vowel of the stem. This rule is formulated below:

72)

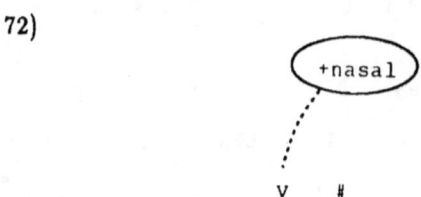

Next, we can formulate the rule of Nasal Assimilation to spread [+nasal] from a vowel adjacent to the conditioning suffix onto a preceding vowel, as long as both trigger and target are linked to the same [+voice] feature, as in (73):

73) Nasal Assimilation:

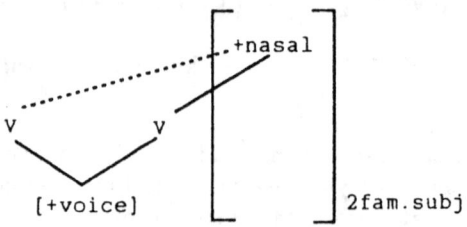

The effect of the condition on the multiply linked [+voice] feature is that any [-voice] segment that intervenes between the trigger and target will prevent the multiple linking that is required in the structural description of the rule, as in (74).

74)

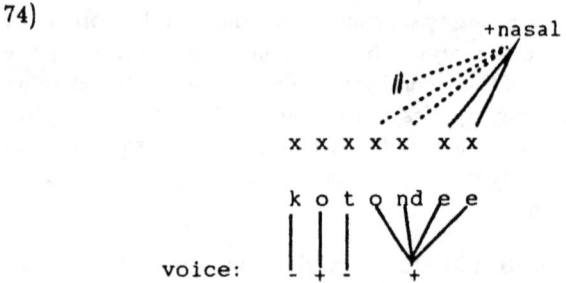

The rule of Nasal Assimilation is blocked from spreading [+nasal] onto the first stem vowel, since it is not linked to the same [+voice] feature as the final vowel that triggers the assimilation rule. An attempt to link all the vowels to the same [+voice] feature would result in the ill-formed structure in (75).

75)

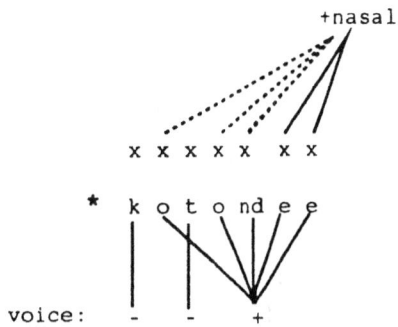

The analysis of Nasal Harmony as a parasitic harmony is possible in Mixtec because both the trigger and target of harmony can be said to bear their [voice] features on the same plane. This result is obtained by first linking the floating [+nasal] feature to the final stem vowel, and subsequently spreading this feature to other stem vowels. Recall that the parasitic harmony analysis of blocking segments was not available for the morphologically governed rule of Regressive Labial Harmony in Warlpiri. Although Labial Harmony spreads [Labial] only onto high vowels, and the non-high vowel /a/ blocks harmony, it was argued that the blocking behavior of /a/ could not be explained by making Labial Harmony parasitic on structures linked to [+high]. In the Warlpiri rule, the harmonic feature is located on a separate morpheme plane, as in Mixtec, but because the feature is linked to a segment belonging to the suffix, harmony must begin by spreading the harmonic feature from the suffixal segment to a stem segment. The trigger and initial target of harmony will not be specified on the same morpheme plane for any distinctive feature, and therefore the linked structure condition can not be formulated. I repeat below an example of the vowel /a/ blocking Warlpiri Regressive Labial Harmony.

76)

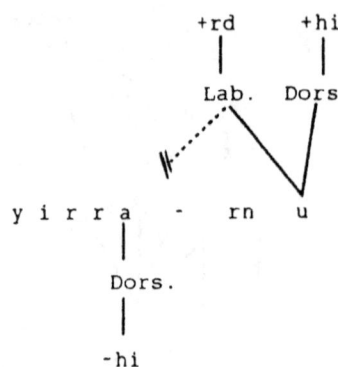

The analysis of Mixtec described above is one way of accounting for the blocking behavior of voiceless stops while maintaining the morpheme plane analysis of morphologically governed harmony. While this is not the only possible analysis of Mixtec, it does serve to illustrate that the morpheme plane analysis of harmony does not preclude an analysis of blocking in morphologically governed harmony. In fact, the Mixtec example does not in itself provide crucial evidence in support of the morpheme plane analysis. Although it is the case that nasal segments do not block nasal harmony, and this fact is explained by adopting the morpheme plane analysis, there is another possible explanation available.

To sketch the alternative analysis, we begin by assuming that the first step in Nasal Harmony is the initial linking of the [+nasal] feature to the final vowel of the stem, as described above. But, instead of saying that Nasal Assimilation is parasitic on linked [+voice] structures, it is possible to say that Nasal Assimilation is constrained by a condition on skeletal adjacency to spread the feature [+nasal] only onto adjacent skeletal positions. This means that nasality will spread from the stem-final vowel onto the immediately preceding consonant. In the case of transparent voiced stops, this is not problematic, since they will always surface as prenasalized stops anyway. Since [+nasal] must continue to spread beyond the transparent voiced continuants, as in (70) we would have to say that these segments actually bear a [+nasal] feature (it is an open question whether they surface with nasal articulation or not when they appear in between vowels nasalized by the harmony process, but the difference would surely be a subtle one at best.)

Morphologically Governed Harmony

Now consider what happens when Nasal Assimilation attempts to spread [+nasal] onto a voiceless consonant. The resulting configuration will be a segment that is specified both as [−voice] and [+nasal]. This configuration of features is non-existent in Mixtec, and in general can be said to be highly marked. We can allow a filter to prevent the association of [+nasal] to the [−voice] segments, in much the same way as a filter was used in Warlpiri to prevent [Labial] from spreading onto a segment specified as [+low]. But if [+nasal] cannot spread onto a voiceless consonant, then by the condition on skeletal adjacency, it cannot spread over the voiceless consonant onto a preceding vowel, as is illustrated in (77).

77)

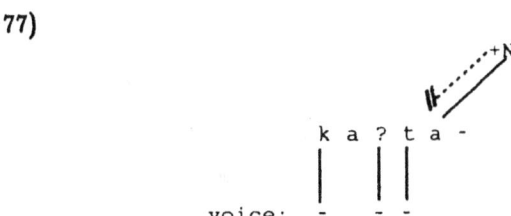

In this example, the first stem vowel cannot undergo harmony because it is not skeletally adjacent to the final stem vowel, which is the only other segment in the word onto which the [+nasal] feature could assimilate.

What about the transparent behavior of stem nasal consonants? They will present no problem if, by adopting the morpheme plane analysis, they bear their nasal specification on a separate plane than the nasal specification that triggers harmony. But, there would also be no problem in assuming, contrary to the morpheme plane analysis, that their nasal specifications were on the same plane as the triggering nasal feature. Consider the derivation of a form with a stem nasal consonant, as in (78), adopting the analysis of Nasal Harmony that imposes a condition on skeletal adjacency.

78)

The first step will be the initial linking of the floating [+nasal] onto the final stem vowel. Next, the first application of the Nasal Assimilation rule will spread [+nasal] onto the nasal consonant /m/. Since this consonant does not bear the feature [−voice], nothing prevents the vacuous application of Nasal Assimilation in this step. But now, it would be possible to allow the harmonic nasal feature to continue spreading by assuming either (i) that the underlying [+nasal] specification on the nasal consonant automatically delinks after Nasal Assimilation; or (ii) the underlying [+nasal] feature of the nasal consonant itself spreads onto the preceding vowel. These two possibilities are illustrated below:

79)

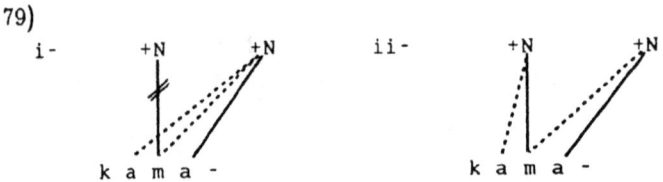

We can see that it is not necessary to assume the Morpheme Plane Hypothesis in order to account for the transparency of nasal segments in Mixtec Nasal Harmony. By invoking markedness filters and a locality condition, devices which are independently required in the theory, we can derive the transparency of these segments. However, this should not be considered a negative result for the Morpheme Plane Hypothesis. It is simply a fact of the theory that for many phonological phenomena, more than one analysis is compatible with the assumptions of the theory. What is important for the discussion of the Morpheme Plane Hypothesis in this thesis is the fact that no morphologically governed harmony system yet examined displays a pattern of blocking that resists explanation assuming morpheme planes. It remains a question for future research whether the morpheme plane analysis of Mixtec Nasal Harmony is the most appropriate analysis, or more generally, whether all morphologically governed phonological rules necessarily operate on multi-planar representations. I adopt here the strong position and claim that all morphologically governed harmonies will be analyzed as in the four examples of this chapter. As a consequence, I am able to formulate a theory of assimilation which has a strong predictive capacity, and perhaps more importantly, a theory which is clearly falsifiable

A final note on Nasal Harmony in Mixtec: the morphologically governed nasal harmony is paralleled by a nasal harmony applying within lexical roots. Whereas the nasal consonants were seen to be transparent to the morphologically governed harmony—a fact explained by the morpheme plane analysis, it is not possible to determine whether nasal consonants block morpheme-internal harmony. By the morpheme plane analysis they should, since by hypothesis they bear their nasal specification on the same morpheme plane as the harmony trigger. However, it is not clear that the necessary trigger for harmony is ever present in roots that contain a nasal consonant. Root-internal harmony is triggered by the final vowel of a root, and roots of the form CVNV always surface with the first vowel oral and the final vowel nasal. Thus, it looks as though root-internal harmony is blocked by the nasal consonant. But there is a local rule assimilating nasality from a nasal consonant onto a following vowel, therefore it is impossible to tell if a final vowel following a nasal consonant is ever underlyingly nasal. In all cases, the failure of the first vowel in CVNV roots to nasalize could be a reflex of a morpheme structure constraint that prohibits nasal vowels from surfacing after nasal consonants, an environment in which vowels will always be redundantly nasal. These facts serve to obscure any distinction which might exist in the blocking phenomena of morpheme-internal nasal harmony, and the nasal harmony triggered by the second person familiar suffix.

4.6 Locality Conditions on Phonological Rules

Adopting the Morpheme Plane analysis of Warlpiri Regressive Labial Harmony necessitated an analysis of the opacity of blocking segments in that systems which invokes a locality condition on harmony. In this section I argue that using the notion of locality in this way does not increase the power of the theory, because the device of a locality condition is otherwise a necessary part of grammar.

The formalism of the multi-dimensional model, discussed in Section 1.2, allows phonological processes to operate at a distance, as long as the two segments involved in the operation are adjacent at some level of the representation. It is a fact that some phonological processes are constrained to operate only on segments that are adjacent on the skeleton, although nothing about the features involved in the process would prohibit a long-distance application. Consider for example the rule of Coronal Assimilation in English (Clements (1985), Sagey (1986)). This rule causes a coronal to assimilate the values for [anterior] and [distributed] from a following coronal, as in the following examples (from Clements (1985)):

80)

	/t/	/d/	/n/
[+ant,−dist]	eighth	hundredth	tenth, enthuse
[−ant,+dist]	white shoes	red shoes	inch, hinge, insure, enjoy
[−ant,−dist]	tree	dream	enroll

English Coronal Assimilation is constrained to operate on segments that are skeletal adjacent, but there is no principled reason why the rule couldn't operate at a distance, across vowels which are not specified for the Coronal node.

A long distance rule involving the assimilation of the Coronal node is described in Schein and Steriade (1986). The Sanskrit rule of *ṇ-Retroflexion*, or *Ṇati*, involves the assimilation of the coronal node from retroflex continuants /r,ṛ,ṣ/ onto coronal nasals.[45] This rule operates at a distance to effect the alternations seen in (81) (from Schein and Steriade 1986). The forms in (i) show the operation of *Ṇati*, while the forms in (ii) show either blocking of assimilation, or absence of a trigger. The rule is blocked by intervening coronal segments, but as long as no such segments occur, the rule will operate at an arbitrary distance.

81) -na-   i-   iṣ-ṇa-   'seek'
     'present'   pṛ-ṇa-   'fill'

                   ii-   mṛd-na-   'be gracious'

     -na-   i-   pur-ṇa-   'fill'
     'passive   vṛk-ṇa-   'cut up'
     participle'   ii-   bhug-na-   'bend'

     -ana-   i-   pur-aṇa-   'fill'
     'middle   kṣubh-aṇa-   'quake'
     participle'   ii-   marj-ana   'wipe'
                         kṣved-ana   'hum'

Ṇati is formulated as in (82):

---

[45]The symbol ṛ represents a syllabic /r/.

82)

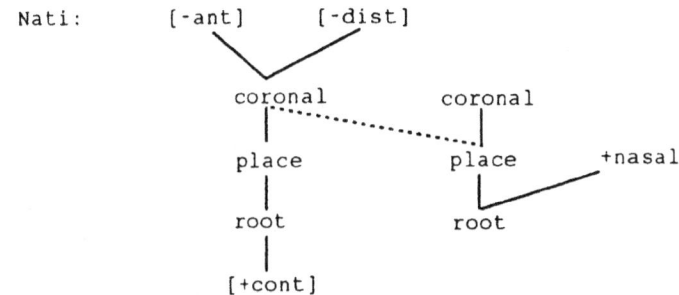

The contrast between English Coronal Assimilation and Sanskrit Ṇati indicates that the locality condition under which a rule operates must be explicitly encoded on the rule itself. English must stipulate that the two segments are skeletal adjacent, while Sanskrit will preserve adjacency only on the Coronal plane. There are many different ways to achieve this encoding. I suggest that if adjacency holds on any plane other than the plane of the assimilating feature, then the rule must explicitly state the locality condition. Thus, Sanskrit Ṇati will be the unmarked case, since adjacency is only relevant on the Coronal plane, and English Coronal Assimilation will be the marked case, requiring an adjacency condition on the skeleton.

Given this view of locality conditions, the analysis of harmony which invokes locality in the form of an adjacency condition is formally identical to the treatment of English Coronal Assimilation. Of course, adjacency need not be defined in terms of the skeletal level. I suggest that any well-defined prosodic level can serve as the level at which adjacency is defined.[46]

In the case of Warlpiri, I defined adjacency at the syllable level. Other well-defined prosodic levels would include the level of metrical structure, encoding metrical feet, and the prosodic levels defined within the syllabic representation—such as Nucleus or Rime.

The local application of harmony seen in Warlpiri and Mixtec

---

[46] Steriade (1987a) reaches a similar conclusion. See also Archangeli and Pulleyblank (to appear), where a theory is developed in which all phonological processes are constrained to apply locally. A&P assume a slightly different formalism than the one adopted here, and their definition of locality differs as a result. The main difference between the A&P theory and the theory developed here is that I allow some phonological rules to apply non-locally. Non-local rule application is used primarily to account for the existence of transparent segments in harmony systems, a phenomena which receives a different treatment in the A&P framework.

can be contrasted with other non-local harmony processes. We have seen one example of non-local harmony in Sanskrit. There is no well-defined prosodic level at which the trigger and target are adjacent (although adjacency must obtain on the harmonic plane). However, there is another interesting way in which locality can be invoked. Consider the application of harmonic spreading in systems that contain a transparent segment. We saw one instance of transparency in the discussion of Menomini Height Harmony in Section 2.2. In Menomini, the low vowel /a/ is transparent to Height Harmony. I analyzed this system by invoking a filter to prohibit the assimilation of [+high] onto /a/, and then by simply allowing harmony to spread beyond /a/, without affecting it. This is an instance of harmony that is not constrained by locality. The assimilation process targets long vowels, but since all short vowels and long /a/ are transparent to harmony, harmony must not be constrained by an adjacency condition stated at the level of syllable structure. Of course, the trigger and eventual target must still be adjacent on the [high] plane, to prevent crossing association lines, but otherwise, there need be no additional level at which an adjacency relation holds between target and trigger. Thus, harmony systems with transparent segments will always be analyzed as non-local processes, in the theory proposed here. Among these will be languages such as Mongolian (Cole and Trigo 1987), Hungarian (Steriade 1986), Finnish (Steriade 1986), and Montañes (McCarthy 1984).

This definition and use of locality addresses the question posed in Section 1.1 concerning the properties of boundedness and locality. I claim that the locality of a rule must be stipulated—it does not follow in any way from the representation—and that locality is stateable only in terms of well-defined prosodic levels of representation. What about boundedness? An unbounded rule is one which can affect more than one segment, given the right phonological input string. Again, I claim that boundedness is not a property that can be derived from the representation of a phonological rule. Harmony processes are unbounded whenever they are not constrained by locality at some prosodic level. A harmony process that is constrained by locality will be unbounded only if iterative application of the rule is allowed. This follows from the adjacency condition that encodes locality. When skeletal or syllable adjacency is required between trigger and target, harmony must be seen as an iterative, chain-like process. This is because adjacency can only be calculated between two elements, and the trigger will only be prosodically adjacent to the first target it encounters. Consider, for example, a harmony rule spreading the feature [+F] onto vowels that is constrained by locality at the level of syllablic representation. Referring to the structure in (83), the trigger, x_1 will only be syllable-adjacent to the target x_3. However, if after this initial application, we allow harmony to reapply, we can calculate syllable adjacency between x_3 and x_5 and allow x_5 to assimilate [+F]. It is in this sense that unbounded local harmony must be viewed as an iterative process. ("R" stands for *Rime*, and "O" stands for *Onset* in (83).)

83)

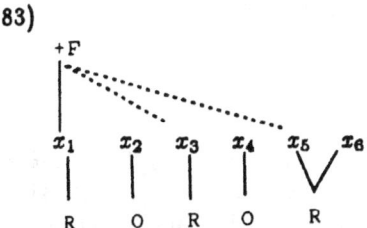

A harmony rule that is subject to locality enforced on the skeleton or at the level of syllable structure will be bounded if it is denied iterative application. This type of rule characterizes mutation and umlaut processes, which generally affect only one segment, but in which the segment need not be skeletally adjacent to the trigger. Examples are the Chamorro umlaut discussed in Section 1.1, German umlaut, and Fula Consonant Mutation (Lieber 1981).

By separating the notions of locality and iterativity, we are able to explain the properties of transparency and opacity in harmony systems, and we are able to formally equate long-distance harmony processes with bounded processes like umlaut and mutation. All of these processes involve the same phonological operation of assimilation, and differ only with respect to conditions on locality and iterativity imposed on the individual rules involved.

Chapter 5

Plane Conflation

Chapter 4 provides several examples of how the Morpheme Plane Hypothesis can explain the distinction between the types of blocking segments found in morphologically governed and non-morphologically governed harmony systems. As McCarthy (1986) shows, the Morpheme Plane Hypothesis also explains the pattern of anti-gemination effects seen in the syncope rules of several languages. Essential for both McCarthy's analysis and mine is the assumption that the multiple planes created by morphological affixation are collapsed into a single plane (or more accurately, family of planes) at some point in the derivation by a process of Plane Conflation. McCarthy, adopting a proposal made by Younes (1983), relates Plane Conflation with the Bracket Erasure Convention proposed in various models of Lexical Phonology (Pesetsky 1979, Kiparsky 1982, Mohanan 1986).

In Section 5.1, I review the empirical evidence for Plane Conflation presented in Chapter 4 of this thesis and in McCarthy (1986). These data suggest that morphologically governed rules apply before non-morphologically governed rules, and that Plane Conflation applies at the juncture of the two rule blocks. The difference between morphologically governed and non-morphologically governed rules is formalized in Lexical Phonology by assigning each to a distinct level in the morpho-phonological derivation. Section 5.2 provides a brief review of Lexical Phonology and an in-depth look at the role of the Bracket Erasure Convention in distinguishing these two levels. Section 5.3 presents data from four languages which argue against the version of Bracket Erasure adopted in Lexical Phonology. These counterexamples show that certain morphological and phonological rules must be able to refer to the internal structure of the stem to which they apply.

I argue that, at most, the Bracket Erasure Convention may apply at the juncture of the lexical and post-lexical levels (defined in Section 5.2.) The implications of these data for McCarthy's use and interpretation of Plane Conflation are discussed in Section 5.3.5. The Bracket Erasure Convention has been claimed to account for certain locality constraints on phonological and morphological rules. In Section 5.4, I propose an explanation of these constraints that does not involve Bracket Erasure, suggesting instead that limitations on the morphophonological parser highly favor grammars in which rules obey a constraint on Adjacency. Section 5.5 considers the role of Plane Conflation in tonal phonology, and discusses the special problem presented by floating tones in formulating the effects of Conflation.

5.1 Evidence for Plane Conflation

5.1.1 Plane Conflation and Harmony

In this section, we examine the role of Plane Conflation in harmony systems. In most of the harmony systems discussed in this thesis, the data is largely indeterminate as to the ordering of harmony with respect to other cyclic or non-cyclic rules in the phonology of a language. There are, however, a few general observations that can be made.

In order to explain why a segment specified for the harmonic feature [F] can block [F] Harmony in some langugages, it is necessary that both the blocking segment and the harmony trigger bear their [F] specifications on the same plane, as in (1):

1) αF βF
    |⋯⋯⋯◂ |
    x x x x   x x x

Adopting the Morpheme Plane Hypothesis, if the blocking segment belongs to a different morpheme than the trigger, the configuration in (1) will only arise if the two morpheme planes are conflated before harmony. However, it is not always straightforward to diagnose an instance of harmony blocking that is attributable to a configuration as in (1). Consider, for example, the blocking phenomenon seen in the Labial Harmonies of Warlpiri, discussed in Chapter 4. The vowel /a/ blocks the harmonic spread of the Labial node. At first glance, one might analyze this by saying that /a/ is specified for a Labial node, which dominates the feature [−round], and it is this

Labial specification which directly blocks harmony, as in (1) (with **F** = [Labial]). However, for various reasons discussed in Section 4.4, I argue for an analysis of the opacity of /a/ which invokes a markedness filter that prevents /a/ from undergoing Labial assimilation, and a locality constraint on harmony that prevents harmony from skipping over non-undergoers. Thus, /a/ does not *directly* block the assimilation of the Labial node on the Labial plane. The kind of explanation of blocking phenomena provided for Warlpiri will be available in any language where the blocking segment represents an asymmetry in the distribution of the harmonic feature in the underlying inventory. The markedness filter derives from such an asymmetry.

In other cases, the analysis of blocking phenomena will depend heavily on which value of the harmonic feature is underlying and which is supplied by redundancy rule. It may appear as though a segment specified as $[-\alpha F]$ is blocking the harmonic spread of $[\alpha F]$, when in fact it is possible to say that only $[-\alpha F]$ spreads harmonically, and $[\alpha F]$ is the redundant feature value. Consider for example the Back and Round Harmonies of Turkish. In Turkish, the root vowels normally condition the backness and roundness of suffix vowels. However, certain suffixes which contain invariant back round vowels condition back round vowels to surface in any following suffixes, even if the preceding root has front unrounded vowels (Clements & Sezer (1982)). In the following examples, the first suffix following the root shows regular harmonic alternations in its first vowel (underlyingly specified only as [+high]), while the second vowel always surfaces as /o/. Any suffix following the first one will contain only back round vowels.

2) gel-iyor-um   'I am coming'
    koš-uyor-um   'I am running'
    gül-üyor-um   'I am laughing'
    bak-Iyor-um   'I am looking'

One explanation would be to say that the [+back, +round] vowel /o/ in the first suffix blocks the harmonic spreading of [−back] and [−round] from the root as in:

3)

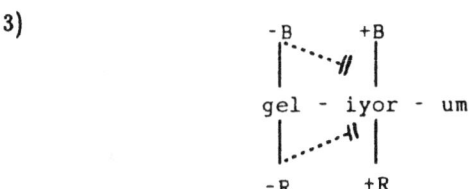

But it is equally consistent with the data to say that only the features [+back] and [+round] spread from vowel triggers, and the "−" values are supplied by redundancy rule. Under this analysis, harmony would apply when only the "+" values are present, as in

4)

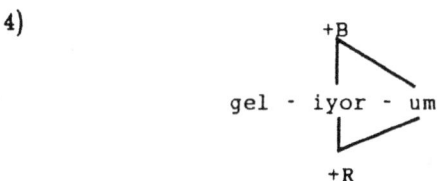

In this case, the invariant suffix vowels are not actually blocking harmony; rather, they represent a marked class of harmony triggers that occur in a suffix instead of a root.

Khalkha Mongolian Round Harmony is one system which does display blocking as in (1). In that system, the feature [+round] spreads from an initial non-high vowel onto non-high vowels, as in (5), repeated here from (4.20) (see discussion in Chapter 4, section 4.2.1). Round Harmony causes alternations between /e/∼/ö/ and /a/∼/o/. A high rounded vowel blocks harmony, as seen in (5ii).

5) i-   erctee   'twisted' (B:252)
       örg-ögd-öx   'to be raised' (S:5)
       sons-ogd-ox   to be heard (S:52)
   ii- dörbüülen   'today' (B:205)
       ogtorguidax   'situated in the sky' (B:112)

In the forms in (5ii), the blocking segment is tautomorphemic with the harmony trigger. A high round vowel will block harmony even if it is hetermorphemic with the harmony trigger, as in (6).

6)   boogd-uul-ax   'to hinder'

Thus, adopting the Morpheme Plane Hypothesis forces us to say that Khalkha Mongolian Round Harmony applies after Plane Conflation.

A second example of the type of harmony blocking illustrated in (1) is found in the ATR Harmony of Bari (Spagnolo (1933), (1960), Yokwe (1978). Every vowel in Bari has a [+ATR] form (i,e,a,o,u) and a [−ATR] form (I,E,A,O,U). A [+ATR] vowel in a root or a suffix will cause other vowels in the same word to surface as [+ATR]. In the absence of a [+ATR] vowel, all vowels in a word surface as [−ATR]. Illustrative examples appear in (7).

7) i- lo-teyok *'stupid'*
       lO-rOk *'nasty'*

    ii- kurit-an *'giraffe'*
        dAk-An *'pipes*

    iii- korop-ti *'leaf-sg.'*
        (cf, kOrOp)

    iv- gwurun-in *'wild-beast-pl.'*
        (cf, gwUrUn)

In addition, some lexically specified low vowels invariably surface as [−ATR] /A/, as is evidenced by the disharmonic roots in (8i). In contrast, other low vowels regularly alternate between /A/ and [+ATR] /a/ (see (7ii)). The invariant /A/ vowel always blocks [+ATR] harmony, whether it is tautomorphemic with the harmony trigger, as in (8ii), or heteromorphemic with the harmony trigger, as in (8iii).

8) i- dikA *'wound'*
        inwAn *'four'*
        kAdi *'house'*
        Akwak *'cobra'*

    ii- rimAt-At *'blood-pl.'*
        (cf, kurit-at *'giraffe-pl.'*)
        yayAl-An *'stupor-pl.'*
        (cf, kopu-an *'blade of hoe-pl.'*)

    iii- pUlEnA-ti *'kidney-sg.'*
        nOlAn-ti *'flour lump-sg.'*
        (cf, ex. (7iii))

The harmonic behavior of a low vowel is not predictable from the phonological or morphological environment. Cole & Trigo (1987) argue that the invariant [−ATR] /A/ vowels must be lexically marked with the feature [−ATR]. This underlying [ATR] feature will block the harmonic spread of [+ATR]—if harmony is ordered after Plane Conflation.

It is not possible to treat the blocking effects of /A/ by employing a markedness filter and a locality condition on harmony, as was done in the analysis of blocking in Warlpiri Round Harmony in Chapter 4. This is because it is not the case that low vowels are in general unable to bear the feature [+ATR]. As mentioned above, in most morphemes, a low vowel will surface as /a/ in the presence of a [+ATR] vowel in the same word. Therefore, low vowels must be included in the class of harmony targets, and must be able to assimilate the harmonic feature.

In both Mongolian and Bari, harmony is a general process which is not sensitive to morphological environment. Harmony is triggered by *any* instance of a segment with the right phonological specifications. In both cases, it is possible to order harmony very late in the derivation. Since both harmony processes apply within roots in a feature-filling manner, harmony could be said to be cyclic.[1] It is difficult to determine whether these rules apply cyclically, but there is nothing about the harmony systems that requires cyclic application.

The third example of a harmony rule directly blocked by a segment which bears the harmonic feature, as in (1), has been discussed already in Chapter 4. Warlpiri Progressive Labial Harmony spreads the Labial node from the vowel /i/ onto high vowels, causing all following /u/ vowels to surface as /i/. This harmony process is blocked by Labial consonants. I argue in Section 4.4 that Progressive Labial Harmony must be a non-cyclic rule, since it applies within roots in a feature-changing manner.

We can contrast the harmonies in Mongolian and Bari, and the Progressive Labial Harmony in Warlpiri, with the Regressive Labial Harmony in Warlpiri, also discussed in Chapter 4. This harmony process is clearly morphologically governed. The Labial node of /u/ spreads regressively from the Past suffix onto stem vowels, but other suffixes with the underlying vowel /u/ do not similarly trigger harmony. Correlating with the morphological sensitivity of the rule is the fact that it is not blocked by heteromorphemic Labial segments. Similarly, the Continuancy/Anteriority Harmony in Wiyot is also mor-

---

[1]As discussed in Kiparsky (1982c) and Harris (1983), cyclic rules are constrained to apply in a derived environment only when they are structure-changing. Structure-building rules, or all rules that fill in features or structure without changing underlying distinctions, may apply cyclically in a non-derived environment.

phologically governed, conditioned by the diminutive and augmentative suffixes, and like Warlpiri, is not blocked by heteromorphemic segments that are specified for the harmonic feature.

It is somewhat less clear whether the Glottal Harmony in Coeur d'Alene and the nasal harmony in Mixtec are morphologically governed rules. In both cases, it might be possible to say that harmony is simply conditioned by a floating glottal or nasal feature, with no particular morphological environment. However, at least in the case of Coeur d'Alene, it is necessary to assume that harmony applies before Plane Conflation, since underlyingly glottal segments do not block harmony.

We have the following facts to account for: the morphologically governed harmonies of Warlpiri and Wiyot, and the (morphologically governed?) Glottal Harmony of Coeur d'Alene must apply before Plane Conflation; whereas the clearly non-morphologically governed harmonies of Mongolian, Bari and Warlpiri must apply after Plane Conflation, and in the case of Warlpiri, non-cyclically. Section 5.2 discusses the formal distinction in Lexical Phonology between morphologically governed rules and rules which are insensitive to morphological structure. For now, it will suffice to say that the morphologically governed rules apply in a block before the non-morphologically governed rules, with Plane Conflation ordered between the two blocks.

The harmony facts do not reveal much about the cyclicity of the rules belonging to each of these blocks, therefore, it is difficult to decide on the basis of these facts alone whether Plane Conflation applies cyclically, or only once before the application of non-morphologically governed phonological rules. However, it is clear what kind of data would argue for cyclic Plane Conflation. Recall the rule of progressive Tongue Root Harmony in Coeur d'Alene (Chapter 4) which spreads the Tongue Root node from a root vowel onto a stressed suffix vowel, as in (9).

9)

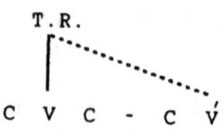

Plane Conflation

Tongue Root Harmony is blocked by a class of consonants which are also specified for Tongue Root articulation. If Tongue Root Harmony applies before Plane Conflation, then a Tongue Root consonant intervening between trigger and target will not block in the configuration in (10).

10)

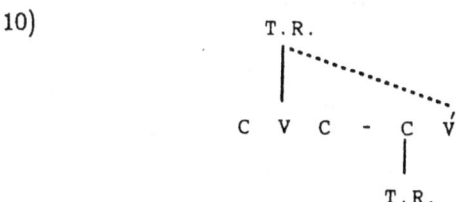

Next consider a situation where a suffix intervenes between the root and the suffix containing the stressed vowel. If this intervening suffix contains a Tongue Root consonant, then harmony will be blocked only if Plane Conflation applies cyclically, aligning the root plane with the first suffix plane, as in (11).

11)

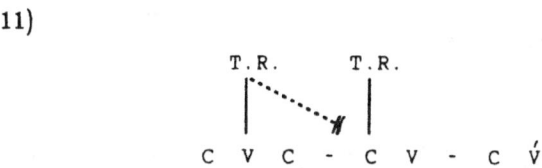

If Plane Conflation applies only after all morphological affixation has taken place then the [+F] consonant would not block harmony, as in (12).

12)

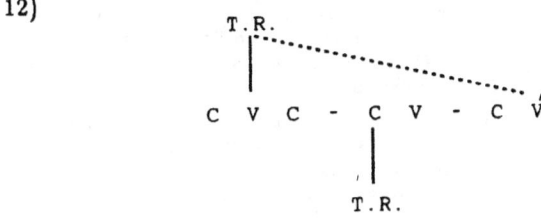

Unfortunately, the forms which would indicate if this harmony applies before Plane Conflation have not yet been found (although preliminary findings do indicate that the rule applies cyclically).[2]

5.1.2 Plane Conflation in McCarthy's Analysis

McCarthy (1986) requires Plane Conflation in the analysis of several distinct phenomena, summarized briefly here. He argues that Plane Conflation applies after syncope in Afar and Tonkawa, but before syncope in Yup'ik Eskimo, Damascene and Iraqi Arabic, and Biblical Hebrew. This argument is based on his analysis of the Obligatory Contour Principle (OCP) acting as a constraint on derivations. McCarthy formulates the OCP as a constraint which prevents the occurrence of adjacent, identical segments on a single phonological plane. If a syncope rule applies to delete a vowel from between two consonants, then the OCP will prevent syncope from applying if the two consonants are identical, and reside on the same plane, as in (13i), but the application of syncope between identical consonants on distinct planes will be allowed, as in (13ii). Note that the output of syncope applying to either structure would be identical on the surface.[3]

---

[2]See the discussion of example (36vi) in Chapter 4. This example seems to indicate that Progressive Harmony is ordered before Regressive Harmony—a rule which was argued to be cyclic on the basis that it fails to apply in non-derived environments. This may be taken as evidence that Progressive Harmony also applies cyclically, assuming a theory where, within a level of derivation, non-cyclic rules follow cyclic rules. The question of cyclicity and morpho-phonological levels is addressed in Section 5.2 on Lexical Phonology.

[3]McCarthy's analysis of these phenomena invoking a universal OCP is not without problems. There appear to be a number of languages which violate the OCP, allowing adjacent identical segments in the representation of roots, and where such sequences of segments are formally distinct from geminates. Odden (1988) presents counterevidence to a universal OCP from Turkish, Chuckchi, Hua, Cuna and Southern Paiute. If the OCP is not a universal, then it simply means that individual languages will have to stipulate the existence of this constraint.

Odden provides further criticism of McCarthy's use of the OCP in explaining anti-gemination effects. His criticisms are based on the fact that some languages permit rules of vowel deletion that create surface violations of the OCP, or rules of vowel insertion that apply only between identical consonants—an environment that should be prohibited by the OCP. None of these criticisms directly undermine McCarthy's use of the OCP in explaining syncope facts, if it is accepted that the OCP will not function as a constraint on phonological derivations in every language.

Plane Conflation

13)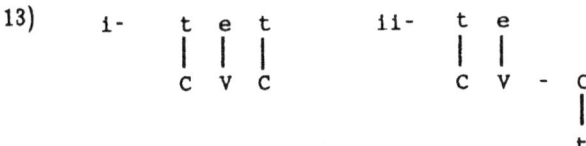

McCarthy provides further evidence for the Morpheme Plane Hypothesis and Plane Conflation, in addition to the evidence from syncope. Unfortunately, several of these examples (Hausa Palatalization, Rotuman /a/-Umlaut and Coalescence, Harga Oasis Arabic Umlaut, and Chaha Labialization) do not in fact clearly support the Morpheme Plane Hypothesis. In all of these languages, a segment occurs in the environment to undergo a phonological rule, and the effects of the rule are realized on other identical segments elsewhere in the word, even though these other segments may not be in an environment where the rule is predicted to apply.

For example, in Hausa, there is a rule which palatalizes a coronal before a front vowel (Gregersen 1967). The environment for palatalization is found in certain suffixes, e.g., the Past Participle /aCCee/, which have the interesting property that the consonant preceding the front vowel is always identical with the final root consonant. In these forms, if the final root consonant is a coronal, as in the root /mat(u)/ 'die', then a coronal will surface in the suffix consonant position, and undergo palatalization. Further, the palatalization of the suffix coronal consonant can be realized on the root coronal, which is not followed by a front vowel in the surface string, e.g, /mač-aččee/ 'dead'.

McCarthy analyzes forms like the Past Participle as involving a rule of total (root-node) assimilation which spreads the final root consonant onto the suffix consonant position, as in (14).

14)

This assimilation must take place when the root and the suffix are represented on separate morpheme planes, as in (14), since otherwise the initial vowel of the suffix would block the root node from spreading. He argues that the anomalous occurrence of palatalization on the root consonant is explained by ordering palatalization before Plane Conflation, as in (15i).

15)

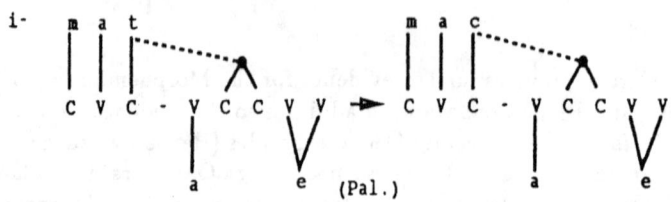

If palatalization were ordered after Plane Conflation, then the long-distance geminate consonant would be broken into two members, as in (15ii), and palatalization would occur only on the suffix consonant.

15)

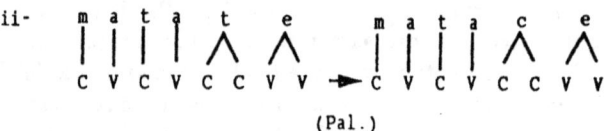

However, this example could be reanalyzed without invoking morpheme planes. We could allow Palatalization to apply only to the suffix coronal, with a regressive harmony rule spreading the palatal feature onto the preceding root coronal. (Odden (1986b) makes the same observation.) Under the harmony analysis, it is not necessary to assume anything about the ordering of Plane Conflation with respect to palatalization, and the representation need not involve more than one phonological plane.[4]

---

[4] I agree with McCarthy that suffixes like the Past Participle in Hausa are best analyzed as involving distinct morpheme planes for the root and suffix, but I do not reach this conclusion on the basis of the palatalization facts alone. Rather, I would argue that the realization of the final root consonant in the suffix consonant position *must* be achieved by *spreading* the consonant melody, which in turn requires that the initial vowel of the suffix be specified on a separate plane from the root melody. The alternative to the spreading analysis would be to say that the root consonant is copied and the copy is associated with the suffix consonant position. However, I do not believe that a copy rule can take a copy of a segment, move it across another segment into the onset of the following syllable, associating it

Plane Conflation

Apart from the difficulties mentioned above, there remain some data in McCarthy's article which do support the Morpheme Plane Hypothesis, and in view of this, we will consider the role of Plane Conflation in his analyses in this section.

McCarthy presents data from several languages which shows that syncope is blocked from deleting a vowel between two tauto-morphemic identical consonants. However, as McCarthy notes, this fact is somewhat puzzling since in some languages which exhibit this constraint, such as Tiberian Hebrew, Biblical Hebrew, and Iraqi Arabic, the tautomorphemic consonants are actually represented as a geminate consonant on the consonant melody plane, as in the example from Tiberian Hebrew in (16).

16)

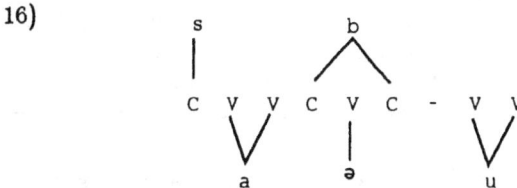

The OCP should not prevent syncope from applying to the representation in (16), deleting the schwa in the second syllable, since the resulting structure does not contain two adjacent identical consonants. The two consonants that surface as /b/ are linked to a single

---

with a skeletal position that is not adjacent to the original segment. I know of no reduplication process which requires such machinery, and I remain doubtful whether the computational resources required to perform this copy-shift operation are otherwise required anywhere else in the analysis of language (see discussion in Section 5.4).

I note also that the spreading analysis explains why CV roots like /so/ 'love' do not spread their consonant in forms like the Past Participle, as in */soyassee/ (with an epenthetic /y/). Since the vowel /o/ (which can't undergo the truncation rule that effects other root final V's) intervenes between the consonant /s/ and the empty C position of the suffix, spreading of the consonant root node can't take place:

```
 s   o
 |   |
 C   V  -  V  C  C  V  V
         a        e
```

This form surfaces as /soyayyee/ 'loved', with epenthetic /y/ in the suffix consonant position (example provided by M.Kenstowicz, and attributed to M. Kidda). Under the uni-planar reduplication analysis, the root consonant can be copied "over" the suffix vowel, and so there is no principled reason why it should not also be able to be copied over the root vowel in CV roots.

consonant melody in (16). However, the fact is that syncope fails to apply in precisely this environment, and McCarthy accounts for this by ordering syncope after Plane Conflation collapses the consonant and vowel melodies onto one plane, as in (17).

17)

The OCP will prevent syncope from applying to the representation in (17); the result of Plane Conflation is that the geminate /b/ has been split into two separate /b/ segments in order to allow the vowel melody for /ə/ to appear on the same plane without crossing association lines. Deleting the /ə/ would result in two distinct but identical consonants appearing adjacent to one another.

An added twist to the Tiberian example is that, whereas syncope is blocked from applying between adjacent identical tauto-morphemic consonants, as in (17), it is not blocked from applying between heteromorphemic consonants. For example, syncope applies to *hin-eni* to derive *hinni* 'behold me'. The problem is that if syncope applies after Plane Conflation, it should treat tautomorphemic geminates on par with heteromorphemic geminates. McCarthy argues that syncope applies before Plane Conflation has collapsed the suffix plane with the stem plane. This entails that Plane Conflation applies twice in Tiberian Hebrew: once after the morphemes comprising the stem have been combined, and once after the suffixes have been added. Syncope is ordered after the first application of Plane Conflation, but before the second. (18) illustrates the derivation of *hinni*.

18)

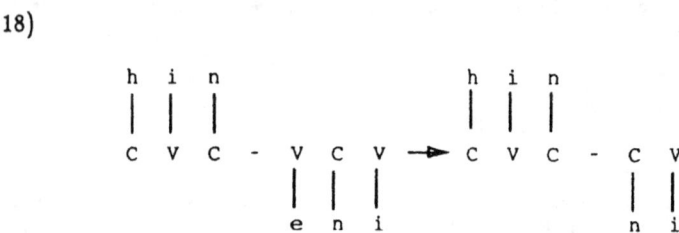

In the case of Yup'ik Eskimo and Damascene Arabic, the application of syncope is prevented between any two identical consonants, tauto-morphemic or hetero-morphemic. In order to extend the OCP explanation of syncope blockage to these cases, syncope must be ordered after Plane Conflation has aligned the stem plane with all affix planes.

For most of his examples, McCarthy does not provide arguments for the ordering of syncope with respect to other cyclic or non-cyclic rules of the language. He does, however, observe that syncope rules which apply only word-internally, and which either exhibit morphological conditioning or precede morphologically governed rules, are ordered before Plane Conflation. Such is the case with syncope in Tiberian Hebrew, Afar, and Tonkawa. On the other hand, the rule of Yup'ik syncope, which must apply after Plane Conflation, is claimed to be ordered very late in the derivation, and is clearly not morphologically governed. The distinction seems to be the same one we observed in the preceding discussion of harmony systems: morphologically governed rules precede Plane Conflation, while non-morphologically governed rules follow Plane Conflation.

McCarthy suggests that the distinction between the syncope rules that apply before and after Plane Conflation is the same as the distinction made in Lexical Phonology between lexical and post-lexical rules, and he proposes that Plane Conflation is ordered between the lexical and post-lexical levels. In Lexical Phonology, a convention on the erasure of morphological boundaries is largely responsible for the characteristic differences between lexical and post-lexical rule application. Following a proposal by Younes (1983), McCarthy proposes that Plane Conflation be equated with Bracket Erasure.

In fact, the Bracket Erasure Convention is said to account for several phenomena in addition to explaining the lexical/post-lexical distinction. Moreover, in Lexical Phonology, Bracket Erasure is said to apply at intervals within the lexical level, as well as at the juncture of the lexical and post-lexical levels. If Plane Conflation is to be equated with Bracket Erasure, then Plane Conflation should also apply within the lexical levels. This would have important consequences for any analysis of a phonological system that invokes morpheme planes. Therefore, it is worthwhile to take a close look at the arguments presented in support of the Bracket Erasure Convention. The next section examines the role of the Bracket Erasure Convention in Lexical Phonology.

5.2 Lexical Phonology and the Bracket Erasure Convention

The theory of Lexical Phonology was born out of a paper by Pesetsky (1979) on the phonology and morphology of Russian. Pesetsky's model was further developed in the work of Kiparsky (1982-1985), Mohanan (1986), Mohanan & Mohanan (1984), and Halle & Mohanan (1985), among others. Although there are significant differences in the versions of Lexical Phonology presented by these authors, I sketch here some of the more general properties of the model.

Lexical Phonology recognizes a distinction between two levels in the application of phonological rules. Phonological rules may apply in the *lexicon* to the output of rules of word-formation, and they may apply *post-lexically* (in the syntax), where words are inserted into phrases. Further, the lexical phonology may be subdivided into various ordered *strata*, which are morphologically defined subdomains of the grammar. Grouping morphological operations into ordered strata is intended to account for ordering constraints on the attachment of morphemes, and for differences in the phonological behavior of groups of morphemes. For example, Mohanan proposes that the Lexical Phonology of Malayalam contains a distinct stratum for the morphological processes of derivation, sub-compounding, co-compounding, and inflection. He argues that a different (but overlapping) set of phonological rules is associated with each of these morphological classes.[5]

Phonological rules are assigned to a set of continuous strata in the lexical and/or post-lexical domains. The diagram in (19) illustrates the interaction of morphology and phonology as defined in the Lexical Phonology model.

---

[5]But see Sproat (1985), Cole (1986), and Christdas (1986) for a criticism of this model. Sproat and Christdas, in particular, present compelling reanalyses of the Malayalam data which indicate that the distinction between sub-compounding and co-compounding is already encoded in the syntactic representations of these structures, and need not be redundantly encoded in the morphology and phonology.

19)
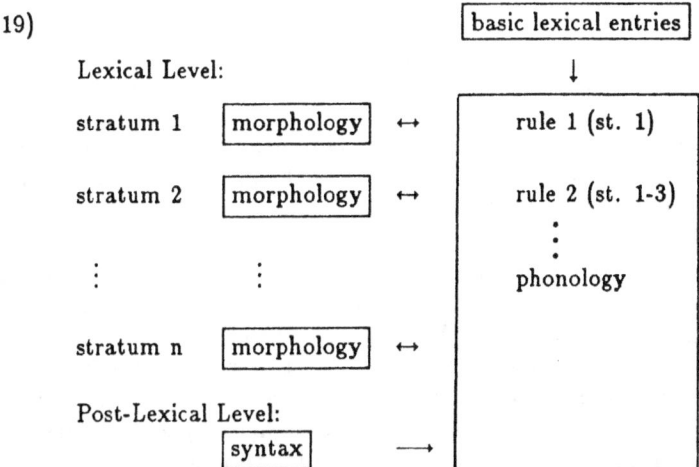

As pictured in (19), a set of lexical phonological rules apply after each morphological operation, where the stratum membership of the morphological operation determines which phonological rules are triggered.

We will be concerned here mainly with the characteristic differences between the lexical and post-lexical domains. Kiparsky (1982) and Mohanan (1982) argue that cyclic rules apply exclusively in the lexical domain.[6] These are the rules that are sensitive to morphological structure, and that frequently exhibit lexical exceptions. In contrast, non-cyclic rules that show no morphological sensitivity are assigned to the post-lexical domain.[7]

Given that there is a domain distinction between the lexical and post-lexical application of phonological rules, how does one determine to which domain a phonological rule is assigned? In Kiparsky (1982) and Mohanan (1982), all rules are assigned to the lexical domain, where they apply cyclically. Morphologically governed rules may apply only in the lexical domain, while other rules may additionally be

---
[6] As discussed in Mascaró (1976), cyclic rules are those rules which are governed by the Strict Cycle Condition. The SCC constrains the application of neutralizing rules to derived environments. A derived environment is created by the concatenation of morphemes, or by the application of a phonological rule. Rules which are not constrained by the SCC are said to be non-cyclic. Non-cyclic rules will apply both within morphemes and across morpheme boundaries, and they may be neutralizing.

[7] Halle & Mohanan (1985) argue that in English certain morphologically-governed lexical rules must be non-cyclic, since they change structure in non-derived environments. They conclude that some non-cyclic rules can apply in the lexical domain. Mohanan & Mohanan (1984) make similar arguments based on their analysis of the consonant system in Malayalam.

assigned to the post-lexical domain, where they apply non-cyclically. If we accept the findings of Kiparsky (1984), Mohanan & Mohanan (1984), and Halle & Mohanan (1985), concerning non-cyclic rule application in the lexical domain, we can not use cyclicity as the sole criterion for determining the domain assigment of a phonological rule. This means that a lexical rule will have the property of being either cyclic *or* morphologically governed.

In Lexical Phonology, the properties distinguishing lexical from post-lexical rule application are said to follow in part from the Bracket Erasure Convention (BEC). The BEC applies at the end of every lexical level to delete internal morphological boundaries. The result of this convention is that all morphological structure internal to a word is absent when the post-lexical rules apply; hence, no post-lexical rule can refer to the internal structure of a word, and all phonological rules with morphological conditions must apply at the lexical level.[8] It is instructive to consider here the origins of the BEC, and the kinds of phenomena it has been said to explain.

Bracket Erasure was first introduced in Chomsky & Halle (1968) (SPE), as part of the definition of cyclic rule application. In their formulation, a cyclic rule applies to the maximal string that does not contain any boundary symbols (brackets). When a new cycle is created, any internal brackets are erased before the application of the first cyclic phonological rule. Pesetsky observes that the BEC convention is incompatible with the Strict Cycle Condition (Mascaró 1976), which prevents cyclic rules from applying to strings which are exhaustively contained in earlier cycles. If all internal brackets are erased at the beginning of every cycle, it would be impossible to distinguish which segments are introduced in the current cycle. Pesetesky proposes to overcome this problem by ordering the BEC at the end of every cycle. I refer the reader to his paper for a complete discussion of these issues, noting only that he is able to maintain this conception of the BEC given that in his theory cyclic phonological rules apply directly after each morphological operation—in contrast to the SPE model, where phonological rules apply only after the entire word has been constructed.

---

[8]Of course, as Mohanan (1986:24) notes, morphological information expressed on the external brackets will still be visible at the post-lexical level, and therefore, it would in principle be possible for a post-lexical rule to be sensitive to such information. Mohanan would like to rule out this possibility, but recognizes that the BEC alone will not achieve this result. He notes that it is not possible to erase all morphological information, even from the external brackets, before entering the post-lexical phonology, since certain information will ultimately by required in order to do lexical insertion into syntactic structures.

As noted by Pesetsky (1979), the cyclic BEC constrains the application of cyclic rules to refer only to those morphological brackets which are created on the current cycle. It seems to be an accurate generalization that morphological boundary information only conditions phonological rules in a local way. Were it not for a constraint such as the BEC, we might expect to see a phonological rule of the sort in (20), which to my knowledge is unattested.

20) $i \longrightarrow \emptyset \quad / \quad \_\_ \ [_N \ i \ [_V$

Pesetsky argues that the BEC also accounts for the adjacency constraint on the application of morphological operations first discussed in Siegel (1974, 1978) and Allen (1978). Allen (1978) formulates the following condition:

The Adjacency Condition: No Word Formation Rule can involve X and Y, unless Y is uniquely contained in the cycle adjacent to X.

This condition is intended to explain why a morphological process attaching an affix to a stem cannot refer to properties of other morphemes deeply embedded in the stem. It is claimed that there are no word-formation rules which, for example, would derive an adjective from a noun *only* if the noun was itself derived from a verb. If the BEC destroys the morphological structure internal to the stem before the derivational affix is attached, then it follows that the affixation rule cannot be sensitive to any properties of morphemes inside the stem which are not also properties of the stem itself.

Mohanan (1982) and Kiparsky (1982) claim that the BEC as a cyclic operation is too strong. They argue that the BEC must apply only at the end of a lexical stratum. In their analyses, all brackets introduced by morphological operations at Stratum N will be visible to morphological and phonological processes assigned to Stratum N. They both cite cases where a morphological rule must make reference to the internal structure of a stem, but only the internal structure that is created by morphological rules applying at the same stratum. The cyclic BEC would not allow any internal structure to be referenced. The Adjacency Constraint allows the identity of the adjacent morpheme to be referred to, but allow this for all cases of affixation. Kiparsky and Mohanan argue that a morphological or phonological process applying at Stratum N can only make reference to properties of an adjacent morheme that is attached at Stratum N.

Mohanan's counterexamples to a cyclic BEC come from the causativization paradigm in Malayalam. He observes five different morphological processes of causativization: (i) Denasalization of root consonant, (ii) Gemination of root consonant, (iii) suffixation of /-ut̲t̲/, (iv) suffixation of /-ikk/, and (v) infixation of /-ipp-/. The first three processes are described as being less productive—they apply only to intransitive verbs, and the choice among them is lexically governed. Processes (iv) and (v) are said to be more general—applying to intransitive and transitive verbs alike. However, there are certain constraints on processes (iv) and (v). While (iv) can suffix /-ikk/ to a verb that has undergone Denasalization (i), as in (21i), it cannot apply to its own output to create double causativized verbs, as in (21ii,iii).

21) i- mayaŋŋ *'to doze'*
    mayakk *'to hypnotize'*
    mayakk-ik'k' *'to cause to hypnotize'*

   ii- paṭh-ik'k' *'to study'*
    * paṭhik'k'-ikk

   iii- d̲ukkh *'grief'*
    d̲ukkhik'k' *'to grieve'*
    * d̲ukkhik'k'ikk *'to make X grieve'*

Mohanan's explanation for this phenomena is to say that the causativization processes in (i)-(iii) belong to Stratum A, and that the processes in (iv) and (v) belong to Stratum B, ordered after A. Stratum ordering explains why processes (iv) and (v) can follow (i)-(iii), but not vice-versa. To prevent /-ikk/ from attaching to a stem already derived by /-ikk/ suffixation, Mohanan argues that /-ikk/ is prohibited from attaching to stems with branching structure ([[X]Y]). The BEC will apply after Stratum A causativization, and therefore a stem which has undergone Stratum A causativization will not have a visibly branching structure at Stratum B, and /-ikk/ is predicted to attach to such a stem, as in *mayakk-ik'k'* (21i). On the other hand, a stem which has undergone /-ikk/ suffixation will have the branching structure [[stem] ikk], which disallows subsequent application of /-ikk/ suffixation. This does not strike me as a particularly compelling argument. Mohanan provides no discussion of the other morphological processes belonging to Stratum B which might support his argument that /-ikk/ is prevented from attaching to any Stratum

B affix. In the absence of such supporting evidence, it appears that the constraint on /-ikk/ suffixation is that it cannot be recursively applied. Given the overall rarity of recursive morphology, it would seem that the statement of such a constraint is an otherwise necessary aspect of grammar, and does not in itself warrant weakening the BEC, as in Mohanan's analysis.

The second argument Mohanan provides for weakening the BEC to apply only at the end of a lexical stratum also derives from the Malayalam causativization paradigm. He observes that the causative morpheme /-ipp-/ appears only internal to the Stratum B causative suffix /-ikk/. He chooses to analyze like this as an infixation operation, presumably based on the fact that /-ipp-/ cannot appear attached to a verb stem without being followed by /-ikk/ (at least not according to the examples he cites). He argues that /-ipp-/ is infixed immediately preceding the last branch of a stem: [[dukkh] ik'k'] 'to grieve' derives [[[dukkh] ipp] ik'k'] 'to make X grieve'. /-ipp-/ cannot infix into causative stems derived by the Stratum A application of /-uṭṭ/ suffixation, a fact which is explained under Mohanan's analysis by the application of the BEC at the end of Stratum A. The BEC destroys the brackets that indicate the necessary "last branch" condition for /-ipp-/ infixation to apply: it is not possible to apply /-ipp-/ infixation to the form [[waṛ uṭṭ] 'to make X come' to derive *waṛipputṭ.

There are alternate analyses of /ipp/ causativization that do not support the stratum-final version of the BEC. One possibility would be to simply stipulate that /ipp/ infixes only before the prefix /-ikk/. This analysis does argue against the cyclic BEC, but it does not support Mohanan's stratum-final version. Alternately, one could claim that /-ippikk/ is an independent causative suffix. Sproat (1985) and Fabb (1988) make similar claims about the existence of "long suffixes" in English, to explain certain violations of the constraint that Stratum 1 suffixes are always internal to Stratum 2 suffixes—eg, /-ability/.

Kiparsky's argument for applying the BEC only at the end of every stratum is based on a constraint on the derivation of denominal verbs in English. Kiparsky notes that verbs derived by zero-affixation from nouns are limited to cases where the noun is itself an underived stem, or where the noun is derived by Stratum 1 affixation, as in (22i).[9] Zero-derived verbs cannot be formed from nouns derived by

---

[9]Stratum 1 suffixes in English are those which trigger application of the cyclic stress rules. Stratum 2 suffixes never affect the stress of the stem. See Kiparsky (1982a) for discussion.

Stratum 2 affixation, as in (22ii).

22) i- to proposition, to engineer, to commission, to reference

   ii- *to singer, *to beating, *to sisterhood, *to alcoholism
        *to nationalist, *to promptness

Kiparsky argues that verbal zero-affixation applies at Stratum II, and formalizes the constraint on this process by stating that the verbal zero affix cannot attach to branching structures. Since the BEC will have applied to the derived nouns in (9i) before they are input to Stratum II, they will not have branching structure, and hence zero-affixation is possible. In contrast, the attachment of any Stratum II suffix prior to zero-affixation will create a branching structure that prohibits zero-affixation.

Sproat (1985) has stated that the generalization on which Kiparsky's argument is based is not very robust, and possibly even false. He notes that some Stratum II suffixes do seem to allow zero-affixation to follow, as in *to sticker*. Sproat goes on to say

> ...bona fide examples involving Stratum I suffixes do not exactly abound. Note the ungrammaticality of the following: *to ungrammaticality, *to religion, *to scientist, *to evasion... If anything, it seems as if Kiparsky's constraint may in fact be applicable to affixed nouns *no matter what their derivational history:* forms like *to proposition, to engineer,* and *to sticker* will simply be exceptional, in that case. *p. 440*

Thus, it seems that Kiparsky's data concerning zero-derived denominal verbs may support the more radical position of abandoning both the cyclic and the stratum-final versins of the BEC. We will see similar arguments in the following section.

Mohanan (1986) argues that the stratum-final BEC is required within the Lexical Phonology framework to account for the fact that certain phonological rules that apply at Stratum n fail to apply to forms created at Stratum $n-1$. For example, there is a rule in English that deletes /g/ before a nasal consonant, as in the words *sign, signing, malign, maligns*. However, this rule must be blocked from applying to forms like *signature, malignant*. Since the rule applies in a non-derived environment in *sign, malign*, it must be a non-cyclic rule. But what then blocks its application in *signature, malignant*?

Mohanan argues that this problem can be solved in Lexical Phonology by stipulating that the rule of /g/-Deletion only deletes a /g/

Plane Conflation

when it precedes a morpheme boundary, as in (23). Further, /g/-Deletion is assigned to Stratum 2, while the affixation of /-ature/ and /-ant/ takes place at Stratum 1. If brackets are erased at the end of every stratum, then after affixation of /-ature/ and /-ant/, the morpheme boundaries separating these suffixes from the stems they attach to will not be visible at Stratum 2. A derivation that illustrates this process follows:

23) /g/-Deletion   g ⟶ ∅ / __ [+nasal]]

    stratum 1:   [sign] [ature]   [sign] [ing]
    affixation: [[sign] [ature]]   —
    BEC :   [signature]   —

    stratum 2:
    /g/-Deletion: n.a.   [sin] [ing]
    BEC :   —   —

    subsequent strata:
    affixation: —   [[sin] [ing]]
    BEC :   —   [sining]

    [signature]   [sining]

This is not a particularly convincing example of the need for the BEC. The rule of /g/-Deletion can be reanalyzed, without mentioning morphological brackets in the structural description of the rule, as a process which deletes a /g/ before an unsyllabified nasal, as in (24).

24) /g/-Deletion (revised)
    g ⟶ 0 / __ N'

Revised /g/-Deletion can be assigned to Stratum 2. When /-ature/ is affixed to /sign/ in Stratum 1, the root final /n/ gets resyllabified as the onset of the following syllable, as *sig.na.ture*. Thus, revised /g/-Deletion (24) will not apply to this form. On the other hand, affixation of /-ing/ in *maligning* does not occur until after Stratum 2, and therefore the /g/ in the root /malign/ will still be unsyllabified at Stratum 2, providing the right environment for /g/-Deletion.

    A thorough discussion of the BEC is found in Sproat (1985), where several more arguments for the BEC are presented and reanalyzed.

Sproat finds that in other cases, the evidence adduced in support of the BEC really only provides evidence for the Strict Cycle condition.

To summarize, we have seen some evidence which suggests that the cyclic BEC is too strong. Certain processes in English and Malayalam require identifying properties of the last morpheme that was attached to a stem. If Plane Conflation is to be equated with the BEC, these findings entail that Plane Conflation does not apply cyclically either. However, there do not appear to be strong arguments in favor of adopting the stratum-final version of the BEC, either. If the BEC does not apply stratum-finally, then it apparently does not apply at all within the lexical derivation. Again, equating Plane Conflation with the BEC entails that Plane Conflation also does not apply internal to the lexical derivation. This result is at odds with McCarthy's analysis of Tiberian Hebrew, and we return to discuss this problem below in Section 5.3.5.

Earlier, it was stated that the cyclic BEC explains certain locality constraints on morphological and phonological rules, namely that neither type of rule makes reference to morphological structure that was created on earlier cycles in the derivation of a word. If we reject the cyclic BEC we lose an explanation for these constraints. We return to the question of explaining the constraints on the accessibility of internal morphological structure in Section 5.4.

We turn now to consider data from four languages which further challenge the BEC. Consideration of these data will lead to a formulation of the locality constraint governing morphological and phonological rules.

5.3 Counterexamples to the BEC

5.3.1 English Derivational Suffixation

The BEC is called into question in the light of Fabb's (1988) analysis of morphological constraints on suffixation in English. In English, there are at least 33 productive derivational suffixes which sometimes combine with one another in word formation. It is a fact, however, that this process of suffix combination is very restricted. Fabb criticizes the treatment of suffixation constraints formulated in Lexical Phonology, and offers an alternative explanation which requires that morphological suffixation processes have access to the internal structure of a stem.

The theory of Lexical Phonology gives a stratum-ordering account of the constraints on suffix combination. Specifically, English suffixes are divided into two ordered strata; Stratum 1 suffixes can be followed by either Stratum 1 or 2 suffixes, but Stratum 2 suffixes can only be followed by Stratum 2 suffixes. The stratum-ordering hypothesis, discussed earlier in Section 5.2, is supposed to account for why Class 1 suffixes like /-ity/ do not attach productively to Class 2 suffixes like /-less/ and /-ed/. Fabb argues convincingly that the stratum ordering hypothesis alone is insufficient to account for the complete set of ordering restrictions observed in English suffixation.

Fabb notes that among 1089 mathematically possible combinations of suffixes, only between 40 and 50 actually occur. Once certain selectional restrictions on the categorial status of a stem, and phonological restrictions on the shape of a stem are taken into account, the actual number of possible combinations reduces to 456. Fabb argues that the ordering constraints imposed by the LP analysis only reduce this figure to 354 possible combinations—still a long way from the limited number of actually occurring combinations.

Fabb presents an alternative analysis of the suffix-combination constraint that reduces the 456 possible combinations to 40 or 50. He claims that

> "...a much more powerful restriction appears to be operative among English suffixes; one which does not seem to have been claimed before. This is that many of the suffixes simply do not attach to already-suffixed words."
> p.15

For example, the Stratum 2 suffix /-age/ attaches to nouns and verbs and creates a noun:

25) $[[\text{parent}]_N \text{ age}]_N$ $[[\text{drain}]_V \text{ age}]_N$
     $[[\text{mile}]_N \text{ age}]_N$ $[[\text{fall}]_V \text{ age}]_N$
     $[[\text{foot}]_N \text{ age}]_N$ $[[\text{advant}]_V \text{ age}]_N$

Were there no further restrictions on /-age/ attachment, we should expect it to attach to any noun or verb which is derived by affixation at either Stratum 1 or Stratum 2. However, it seems that /-age/ is one of the suffixes that never attaches to a derived stem. If the BEC were to apply at the end of every cycle, derived stems would be indistinguishable from non-derived stems, which would make the constraint on /-age/ suffixation impossible to formulate. Even if the BEC were to apply at the end of every stratum, we should expect to see some examples of /-age/ attaching to a derived stem. Any Stratum 1 nominalizing or verbalizing suffix should be able to be followed by /-age/, since stems derived by affixation at Stratum 1 are indistinguishable from non-derived stems at Stratum 2. The examples in (26) illustrate that /-age/ fails to attach to Stratum 1 affixes.

26) * [[[inhabit]$_V$ ant]$_N$ age]$_N$
     * [[[combat]$_V$ ant]$_N$ age]$_N$
     * [[[deni]$_V$ al]$_N$ age]$_N$
     * [[[refuse]$_V$ al]$_N$ age]$_N$
     * [[[California]$_N$ an]$_N$ age]$_N$
     * [[[magic]$_N$ ian]$_N$ age]$_N$
     * [[[compli]$_V$ ance]$_N$ age]$_N$
     * [[[reli]$_V$ ance]$_N$ age]$_N$
     * [[[substant]$_N$ iate]$_V$ age]$_N$
     * [[[anim]$_N$ ate]$_V$ age]$_N$

Fabb combines the constraint on suffix combining with other selectional restrictions to arrive at 40 predicted, and actually occurring suffix combinations. However, in order for his analysis to succeed, it must be possible to distinguish derived stems from non-derived stems, and this requirement is inconsistent with the stratum-final or cyclic version of the BEC.

5.3.2 Seri

The complex phonology of Seri, presented in Marlett (1981) provides more evidence against the BEC. Seri, a Hokan language spoken in northwestern Mexico, has a very rich prefix morphology, with several phonological rules operating exclusively in the prefix domain. The prefixes are ordered by the template shown in (27).[10]

27)   Oblique-Directional- Object- $\left\{ \begin{array}{l} \text{Subject-Mood} \\ \text{Imperative} \\ \text{Infinitive} \end{array} \right\}$ -Neg.-Root

The segment inventory of Seri is given below. A full treatment of the syllable structure of Seri is beyond the scope of this discussion, but I draw the reader's attention to the fact that Seri allows very complex syllables, with up to four consonants in both onset and coda position, three of which can be obstruents.

---

[10]Not all prefixes are indicated in (27), but only the ones relevant for the arguments of this section. All data in this section is taken from Marlett (1981).

Consonants

stops	p	t		k	kw		
fricatives	f	s	š	x		X	Xw
	W	L					
nasals	m	n					
lateral		l					
glide			y			?	

Vowels

	Front	Back
High	i i:	
Mid		o o:
Low	e e:	a a:

Note that the low vowel /e/ is phonetically [æ].

In this section we will look at one morphological process and two phonological rules in Seri which require knowledge of the internal structure of the stem in order to apply. I argue that these processes are counterexamples to the BEC applying within the lexical derivation.

Imperative allomorphy

The 2nd person imperative prefix has several allomorphs. It appears as /k − / when preceding the negative prefix /m-/ (28i) or before short low vowels (28ii), as /∅/ when it both follows the 3rd person oblique prefix and precedes a short low vowel (28iii) or in some intransitive verb forms (28iv). When the 2nd person imperative prefix immediately follows the 1st person sg. object prefix /ʔim-/ a special suppletive form /ʔpo-/ occurs which replaces both prefixes (28v). In all other environments the 2nd person imperative prefix appears as /ʔ-/ (28vi).[11]

28) i- k-m-ataX   'don't go!'
       k-m-o-tis   'don't point!'
    ii- k-ataX   'go!'
        k-emen   'winnow it!'
        ʔe-k-aškam   'come (pl.) to me!'

---

[11] The forms in (28iii) represent an intermediate stage in the derivation, before application of a rule which deletes a short low vowel before a vowel. The actual surface forms are *ko:mɨk* and *ko:taX*. The forms in (28iv) further undergo an ablaut rule which lowers the initial vowel.

iii- ko-∅-amxk   'take it to him!'
      ko-∅-ataX   'go like a donkey!'
iv-   ∅-oit   'dance!'
      ∅-o:s   'sing!'
      ∅-o-sanx   'carry on your back!'
      ∅-a:npX   'go home!'
v-   ʔpo-sanx   'carry me on your back!'
      ʔpo-o:kta   'look at me!'
      ʔpo-i:pxk   'wrestle me!'
      ʔpo-št   'tattoo me!'
vi-   ʔ-i:m   'sleep!'
      ʔ-o:kta   'look at it!'
      ʔ-a:fk   'pound it!'
      ʔ-mai   'be quiet!'

To account for the forms in (28i), the imperative rule must be able to identify the following morpheme as the negative prefix. Note that in the same phonological environment, where the /m/ does not belong to the negative morpheme, the allomorph /ʔ-/ is selected, as in the form *ʔ-mai* (28vi). This fact alone demonstrates that the cyclic version of the BEC cannot be upheld in Seri. However, advocates of Lexical Phonology might argue that the imperative prefix and the negative prefix belong to the same stratum, and so the brackets identifying these morphemes will not be erased until after the imperative prefix has been added. So this form is not provably a counterexample to the stratal version of the BEC.

The allomorph /k-/ in (28ii) can be determined given the phonological environment alone. The zero allomorph in (28iii) could be said to derive from a phonological rule which reduces the sequence *koka* to *koa*; it just so happens that this sequence of segments will not be encountered elsewhere in the prefix morphology. Were we not able to formulate a phonological environment for this allomorphy rule, then it would be another counterexample to the cyclic BEC. The rule would have to make reference to both the 3rd person oblique prefix and the 2nd person imperative. The other zero allomorph in (28iv) is not problematic, since the allomorphy rule would only need to determine that the stem to which the imperative prefix is attached is intransitive, and that the initial stem segment is a short low vowel.

The most problematic form is the special allomorph which represents both the 2nd person imperative and the 1st person sg. object prefixes. If the imperative prefix in the forms in (28v) were not preceded by the 1st person sg. object prefix, then the "elsewhere" allomorph /ʔ-/ would be chosen. We can say that /ʔ-/ is actually inserted when the imperative prefix is attached to the stem, and that it gets deleted by a rule of /ʔ-/-Deletion and replaced with the combined form /ʔpo-/ when the object prefix is attached.[12]

It does not seem that the environment for /ʔ/-Deletion can be phonologically stated. The 1st person sg. object prefix can precede other prefixes with an initial /ʔ/, such as /ʔ-/~/ʔp-/ *1sg. subject*, /ʔi-/~/ʔa-/~/ʔati-/ *1 poss.*, /ʔi-/ *nom.*. Although I was not able to locate the relevant forms, Marlett makes no mention of special allomorphy in any of these environments. Since Marlett is otherwise very thorough in describing prefix allomorphy, I will assume that the process which deletes the /ʔ-/ imperative prefix before the 1sg. object prefix is particular to this morphological sequence.

A cyclic application of the BEC would not allow the allomorphy rule for /ʔpo-/ in (28v) to be stated. The allomorphy rule needs to identify the presence of the imperative prefix, yet given a cyclic BEC, the imperative prefix would no longer be morphologically identifiable. In this case it is possible to show that stratum-final application of the BEC will also run into problems. It is possible to show that the object prefix does not belong to the same stratum as the imperative prefix by any criterion for stratum membership used in Lexical Phonology. Therefore, even by allowing the BEC to apply only at the end of a stratum, the brackets identifying the imperative prefix would not be present when the object prefix is added.

The arguments for assigning the imperative and object prefixes to distinct lexical strata is based on the phonological behavior of the object (and subject) prefixes in comparison to the other prefixes in Seri. As mentioned above, there are several phonological rules which operate in the prefix domain. Three such rules are /o/-Epenthesis, /i/-Deletion and Vowel Deletion. Each of these rules is triggered by a wide variety of prefixes, but systematically fails to apply when

---

[12] Alternately, we might assume that both prefixes are attached simultaneously, and that there is no stage at which a phonologically separate imperative prefix is present. I am adopting a framework here in which morphological operations apply sequentially, and are potentially followed by phonological rules applying after each morphological operation. Of course, in a framework where all morphology precedes the application of phonological rules (as in SPE), nothing like the BEC applying in the morphological derivation could be maintained in the first place. This is because in such a theory, the phonology would have to be able to see the boundaries between morphemes in order to determine the existence of phonological cycles. Halle (1990) and Odden (1990) both propose models in which phonology and morphology are independent components of grammar, with morphology feeding phonology.

its environment is created by attachment of the object prefixes. In (29), (30) and (31), I briefly illustrate the application of each of these rules. The last two examples under each rule show that the object prefix does not trigger the rule.

29) *o-Epenthesis:* ∅ ⟶ o / C__ mC
(*before an unsyllabified /m/*)

    i- mi-msisi:n   UR: Mood-Root
       m-msisi:n   (i-Deletion (30))
       momsisi:n   (o-Epenthesis)
       '*he is pitiable*'

    ii- k-m-tis   UR: Imp-Neg-Root
        komtis   (o-Epenthesis)
        '*don't point at it*'

    iii- ʔim-mi-kašni   Obj-Mood-Root
        ʔim-m-kašni   (i-Deletion (30))
        ʔimimkašni   (i-Epenthesis)
        '*it bit me*' (cf, * ʔimomkasni)

    iv- ʔim-m-tkm-a:-patxk-is UR: Obj-Subj-Aug-Root-is
        ʔimtkma:patxkis   (Degemination)
        '*OK, untie me!*' (cf, * ʔimomtkma:patxkis)

30) *i-Deletion:* i ⟶ ∅ / C__C

    i- si-meke   UR: Mood-Root
       smeke   (i-Deletion)
       '*lukewarm*'-*irrealis*

       (cf., ʔ-si-amXo UR: Subj-Mood-Root
         ʔ-si-amXo   (I-Deletion n.a.)
         ʔ-si:-mXo   (Short Low Vowel Deletion)
         '*shall I say?*'

    ii- k-i-tis   UR: Nom-OM-Root
        ktis   (i-Deletion)
        '*he who points at it*'

    iii- maši-k-noptotkaʔa UR: Obj-Nom-Root
        '*we are hitting you*' (cf, * mašknoptotkaʔa)

    iv- ʔiši-po-šaXw   UR: Obj-Mood-Root
        '*he told us*' (cf, * ʔišpošaXw)

31) *Vowel Deletion*: V ⟶ ∅ /__V

    i- po-i:m   UR: Mood-root
        pi:m   (Vowel Deletion)
       'sleep'-irrealis

    ii- ?-si-i-kapot UR: Subj-Mood-Verbalizer-Root
       ?-si-i-kapot (i-Deletion n.a.)
       i?sikapot   (Vowel Deletion)
       'I have-jacket'

    iii- ma-i?a-st   UR: Obj-Inf-Root
       'to tattoo you' (cf, *mi?ast)

    iv- ma-i?a-tis   UR: Obj-Inf-Root
       'to point at you' (cf, *mi?atis)

Within the Lexical Phonology framework, the failure of the object prefixes to trigger the phonological rules described above can be explained by assigning these prefixes to a lexical stratum where the rules in question do not apply. The imperative prefix triggers /o/-Epenthesis (29ii), and so must belong to a stratum in which /o/-Epenthesis applies (the imperative prefix does not create the environment necessary for the other two rules to apply). If the imperative prefix is assigned to a different stratum than the object prefix, then the brackets identifying the imperative prefix will be deleted by stratum-final application of the BEC, before the object prefix is attached. Since it is necessary to identify the imperative prefix for the rule of /?po-/ allomorphy, we must conclude that the BEC neither applies at the end of every lexical stratum, nor at the end of every cycle.[13]

---

[13] One might argue that the stratal BEC could be maintained if we allowed both the object and imperative prefixes to be assigned to the same stratum, and merely encoded the exceptionality of the object prefixes directly in the statement of all the relevant phonological rules. This analysis misses the generalization that the object prefixes *uniformly* fail to trigger the phonological rules that otherwise apply almost exceptionlessly throughout the prefix phonology. Also, it weakens the theory of Lexical Phonology if stratum membership cannot be determined on the basis of the phonological behavior of a morpheme in all cases. The only other way that stratum membership can be determined is by constraints on the relative ordering of morphemes. By either evaluation method, the object and imperative prefixes should belong to distinct strata in a Lexical Phonology analysis of Seri. See Cole (1987) for a slightly different analysis of this phenomenon, which adopts the version of Lexical Phonology formulated in Halle & Vergnaud (1986).

/k/-Epenthesis

The second argument against the BEC from Seri relates to the rule of /k/-Epenthesis. This rule has the odd characteristic of inserting a /k/ between a coronal consonant /t,s/ and a /m/ belonging to a prefix, if the coronal is not word initial. Its effect is to create an alternation in three mood suffixes: /t-/~/tk-/ *realis*, /tm-/~/tkm-/ *abilitative*, and /si-/~/sk-/ *irrealis*.[14] The application of /k/-Epenthesis is illustrated in (32i) (the inserted /k/ is underlined). (32ii) shows that /k/-Epenthesis fails to apply if the coronal consonant is word-initial. (32iii) shows that /k/-Epenthesis fails to apply if the /m/ is root-initial.

32) i- ma-tm-akatX?o   UR: Obj-Mood-Root
        matk̲makatX?o
        '*it didn't leave you*'

    ?-t-m-amšo?o   UR: Subj-Mood-Neg-Root
    i?tk̲mamšo?o
    '*I don't want*'

    ?a-tm-o-ko:šX   UR: Subj-Mood-Detran-Root
    ?atk̲moko:šX
    '*Let's rob*'

    ?p-si-m-apXtim-Xo   UR: Subj-Mood-Neg-Root-Emph
    ?p-s-m-apXtim-Xo   (i-Deletion)
    i?psk̲mapXtimXo   (k-Epenthesis)
    '*I'm not going to pack!*'

    ii- t-m-afp   UR: Mood-Neg-Root
        '*he didn't arrive*' (cf, *tk̲mafp)

    tm-a:?-Xap   UR: Mood-Pass-Root
    '*it can be dug up*' (cf, *tk̲ma:?Xap)

    si-meke   UR: Mood-Root
    s-meke   (i-Deletion)
    '*if it were lukewarm*' (cf, *sk̲meke)

---

[14]The enviroment for /k/-Epenthesis, a coronal-m sequence, is only created by one prefix combination that does not involve one of these mood prefixes. The directional prefix /nt − /, when followed by the negative prefix /m-/, does not trigger /k/-Epenthesis. There are several ways this could be accounted for. One solution would be to view /k/-Epenthesis as an allomorphy rule which applies only to the mood prefixes listed above. Alternately, a Lexical Phonology analysis of these facts might assign the directional prefix to a separate stratum than the one which contains the mood prefixes.

iii- i-t-mis   UR: Obj-Mood-Root
     'it resembles it' (cf, *itkmis)

     ?p-si-masoL   UR: Subj-Mood-Root
     ?psmasoL   (i-Deletion)
     'should I be yellow?' (cf, *?pskmasoL)

The failure of /k/-Epenthesis to apply if the coronal is word-initial cannot be said to follow from general constraints on syllable structure in Seri. Words like *t-kma:mat* 'is it a female?' illustrate that the sequence *coronal-k-m* is otherwise a well-formed onset in the language. It must therefore be part of the structural description of the rule that the coronal consonant *not* be word-initial. Thus, there are two conditions on epenthesizing a /k/ in a *coronal-m* sequence: (i) a morpheme must precede the mood prefix that contains the coronal consonant, and (ii) the /m/ must be part of a prefix.

The problem for the BEC is that in order for condition (ii) to be met, the brackets identifying the root must be still be present when /k/-Epenthesis applies. If the BEC were to apply cyclically, then the root brackets would always have been deleted by the time the morpheme is added which precedes the coronal consonant, fulfilling condition (ii). Moreover, even assuming stratum-final application of the BEC, the root brackets will in many cases have been erased before /k/-epenthesis applies, since in many cases the morpheme preceding the mood prefix belongs to a different stratum than the mood prefix. I show this next.

Notice in (32i) that /k/-Epenthesis can apply after the subject and object prefixes are added; these prefixes precede the mood prefix and fulfill condition (i). In the preceding discussion of imperative allomorphy, I argued that the object prefix belongs to a different stratum than the other prefixes. The object prefix fails to trigger three phonological rules that are regularly triggered by other prefixes, as illustrated by the forms in (29iii,iv) (30iii,iv) and (31iii,iv). Contrast with those examples the following forms, which show that the mood prefixes regularly trigger the rules of /o/-Epenthesis (33), /i/-Deletion (34), and Vowel Deletion (35).

33)   /o/-Epenthesis:
        t-m-panšX   UR: Mood-Neg-Root
        tompanšX
        'didn't he run?'

ko-m-si-m-xi:it   UR: Obl-Subj-Mood-Neg-Root
ko-m-s-m-xi:it   (i-Deletion)
ko-m-sk̲-m-xi:it (k-Epenthesis)
komsko̲mxi:it   (o-Epenthesis)
'your moving to it'

i-t-m-pi   UR: Obj-Mood-Neg-Root
i-tk-m-pi   (k-Epenthesis)
itko̲mpi   (o-Epenthesis)
'didn't he taste it?'

34) /i/-Deletion:
mi-ʔe:mt   UR: Mood-Root
mʔe:mt
'it stank'

si-m-i:x   UR: Mood-Root
smi:x
'won't there be?'

si-šatX-Xo UR: Mood-Root-Emph
sšatXXo
'will get thorns'

35) Vowel Deletion:
mi-o:m   UR: Mood-Root
mo:m
'he lies'

si-a:-tikpan-is UR: Mood-Aug-Root-is
sa:tikpanis
'he'll work'

ko-si-itoix   UR: Obl-Mood-Root
kwsitoix
'will (pl.) leave?'

/k/-Epenthesis applies after the subject prefix is attached, and like the object prefix, the subject prefix also fails to trigger /o/-Epenthesis, as shown in (36). (The surface forms in (36) are derived by application of the phrase-level rule of /i/-Epenthesis.)

36) ?p-mi-?ak   UR: Subj-Mood-Root
    ?p-m-?ak   (i-Deletion)
    i?pim?ak   (i-Epenthesis)
    'I am blind' (cf, * i?pom?ak)

    m-mi-?ak   UR: Subj-Mood-Root
    m-m-?ak   (i-Deletion)
    mim?ak   (i-Epenthesis)
    'You are blind' (cf, * mom?ak)

(It is not possible to determine if the subject prefix triggers /i/-Deletion or Vowel Deletion, since the environments in which these rules apply are never created by attaching the subject prefix.)

The subject and object prefixes fail to trigger the phonological rules that are triggered by the mood prefixes, and therefore, in a Lexical Phonology analysis they would be assigned to a separate stratum—we'll call it Stratum 2. Stratum 1 will contain the mood prefixes, together with all of the other prefixes that precede the subject and object prefixes—all of which have similar phonological behavior. The rules of /o/-Epenthesis, /i/-Deletion, and Vowel Deletion will be assigned to Stratum 1, but not to Stratum 2. The rule of /k/-Epenthesis will be assigned at least to Stratum 2. If the BEC were to apply at the end of every stratum, then at the end of Stratum 1 the brackets identifying the root morpheme would be erased, and any application of /k/-Epenthesis in Stratum 2 would not be able to distinguish a /m/ in a prefix from a root-initial /m/. This means that /k/-Epenthesis applying at Stratum 2 would incorrectly insert a /k/ before a root initial /m/ in forms like * ?pskmasoL, from underlying ?p-si-masoL (cf, (32iii)). I conclude that the BEC can neither apply at the end of every cycle, nor at the end of every stratum in Seri.

Agreement as Infixation

In the preceding two sections, I presented data which showed that the object and subject prefixes fail to trigger phonological rules that the other prefixes trigger. One possible analysis of these facts is to say that the object and subject prefixes are not part of the lexical morphology/phonology in Seri, but that they are inserted into words from argument positions in the syntax. Motivation for this analysis comes from the fact that the overt subject and object pronouns in argument positions cannot normally co-occur with the word-internal subject and object prefixes. This analysis does nothing to save the

BEC—it will remain problematic that the phonological rule of /k/-Epenthesis and the allomorphy rule for the imperative prefix, which are triggered by the subject and object prefixes, require knowledge of the internal structure of the stem. Certainly all internal brackets will have been erased at the end of the lexical morphology/phonology, before the subject and object prefixes are inserted.

To complicate matters further, there are three different positions in the morpheme template where the subject prefix can appear. A special subject prefix indicating 1st person restrictive subject follows the negative prefix, a prefix indicating an unspecified subject follows the mood prefix, and the rest of the subject prefixes appear preceding the mood prefix, as illustrated in (37).

37) Subj. - Mood - Unspec.Subj. - Neg. - 1st Restric. Subj. — ... — Root

Only one of these three subject positions may be filled. If we adopt the analysis that the subject (and object) prefixes are inserted into the word in the syntax, then it is clear that the internal structure of the stem must still be visible, since the environment into which the subject prefix is inserted is morphologically defined, dependent on which subject prefix is inserted.

5.3.3 Ci-Ruri

The Bantu language Ci-Ruri provides another counterexample to the BEC. The relevant data concerns the unusual tonal phonology associated with the Present Continuous verb tense. This aspect of Ci-Ruri phonology has been analyzed by Massamba (1984) and Goldsmith (1982, 1984, 1986).

Goldsmith (1986) attributes the following structure to the Present Continuous verb forms:[15]

38) Subject Tense Object Radical Extensions Final-Vowel
$$\underbrace{\qquad\qquad\qquad\qquad\qquad}_{stem}$$

The Radical, all Extensions, and the Final Vowel together comprise the *stem*.

---

[15]The template in (38) actually reflects a slightly marked order. When the subject prefix is a Class 1 (3rd person sg. human) subject, it appears word-initially and with no lexical H-tone, as in (38). However, all other subject prefixes appear in second position, following the tense prefix, and they always bear a lexical H-tone. Since the tonal properties of the Present Continuous tense are a little easier to observe when the subject prefix is not tone-bearing, all the examples in this section have the Class 1 subject and the morpheme order in (38).

Roots fall into two classes: those which bear a lexical H-tone, and those which are lexically toneless. The latter class surfaces with a default L-tone (unless they acquire a H-tone by application of a phonological rule). The lexically specified H-tone always surfaces on the first vowel of the root.[16]

The Present Continuous tense is marked in three ways: (i) by the presence of a tense prefix, (ii) by a H-tone inserted on the final vowel of underlyingly toneless stems, and (iii) by the application of a special tone spreading rule which spreads a H-tone on the final vowel to the initial vowel of a stem which contains more than three syllables.[17] The following examples illustrate these features.[18] The examples below are schematic, and are to be read as follows: /ka/ is the subject prefix, /a/ is the tense prefix, and V...V represents the stem, where each V stands for an entire syllable, and the last V always represents the Final Vowel (see (38)).[19]

---

[16] There are many more details to the tonal system that I am suppressing here for ease of exposition. For instance, there is a phrase-level rule which shifts all tones one syllable to the right, except the tone on a penultimate syllable. All of the examples shown in this section represent the placement of tones before this tone-shifting rule. Other simplifications will be footnoted at appropriate places in the text that follows.

[17] This spreading rule affects the H-tone inserted by the rule in (ii), but it also spreads a H-tone which can appear on the final syllable of a H-tone stem by the Two Prestem High Rule (Goldsmith 1986). Two Prestem High applies in *all* tenses, and inserts a H-tone on the final syllable of a stem just in case the stem is preceded by two subject/object prefixes which bear H-tones. Whether a final H-tone derives from (ii) or from the Two Prestem High Rule, the spreading of the H-tone from the final syllable to the initial syllable of stem is unique to the Present Continuous tense.

[18] In the appendix to this section, I provide the full paradigm for the Present Continuous tense, adopted from Goldsmith (1986).

[19] In the second example in (39ii), I have suppressed a complexity in the paradigm: the H-tone inserted on toneless stems by the Present Continuous tense prefix surfaces on the final vowel, *except* on trisyllabic stems. Trisyllabic toneless stems surface with the inserted tone on the penultimate syllable. Thus, the second form in (39ii) should actually read *ka-a-VV́V*.

39) i- H-tone stems: tense prefix, no inserted tone
ka a V́ V
ka a V́ V V

ii- Toneless stems: tense prefix, inserted tone
ka a V V́
ka a V V V́

iii- Toneless stems: tense prefix, inserted tone, tone spread
ka a V́ V V V́
ka a V́ V V V V́

The forms in (39i) and (39ii) show the contrast between H-tone and toneless stems: only the toneless stems surface with an extra H-tone, due to the presence of the tense prefix. The forms in (39iii) illustrate how the H-tone placed on the final syllable of the stem by the tense prefix is spread (or copied) onto the initial stem syllable. I stress here that the occurrence of an extra H-tone on the final and initial syllables of toneless stems is a special property of the Present Continuous tense, and is not observed in any other morphological form.

The problem for the BEC is apparent at this point. The rule which inserts a H-tone on the final syllable of a toneless stem is morphologically governed by the Present Continuous tense prefix. In order for this rule to apply, it must determine if the stem has a lexical H-tone. But in order to make this determination, the rule must be able to identify the boundaries of the stem. It would not be correct to say that the rule inserts a H-tone on a word that bears no H-tone, since the H-tone insertion rule applies to all toneless stems, even if they are preceded by object prefixes, which bear a lexical H-tone, as in (40) (the object prefix is marked as OB.).

40) Toneless stems:
ka a ÓB V V́
ka a ÓB V V V́
ka a ÓB V́ V V V́
ka a ÓB V́ V V V V́

If the BEC were to destroy the stem boundary before the tense prefix was added, then the H-tone insertion rule would not be able to distinguish a toneless stem that is preceded by a H-tone object prefix, as in (40), from a H-tone stem. Both types of stems would contain some H-tone on a non-final vowel. Since the H-tone insertion rule needs to be sensitive to whether or not a non-final H-tone is linked to the stem, it is essential that the stem boundary be present when the tense prefix is attached.

The BEC is also problematic for the rule which spreads a H-tone from a final syllable onto the initial stem syllable. This spreading rule is governed by the tense prefix, yet it must be able to see the boundaries of the stem to determine which syllable is stem-initial. Note that the spreading rule applies to stems of more than three syllables, and is insensitive to the presence of the extra syllables contributed by the (optional) object prefixes which may occur between the tense prefix and the stem.

These facts clearly rule out the possibility that the BEC applies cyclically. What about the stratum-final version of the BEC? It is not yet clear to me how many lexical strata are present in Ci-Ruri, nor where stratal divisions should be made. But if there are any stratal divisions at all, they would probably assign the tense prefix to the outer stratum. I make this conjecture on the basis of two facts. First, the tense prefix occurs as the outermost prefix in all cases except where the Class 1 subject prefix exceptionally occupies the outer position. Therefore, if stratum-ordering accounts at all for the linear order of morphemes, then the tense prefix will belong to a stratum which is ordered after prefixes which are closer to the stem. Second, there is phonological rule—the Two Prestem High Rule, (described in footnote 17 above)—which is triggered by the object and subject prefixes, but not by any tense prefix. The distinction between the tense prefixes and the subject and object prefixes with respect to this rule can be achieved by assigning the subject and object prefixes to Stratum 1, which will be the domain of the Two Prestem High rule, and assigning the tense prefix to Stratum 2. But this division of strata entails that all brackets identifying the stem, subject and object prefixes will be destroyed by the time the tense prefix attaches, at Stratum 2. Thus the H-tone insertion rule triggered by the Present Continuous tense prefix would not be able to distinguish H-tone stems from toneless stems. These facts then lead us to reject both the cyclic and stratum-final application of the BEC in Ci-Ruri.

Appendix to Ci-Ruri

Following is a complete schematic paradigm of the tonal phonology associated with the Present Continuous Tense (from Goldsmith 1986). The first table illustrates forms with a Class 1 subject, in which the tense prefix follows the toneless subject marker. Table 2 illustrates forms with a non-Class 1 subject, in which the tense prefix precedes the H-tone subject marker. Note that the tense prefix is /a-/ in Table 1, and /e-/ in Table 2 (reflecting the application of a back assimilation rule). OM=Object marker, ní=Subject Marker.[20]

CLASS 1 SUBJECT		
No Object Marker	1 Object Marker	2 Object Markers
High Tone Stem:		
ka a V́ V	ka a ÓM V V	——
ka a V́ V V	ka a ÓM V V V	ka a ÓM OM V V V́
ka a V́ V V V	ka a ÓM V V V V	ka a ÓM OM V V V V́
ka a V́ V V V V	ka a ÓM V V V V V	ka a ÓM OM V V V V V́
Low Tone Stem:		
ka a V V̇	ka a ÓM V V̇	——
ka a V V̇ V	ka a ÓM V V̇ V	ka a ÓM OM V V V̇
ka a V̇ V V V̇	ka a ÓM V̇ V V V̇	ka a ÓM OM V V V V̇
ka a V̇ V V V V̇	ka a ÓM V̇ V V V V̇	ka a ÓM OM V V V V V̇

Table 1

NON-CLASS 1 SUBJECT		
No Object Marker	1 Object Marker	2 Object Markers
High Tone Stem:		
e ní V V	e ní OM V V́	——
e ní V V V	e ní OM V́ V V́	e ní OM OM V́ V V́
e ní V V V V	e ní OM V́ V V V́	e ní OM OM V́ V V V́
e ní V V V V V	e ní OM V́ V V V V́	e ní OM OM V́ V V V V́
Low Tone Stem:		
e ní V V̇	e ní OM V V̇	——
e ní V V̇ V	e ní OM V V̇ V	e ní OM OM V V̇ V
e ní V̇ V V V̇	e ní OM V̇ V V V̇	e ní OM OM V̇ V V V̇
e ní V̇ V V V V̇	e ní OM V̇ V V V V̇	e ní OM OM V̇ V V V V̇

Table 2

---

[20]I have corrected what I believe to be a typo in Goldsmith's data. He gives the following forms for L-tone stems with a Class 1 subject and no Object Marker: *ka a V V́ V V̇* and *ka a V V́ V V V̇*. The H-tone on the second stem vowel does not accord with any of the tone rules he discusses, which predict instead a H-tone on the initial stem vowel.

5.3.4 Sekani

Hargus (1985) provides several counterexamples to the stratum-final version of the BEC in her dissertation on Sekani, an Athabaskan language.[21] She states,

> In Sekani, a number of rules which apply on level 3 or later are sensitive to the distinction between stems [the output of level 1 (JC)] and affixes, thus presenting a problem for this version of the Bracketing Erasure Convention. The contexts of the Sekani rules crucially refer to an earlier, non-adjacent level.

For example, Hargus presents the rule of Perambulative Reduction, formulated as in (41).

41) k'èna ⟶ k'an / __ (C) [(clf) stem]

This rule has the effect of collapsing the perambulative prefix /k'è-/ and the customary prefix /na-/ into the form /k'an-/ when they either directly precede the verb stem (verb plus optional classifier) or when a single consonant intervenes between them and the verb stem. Perambulative Reduction is exemplified in (42).

42) k'è-na-d-beh   UR: Per.-Cust.-Class.-Stem
     k'an-d-beh   (Perambulative Reduction)
     k'ąbeh   (other rules)
     he/she swims around

     k'è-na-s-d-beh   UR: Per.-Cust.-Subj.-Class.-Stem
     k'an-s-d-beh   (Perambulative Reduction)
     k'ąsbeh   (other rules)
     I swim around

Perambulative Reduction is blocked from applying if any prefix other than a single mono-consonantal prefix precedes the verb stem. In such cases, the customary prefix /na-/ deletes, as seen in the following examples:

---

[21] The relevance of the Sekani data for the Bracket Erasure Convention has also been noted by Sproat (1985).

43) k'è-na-ts'ə-d-beh   UR: Per.-Cust.-Subj.-Class.-Stem
    —   (Perambulative Reduction n.a.)
    k'èts'əbeh   (/na-/-Deletion, other rules)
    'we swim around'

    k'è-whè-nə-l-s-d-dah
    UR: Per.-Cust.-Incp.   -Der.-Der.-Subj.-Class.-Stem
    —   (Perambulative Reduction n.a.)
    k'èwhènèsdah   (/na-/-Deletion, other rules)
    'I start to walk around'

Hargus argues that both the perambulative and the customary prefix belong to Stratum 4, which means that Perambulative Reduction must apply at stratum 4. However, at Stratum 4, the brackets identifying the verb stem (output of Stratum 1) would have been erased by Stratum-final Bracket Erasure. Hargus' solution to this problem is to stipulate that Stratum 1 brackets are invisible to Bracket Erasure. She argues that other rules of Sekani are similar to Perambulative Reduction in needing to identify the verb stem boundary at later levels. Of course, allowing certain morpheme boundaries to be exceptions to Bracket Erasure weakens the entire theory. Unless there were some way to predict what kinds of brackets could be exceptions to Bracket Erasure in any language, the BEC loses its capacity to constrain grammars in any interesting way. It would seem that the Sekani data seriously challenges the idea that the BEC applies at all within the lexical phonology.

5.3.5 Discussion

The data presented in the preceding four sections suggests rather strongly that the BEC cannot be maintained as either a cyclic or stratum-final operation that destroys morphological boundaries during the lexical level of derivation. It is still possible, however, to allow the BEC to apply once after all morphological operations have taken place, and before the application of the phrase-level (post-lexical) phonological rules. Ordering the BEC at this juncture will provide the explanation for why only lexical rules can access (a limited amount of) internal morphological structure. Recall from the discussion earlier in this chapter that for the morpheme-plane analyses of syncope and harmony systems to succeed, it is necessary to collapse morpheme planes at the end of the lexical phonology. We can tentatively conclude that Plane Conflation is the formal mechanism that effects

Bracket Erasure, and that this process is ordered at the end of the lexical phonology.

The only facts which are inconsistent with this conclusion are the facts concerning Tiberian Hebrew. McCarthy claims that Plane Conflation takes place twice in the course of derivation in this case: once after the "non-concatenative" stem morphology, and once again after the "concatenative" affixing morphology.[22] It is interesting to note that even assuming McCarthy's analyses, Plane Conflation cannot apply at this juncture in all Semitic languages. In the same article, he provides an analysis of Arabic Metathesis in which it is essential that the consonant and vowel melodies of the stem are still on separate planes when the affixing morphemes are added. In the Arabic example, the affixing morphemes are a derivational prefix and infix, and an inflectional suffix. Therefore, if McCarthy's analysis of the Tiberian Hebrew facts is justified, it would seem to be necessary to allow Plane Conflation/Bracket Erasure to be ordered within the lexical derivation as a special property of some languages. Alternately, we could maintain a distinction between Plane Conflation and the BEC, by constraining the BEC to apply only at the end of the lexical phonology as a non-parametric property of Universal Grammar, while allowing Plane Conflation to apply after every cycle, or after every lexical stratum. The choice between these alternative theories will remain open here.

Recall from the discussion in Section 5.2 that the cyclic BEC was offered as an explanation for why morphological and phonological rules do not make reference to morphological structure created on earlier cycles. We have seen evidence that the cyclic BEC is too strong a constraint, but it is significant that none of the counterexamples to the BEC involve calculating relations between elements that are ar-

---

[22]McCarthy suggests a typological distinction between these two kinds of morphology. However, under the "autosegmental" analysis of non-concatenative morphology that he introduces in McCarthy (1981), this distinction is not so clear. The special property of the non-concatenative stem morphology is that the morphemes involved either contribute strictly melodic structure, or strictly syllabic (C/V) structure, where the melodies are linked to the C/V positions by general rules of association. On the other hand, the concatenative morphology contributes melodies and syllabic structures that are pre-associated. If Semitic languages can make a typological distinction between these two types of morphemes, then we should expect to find similar distinctions being made in any language which employs morphemes that consist only of floating features, or extra skeletal positions (as in reduplicative morphology). It is not evident that other languages exploit these distinctions; thus, it remains an open question whether it is possible to make a formal distinction between 'partially-specified' and 'fully-specified' morphemes, assigning each type of morpheme to distinct lexical strata.

bitrarily distant in the morpho-phonological representation.[23] Thus, there is reason to believe that some type of locality constraint governs the accessibility of morphological structure in morphological and phonological rules. I offer a formulation of this constraint in the next section that allows the rules presented in the previous section to be formulated, while in general constraining rules from making reference to all aspects of the internal morphological structure of a word.

5.4 Adjacency in Phonology and Morphology

If the internal structure of a word is visible throughout the lexical derivation, then why don't we see languages exploiting this depth of structure in phonological and morphological rules? We should expect to see phonological rules like

$$e \rightarrow a \ / \ \_\_[_N \ a \ldots [_V$$

or rules of allomorphy like

$$\text{Imperative} \rightarrow /\text{ka} - / \ / \ \_\_[\text{ Subj. } [\text{ Neg.}$$

In fact, even among the counterexamples to the BEC discussed above, no such rules are found. The example from English suffixation constraints requires that a suffix be able to identify the adjacent morpheme; in certain cases suffixation is prohibited if the adjacent morpheme is a suffix. There were two examples from Seri: an allomorphy rule and a phonological rule, which can be formulated as

1sg.Object allomorphy: $/\text{?im-}/_{1sg.Obj.} \rightarrow /\text{?po}/ \ / \ \_\_ \ [\text{ Imp.}$

Imperative allomorphy: $/\text{?-}/_{Imp.} \rightarrow \emptyset \ / \ [\text{ 1sg.Obj. } [\_\_$

K-Epenthesis: $\emptyset \rightarrow k \ / \ X \ [\text{coronal}] \ \_\_ \ m$

        condition: (i) /m/ not in root
                    (ii) coronal not word-initial

---

[23]The Ci-Ruri example involves a dependency between two morphemes that are separated by an arbitrary number of syllables and morphemes, but since both of these morphemes are at the periphery of a morphological constituent, this example does conform to a locality constraint on morphological and phonological rules that is discussed in the next section.

In Ci-Ruri we saw a dependency between the tense prefix and the stem, which are at opposite ends of the word at the stage when the tense prefix is added. Finally, the rule of Perambulative Reduction in Sekani, like the English example, required being able to identify whether the adjacent morpheme was an affix, or a bare stem. None of these cases involve calculating the identity of more than one morpheme internal to the stem, and none of them except Ci-Ruri involve calculating the location of a morpheme that is not adjacent to the trigger of the rule.

5.4.1 Adjacency in Morpho-phonological Parsing

Given the absence of rules which make access to deeply embedded morphological structure, it would appear as though some sort of locality constraint limits the accessibility of morphological structure. But we do not yet have an explanation for why such a constraint should exist or what it derives from. Considering the problem from the perspective of morpho-phonological processing sheds some light on this question. Phonological and morphological rules are utilized in two distinct linguistic functions—word-generation, and word-processing (or *parsing*). Word-generation consists of building a word from the inside out, by applying morphological and phonological rules first to the root and subsequently to every morpheme added to the root, ultimately deriving a surface string from the underlying representations. The analysis performed by linguists usually adopts this perspective. On the other hand, word-processing involves looking at a surface string of segments and figuring out (i) the underlying string of segments, and (ii) the underlying morphological structure. These two tasks are often mutually dependent; if a phonological rule is morphologically-governed, then it will be necessary to determine the morphological environment before the underlying form of a surface segment can be calculated. On the other hand, it is often necessary to "undo" phonological rules and identify the underlying segments before the identity of a morpheme can be determined. While the details of how the human parser performs these functions are unknown to us, it is clear that morphological and phonological parsing go hand-in-hand. I make this point here to stress the complexity of the word-parsing task.

Barton (1987) discusses the computational complexity of morpho-phonological parsing in the KIMMO model (see Koskenniemi (1983) and Kartunnen (1983)). He focuses on the problem of long-distance phonological dependencies of the sort found in harmony systems. Harmony systems present a great challenge to parsing systems, because for a given segment x_i, the surface representation of x_i may be dependent on the presence of a segment x_j that is arbitrarily far away, if x_j is a trigger of a harmony rule that targets x_i. If the parser operates only on a linear representation of surface segments, as does the KIMMO parser, then the parser must perform a series of back-and-forth searches, going from target to trigger and back to target, to calculate the underlying representation of segments in harmony systems. Parsing harmony systems using models like KIMMO is computationally very hard, as Barton shows, and the amount of time required to parse a word can increase exponentially with the length of a word. The arguments presented by Barton show that the approach to parsing adopted in the KIMMO model is inadequate to account for the fact that humans can observably parse languages with harmony rules as efficiently as languages without harmony.

The computational problem of parsing in KIMMO can be overcome if we allow parsing to operate on the multi-dimensional phonological representations adopted in this thesis. The crux of the problem for KIMMO parsing is that the trigger for a phonological rule may be arbitrarily far from the target of the rule, if distance is calculated on the skeleton. However, as discussed in Chapters 1 and 2, the analysis of harmony in multi-dimensional phonology assumes that the trigger and target of harmony must always be *adjacent* on the plane of the harmony feature. If all calculations about the underlying representation of a segment can be made on the basis of features and segments that are adjacent at some level of representation, then parsing becomes computationally much simpler.[24] By guaranteeing that all relations calculated by the parser will be between adjacent elements, where adjacency is defined relative to a particular plane in the phonological representation, it is possible to put a much stricter upper limit on the amount of time (relative to word length) required to parse a word in any human language. This is a significant advance towards explaining how humans perform the complex task of parsing with what amounts to amazing rapidity.

5.4.2 The Adjacency Constraint

The KIMMO parsing problem nicely illustrates the interaction between processing constraints and grammatical constraints. From a

---

[24]This is not to say that it is a trivial task to build a parser that operates on multi-dimensional representations—on the contrary, it is a challenging problem that has not received a great deal of attention in the literature on computational linguistics.

computational perspective, it is highly advantageous to constrain phonological relations such that they may obtain only between elements which are adjacent in the phonological representation. Time-efficiency is sacrificed whenever the parser has to go back and forth across an arbitrary number of elements to calculate a relationship between two elements.

In light of this, it should be clear now why we do not observe phonological and morphological rules which make reference to embedded morphological structure, as in the hypothetical examples given at the beginning of this section. Those examples involved making reference to a morpheme boundary which was not adjacent to the morpheme or phonological segment being targeted by the rule. Consider again the hypothetical rule

$$e \rightarrow a \: / \: \_\_ \: [_N \: a \ldots [_V$$

Imagine the task of a parser analyzing a word in a language which incorporates this rule. Whenever the parser sees a surface character /a/, it must determine whether this rule has applied, in which case it will posit an underlying representation with /e/. In order to make this determination, the parser must scan forward, checking first to see if the adjacent segment is the vowel /a/, which is the initial segment of a N-stem. This calculation may not be simple, but since it involves only the segment adjacent to the target of the rule, it can be calculated fairly efficiently. But before the parser can decide if the rule has applied, it must also check to see if somewhere in the word there is a morpheme with the labelled bracket $]_V$. The parser has to scan forward from the target of the phonological rule, searching an arbitrary number of phonological segments and morpheme boundaries for the conditioning V-boundary. Note that many computations may have to be performed during this search, and any individual computation may involve additional back-and-forth searches of its own. In the best case, the parser will succeed in finding the V-boundary and go back to the target of the rule and identify its underlying form. But making this final determination may involve many back-and-forth searches, and will potentially become more complex the farther the V-boundary is from the target. In short, allowing a phonological or morphological rule to access any morpheme boundary contained in the stem allows for severe violations of adjacency.

Now consider the counterexamples to the BEC discussed above. With the exception of the Ci-Ruri example, none of them involve calculating relationships between elements that are not adjacent at some level of representation. Leaving aside the Ci-Ruri example for

the moment, we can formulate a condition on strict adjacency that
applies to morphological and phonological processes alike.

(44) *Adjacency Constraint* (preliminary): In order to state
a dependency between two elements X and Y in a phonological or morphological operation, X and Y must be adjacent at some level in the phonological or morphological
representation of the word.

Consider the following representation:

$$\ldots x_1 \; x_2 \;]_\alpha \; [_\beta \; x_3 \; x_4 \ldots$$

where $x_1 - x_4$ are elements on some phonological plane (ie., a skeletal
position, a class node (eg., labial, dorsal), or a distinctive feature),
and $]_\alpha \; [_\beta$ are morpheme boundaries, which are projected at all levels of
phonological representation. Then the following adjacency relations
hold: x_n is adjacent to x_{n-1} and x_{n+1}; x_2 and x_3 are both adjacent
to $]_\alpha$ and $[_\beta$.

The Adjacency Constraint has the following effects: (i) No phonological rule can target a segment unless the segment conditioning the
rule is adjacent to the target, relative to a prosodic level or some
feature plane. (ii) No morphological affixation rule can be sensitive
to the presence of a morpheme in the stem unless the morpheme is
adjacent to the morpheme being attached. (iii) No phonological rule
can be governed by a morpheme unless that morpheme is adjacent to
either the target or trigger of the phonological rule.

The effect in (i) is needed to rule out any phonological process
which might involve non-adjacent segments.[25] For instance, based on
empirical observation, we want to exclude the possibility of formulating a rule which copies a segment onto a skeletal position arbitrarily
far away, or a rule of dissimilation in which the trigger and target are
not adjacent on the plane of the dissimilating feature. And of course,
the Adjacency Constraint accounts for the "no crossing lines" constraint on assimilation processes (see discussion of harmony processes
in Chapter 1).

---

[25] Archangeli & Pulleyblank (to appear) discuss the need to constrain phonological processes to operate only locally, and develop a theory where adjacency
must hold between any two items involved in a phonological rule. Their theory adopts a slightly different phonological representation than the one adopted
here (see Section 1.3), and they define adjacency in slightly different terms. But
generally speaking, their Locality Condition (A&P p.80) has the same effect for
phonological rules as the Adjacency Constraint proposed here.

The effect in (ii) is essentially that described by Allen (1978), and in fact the (preliminary) Adjacency Constraint in (44) is just a generalized version of her Adjacency Constraint.

The effect in (iii) is required to explain why morphologically governed rules always operate locally, as observed by Lieber (1981). Extensive discussion of the locality of morphologically governed rules was presented in Chapter 3, where I argued on empirical grounds that it is necessary to prohibit a morpheme boundary from being the context for a phonological rule unless it is adjacent to either the trigger or target of the rule (where adjacency can be calculated on the skeleton or in terms of syllable structure). The observation is that there are no phonological rules which, for example, lengthen all vowels in a word in the presence of a certain morpheme, or which perform across-the-board deletion or epenthesis just in case a particular morpheme is being attached to the stem. Rules which operate in an across-the-board fashion are characterized by the fact that they are insensitive to morphological structure. The Adjacency Constraint can be considered the formal mechanism by which we can rule out the treatment of morphologically governed harmony as conditioned by a rule of the sort in (45), repeated from Chapter 3.

45) (=ex.3.4) $C_{input} \longrightarrow C_{output}\ /\ [\ldots \underline{\quad} \ldots]_{diminutive}$

How do we accomodate the Ci-Ruri example, where the rules inserting and spreading a H-tone are morphologically governed by the tense prefix, but the tense prefix is in no way adjacent to the target of the rule? Consider the morphological structure of the Ci-Ruri verb at the stage where the tense prefix is being added.

46)
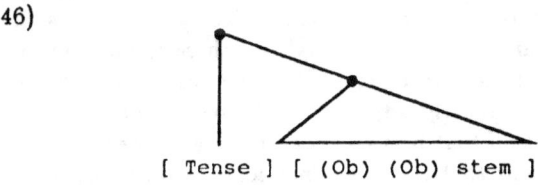
[Tense] [(Ob) (Ob) stem]

We adopt the hierarchical representation in (46) to reflect the order in which the affixes are added to the root (see also Williams (1981) for a discussion of headship and percolation in the morphological constituent structures of words). It is significant that while the stem is not adjacent to the tense prefix, it is also not embedded in the middle of the word. It appears at the periphery. Further, in the morphological structure in (46), the tense prefix c-commands the constituent that contains the stem. Evidently what is needed is a relaxation of the Adjacency Constraint such that only a morpheme which is at the periphery of a consituent is accessible to a morphological rule attaching an affix to that constituent. We can employ the Adjacency Constraint in (47) by redefining the notion of *adjacency* in the following way:

(47) **Adjacency**: In a morphological or phonological representation, X is **adjacent** to Y iff (i) X is a phonological feature or segment, and X is adjacent to Y on some level in the phonological representation; or (ii) X is a morpheme, and X is m-adjacent to Y.

(48) **M-Adjacency**: A morpheme X is m-adjacent to a morphological or phonological element Y iff X m-commands Y.

(49) **M-command**: a morpheme X **m-commands** a morpheme or phonological segment Y only if Y is at the periphery of a constituent ϕ, and X c-commands ϕ.

In the following structure

$$[\ X\ ]\ [\ Y_i \ldots Y_j\ ]_\phi$$

the morpheme X is **m-adjacent** to Y_i and to Y_j, but only linearly adjacent to Y_i. Therefore, X can condition a phonological or morphological rule that targets Y_i or Y_j.

How does the definition of Adjacency, and in particular M-adjacency, accord with the constraints on morpho-phonological parsing discussed above? Referring again to the structure above, there is no problem in allowing X to be adjacent to Y_i, since the parser can always relate two elements that are linearly adjacent. But how do we reconcile the m-adjacency relation that licenses a dependency between X and Y_j with the requirement that the parser not conduct back-and-forth searches on a string? Evidently, what is at stake here is the ability of the parser to identify peripheral segments without needing to search the entire string in a linear sequential manner. If we make the additional assumption that the parser can identify the initial and final elements of the string that it is analyzing, then the inclusion of the m-adjacency relation into the Adjacency Constraint should not pose any problems. This assumption obviously entails that parsing does not necessarily apply 'on-line' in a linearly sequential manner, as is commonly assumed. While it is beyond the scope of this discussion to develop and defend a particular model of morpho-phonological parsing, I note here that I am aware of no empirical evidence that supports the assumption that morpho-phonological parsing operates entirely left-to-right sequentially. It seems entirely plausible to assume that at least some stage of parsing applies only after the entire word has been input, in which case initial and final elements will always be identifiable.

All of the rules examined in Section 5.3, which are counterexamples to the BEC, conform to the revised Adjacency Constraint. The English derivational suffixation rules involve identifying the (linearly) adjacent morpheme. The two allomorphy rules of Seri involve dependencies between (linearly) adjacent morphemes. The Seri rule of /k/-Epenthesis is not morphologically governed, but requires only that properties of phonological elements that are string adjacent be identified. The Ci-Ruri rule involves a dependency between a prefix and the stem, where the prefix is m-adjacent to the stem. In Chapter 6 we will see two more examples of phonological rules which are morphologically governed, and in which the triggering morpheme is m-adjacent, but not linearly adjacent, to the target of the rule.

What are the kinds of rule that the revised Adjacency Constraint excudes? Both of the hypothetical rules given at the beginning of this section would be excluded. Let's consider them once more here. The phonological rule

$$e \rightarrow a \: / \: \_\_[_N \: a \ldots [_V$$

is excluded because it states a dependency between the target /e/ and the morpheme boundary $[_V$, but these two elements are not adjacent. The morpheme V is clearly not linearly adjacent to /e/; V does not m-command /e/, so it cannot be m-adjacent to /e/ either. Therefore, the rule violates the Adjacency Constraint. The Adjacency Constraint is also violated in the hypothetical allomorphy rule

$$\text{Imperative} \rightarrow /\text{ka} - / \: / \: \_\_[\: \text{Subj.} \: [\: \text{Neg.}$$

since the Imperative morpheme is not linearly adjacent or m-adjacent to the conditioning Negative morpheme.

5.4.3 The Adjacency Constraint and Plane Conflation in Ci-Ruri

The observant reader may have noticed a rather significant hitch in the analysis of Ci-Ruri offered earlier. Recall that there are two rules

conditioned by the tense prefix which need to identify the boundaries
of the stem. I argued that the dependency between the tense prefix
and the stem is well-formed, since the tense prefix is m-adjacent to
the stem, satisfying the (revised) Adjacency Constraint. However, as
noted in Section 5.3.3, the stem is not actually a single morpheme;
rather, it is composed of a root, several optional extensions, and an
obligatory Final Vowel, as in (50).

50) Root - (Extension)* - Final Vowel

Of the two phonological rules governed by the tense prefix, one targets the initial syllable of the root, while the other targets the Final
Vowel, but must refer to the tonal properties of the initial syllable of
the root. The problem is that the tense prefix will not be adjacent
to the root, given the definition of (m-)adjacency provided above. I
repeat here the morphological structure that is created by prefixation
of the tense morpheme.

51)
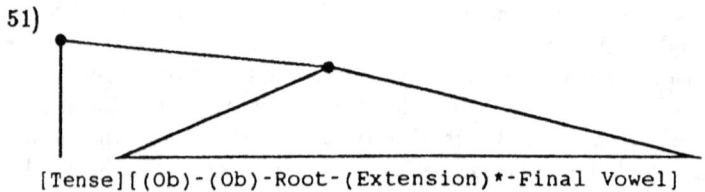
[Tense][(Ob)-(Ob)-Root-(Extension)*-Final Vowel]

If we assume that no brackets are erased before the tense prefix is
attached, then the root will be identifiable, but deeply embedded in
the constituent to which the tense prefix attaches. The tense prefix is
clearly not m-adjacent to the root, and therefore should not be able
to target or refer to a property of any specific segment within the
root.

There are two possible explanations for this problem. One is that
the internal morphological structure of the stem (=Root-Extension-
Final Vowel) is erased by the time the tense prefix is attached. If
the internal structure is not present, then the stem will function as
a single morphological constituent, and any morphological or phonological property of the stem will be accessible to a rule governed by
the tense prefix. This analysis entails that the BEC may in fact apply
internal to the morphological derivation in some languages. This case
is in some ways analogous to the Tiberian Hebrew example, where
Conflation is argued to apply after the stem morphology, but before
the "affixing" morphology.

Another explanation would be to say that Plane Conflation—but not Bracket Erasure—applies after the stem morphemes have been concatenated, and collapses all stem morphemes onto one plane. Then, we could reformulate the rules governed by the tense prefix to be sensitive not to a particular morphological boundary, but rather, to a planar representation. For example, the rule that spreads a H-tone on a final vowel to the initial vowel of the root could be reformulated to spread the H-tone to the leftmost periphery of its plane, as in (52).

52) H-tone Spread:

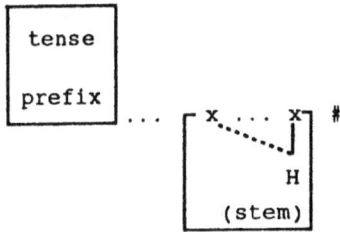

This analysis entails allowing Plane Conflation to apply internal to the lexical derivation, perhaps only as a special property of certain languages. Note that Plane Conflation could not apply cyclically in this analysis, since it would be crucial that the object prefixes not be represented on the same plane as the stem at the time that the tense prefix is added. Cyclic Plane Conflation would put all the object prefixes on the same plane as the stem morphemes, in which case the rule of H-tone Spread would incorrectly spread the final H-tone onto the first vowel of the first object prefix. The two solutions sketched here really only differ in whether the morphological integrity of the stem is attributed to the application of the BEC or Plane Conflation internal to the lexical derivation.

What we want to avoid saying is that Ci-Ruri violates the Adjacency Constraint that in other cases prevents phonological and morphological rules from referring to properties of a morpheme deeply embedded in a word. This would be an undesirable conclusion, since it is true that the vast majority of known rules do in fact conform to the Adjacency Constraint.

To summarize, we saw that by rejecting the BEC on the basis of the counterexamples presented in Section 5.3, we lose an explanation for why phonological and morphological rules are prohibited from referring to morphological structure deeply embedded in a word.

I argued that this constraint follows from limitations on the morphophonological parser that make it difficult for the parser to calculate relations between elements that are not adjacent at some level of representation. The adjacency relation applies strictly to phonological elements, but was seen to be too strong for morphological elements. Instead, the relevant adjacency relation for morphemes has to be stated in terms of morphological c-command and peripherality. The revised Adjacency Constraint supports treating the cases of morpheme-plane harmony discussed in Chapter 4 as morphologically governed assimilation processes. The alternative analysis, which employs a mapping function of the sort $X \longrightarrow Y$, violates the Adjacency Constraint, since the morphological context for the rule to apply may be arbitrarily far from the target segment.

5.5 Floating Features and Morpheme Planes in Tonal Phonology

Consider the bi-planar representation in (53):

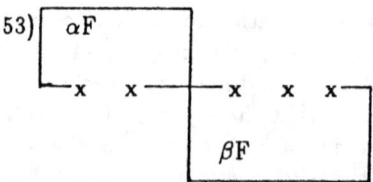

This representation encodes the concatenation of two morphemes, each of which contains a floating [F] feature. An interesting question arises as to whether these two floating features are ordered with respect to one another. In the analysis of morpheme-plane harmony in Chapter 4, I assumed that the relations between a feature and skeletal positions on one morpheme plane were independent of the relations between the identical feature and skeletal positions on another morpheme plane. This assumption about the independence of planes allows a feature on one plane to "skip over" segments which are linked to the identical feature on another plane. We could extend the independence of planes hypothesis to floating features, saying that a floating feature on one plane is not ordered with respect to any features on other morpheme planes. However, assuming that there is no ordering relation that can be imposed between heteromorphemic floating features presents a puzzling situation for Plane Conflation. If the two floating features in (53) are not linked to skeletal positions before Plane Conflation applies, then how does Plane Conflation decide which [F] feature comes first in the uni-planar representation, where ordering relations are imposed between every [F] feature?

Or consider what happens when a floating feature is introduced under affixation, as in (54):

54)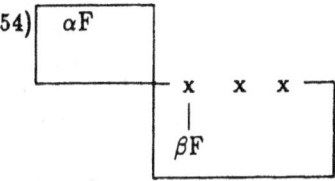

If no ordering relations are imposed on heteromorphemic identical features, then would it be possible for the floating feature $[\alpha F]$ to serve as the context for a rule targeting the linked feature $[\beta F]$? Certainly, the environment for such a rule couldn't be stated strictly in terms of phonological properties since, by hypothesis, $[\alpha F]$ neither precedes nor follows $[\beta F]$.

Questions like these arise immediatly when one looks at problems in tonal phonology. Tonal phonology frequently involves floating tone features, and association rules linking tone features from various morphemes to skeletal positions. Consideration of certain tonal phenomena provides the empirical basis for concluding that heteromorphemic features can in fact be ordered prior to Plane Conflation, even if such features are still floating at the time Plane Conflation applies. In this section we will review some facts about the tonal phonology of Tiv, as they are presented and analyzed in Pulleyblank (1986).

Pulleyblank (1986) presents a very compelling analysis of the tonal phonology of Tiv in which he argues that tones are not linked to segments in the underlying representation of morphemes. Instead, tones get linked by cyclic application of the Association Conventions.

In discussing the tonal phonology of verb forms, Pulleyblank (p.68) observes that all verb stems can be characterized by one of the templates in (55):

55) H-stem verbs: L-stem verbs:

$$\begin{bmatrix} V \quad (V) \quad (V) \\ H \end{bmatrix} \quad \begin{bmatrix} V \quad (V) \quad (V) \\ L \end{bmatrix}$$

That is to say that all verb stems will be either monosyllabic, disyllabic or trisyllabic and bear either a High or Low tone. The floating tones in (50) are linked to tone-bearing segments (vowels) by the Association Convention in (56):

(56) *Association Convention:* Tones are linked to tone-bearing units one-to-one, from left to right.

The fact that it is possible to predict which vowel the underlying tone will link to is strong evidence in favor of leaving underlying tones unlinked. If tones were prelinked in underlying representation, then we should expect to see contrasts between stems in which the tone was linked to the first vowel and stems in which the tone was linked to the second or third vowel.

Now let's consider what happens when affixes are added to a verb stem. Pulleyblank analyzes the General Past prefix as consisting only of a floating low tone. Its effect is to cause a downstep on the initial vowel of a H-tone stem; it has no overt effect on L-tone stems. He gives the following examples:

57) General Past

	H-stem		L-stem	
1 syllable:	!vá came	H	dzà went	L
2 syllable:	!úngwà heard	HL	vèndè refused	LL
3 syllable:	!yévèsè fled	HLL	ngòhòrò accepted	LLL

Consider the derivation of the H-tone stem !yévèsè. Pulleyblank argues that the stem tone associates on the first cycle. Then, on the second cycle, the floating L-tone prefix is added, as in (58).

58)

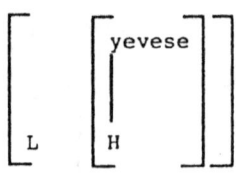

This floating L-tone provides the context for the rule of Downstep, which Pulleyblank formulates as in (59) (the floating tone is circled).

59) Tiv Downstep: H ⟶ !H / L __

Pulleyblank's analysis is done in a framework which does not incorporate the Morpheme Plane Hypothesis. Therefore, the tone features from all morphemes occur on the same tone plane. His formulation of Downstep in (59) reflects this fact. Now let's consider what the derivation would look like under the Morpheme Plane Hypothesis. On the second cycle, we would have the configuration in (60).

60)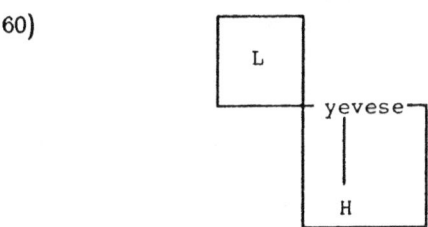

We are confronted now with two problems: First we must prevent the floating L-tone from associating with the second syllable of the stem, by automatic application of the association convention.[26] In order to prevent this association, we must order Downstep before the association convention, which entails that association can not apply automatically every time a floating element is introduced in the derivation. Since association is cyclic in Tiv, Downstep must also be cyclic. We can interpret this to mean that Downstep applies before Plane Conflation (we return below to consider the alternate ordering). So, the second problem lies in reformulating Downstep in such a way that a floating L-tone can trigger downstep of a linked H-tone that is on a separate morpheme plane. Note that Downstep must also apply to a derived form in which a floating L-tone occurs on the same plane as a linked H-tone, as in (61).

61)

---

[26] Pulleyblank argues that association in Tiv is one-to-one from left-to-right.

In (61), the lexical L-tone associated with the root *gbisé* 'type of tubor' is delinked when the root is preceded by the plural prefix *á*. The derived floating L-tone then provides the context for Downstep, and the form surfaces as *ágbís!é*.

In order to include both (60) and (61) in the domain of Downstep, we must reformulate Downstep in such a way that both tautomorphemic and heteromorphemic floating tones can trigger Downstep. This entails that a floating heteromorphemic L-tone must technically precede the linked H-tone, and provide the context for Downstep. In other words, we must assume that a floating tone can be ordered with respect to a heteromorphemic (and therefore hetero-planar) tone, prior to Plane Conflation. I formulate the pre-Conflation rule of Downstep in (62).

62) Downstep (pre-Conflation):

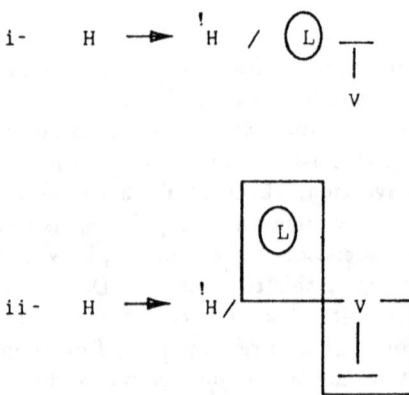

(62i) will downstep a H-tone if a floating L-tone precedes it on the same plane. (62ii) will downstep a H-tone if it is at the left edge of a morpheme which is preceded by a morpheme that contains a floating L-tone. Clearly, these two rules could be collapsed once the appropriate definition of precedence is determined. What we need to rule out is the possibility of a floating L-tone downstepping a heteromorphemic linked H-tone when another tone intervenes between them, as in the representation of *ngòhóróǹ* 'used to accept' in (63).

63)

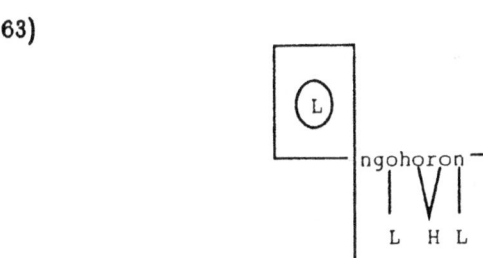

Although the floating L-tone does precede the linked H-tone in (63), it does not trigger Downstep, presumably because a linked L-tone intervenes. Evidently, what is required is a definition of *precedence* that specifies that the floating L-tone in (63) precedes all tones belonging to the morphological constituent to which it is attached. If the floating L-tone precedes the linked L-tone, and the linked L-tone precedes tha linked H-tone, then the floating L-tone cannot immediately precede the linked H-tone, and cannot therefore provide the context for Downstep. We know that the morpheme that introduces the floating L-tone precedes the stem, since the morpheme is designated as a prefix. The fact that the floating L-tone belonging to the prefix must also technically precede elements belonging to the stem means that the precedence relations defined in the morphological structure carry over into the phonological representation.

Note that the precedence relations of the morphological structure can be overridden by precedence relations which are defined in the phonological representation. For example, in the case of Coeur d'Alene Glottal Harmony, a floating glottal feature introduced by a reduplicative prefix can end up linked to a sonorant consonant very far away from the prefix, as in (64) (the floating glottal feature is circled):

64)

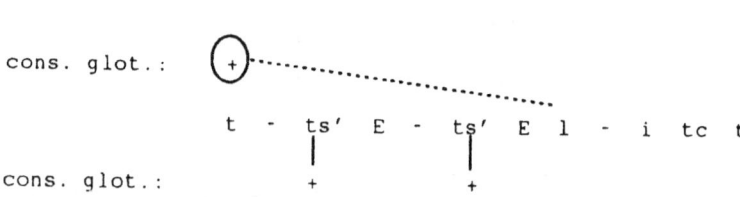

By the reasoning used in the discussion of Tiv Downstep, the floating glottal feature should technically precede all stem segments. Yet, after association, that glottal feature will be linked to a segment (/l/) which obviously cannot be said to precede all stem segments. Therefore, we must assume that the morphological precedence relations which would order the harmonic glottal feature before all stem segments are overridden once that feature becomes linked to some segment in the phonological representation. It will always be possible to define precedence relations between a linked feature and any segment in a string, since precedence can always be defined between any two skeletal positions, regardless of whether they are tautomorphemic or heteromorphemic.

The formulation of Downstep in (62) assumes that Downstep precedes Plane Conflation. The difficulty with (62) lies in formulating the correct definition of precedence that can take into account floating tones on more than one plane. This difficulty can be overcome if we allow Plane Conflation to apply cyclically, before cyclic Downstep.[1] After Plane Conflation, the floating L-tone trigger of Downstep will always be on the same plane as the linked H-tone target. If we order Downstep after Plane Conflation, then the formulation of Downstep given by Pulleyblank (59) will account both for Downstep triggered by a heteromorphemic L-tone and for Downstep triggered by a tautomorphemic L-tone. Of course, in order to apply Plane Conflation cyclically, before the association convention has linked floating tones, we must be able to determine the ordering relations between a floating tone on one morpheme plane and any tones on other morpheme planes. Consider the input to Plane Conflation in (65):

65)

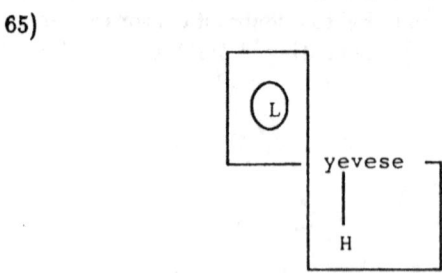

---

[1] Ordering Plane Conflation in the cyclic phonology means abandoning the notion that Plane Conflation is the same process as Bracket Erasure, which I argued above cannot universally apply internal to the lexical morphology and phonology. While none of the harmony or syncope systems discussed above provides evidence for cyclic Plane Conflation, we can not *a priori* rule out this possibility.

Plane Conflation

We want Plane Conflation to create the configuration in (66).

66)

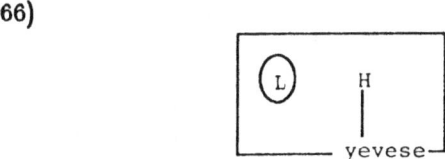

Clearly, Plane Conflation must be able to determine that the floating L-tone precedes the linked H-tone in the bi-planar representation in (65) before it can produce the uni-planar representation on (66). Therefore, like the analysis of post-Conflation Downstep, pre-Conflation Downstep also requires that morphological precedence relations carry over into the phonological representation. There is no evidence at this point on which to choose between the two formulations of Downstep in (59) and (62), and so it must remain an open question whether Plane Conflation is ever actually required to apply at stages prior to the end of the lexical phonology.

5.6 Summary

We began this chapter by examining the role of Plane Conflation in the analyses of harmony and syncope systems that invoke morpheme planes. With the exception of Tiberian Hebrew, there is evidence only for allowing Plane Conflation to apply once, at the boundary of the lexical and post-lexical levels. In light of McCarthy's suggestion that Plane Conflation be equated with Bracket Erasure, we examined the role of Bracket Erasure in various phonological analyses, concluding that the arguments for allowing Bracket Erasure to apply at any stage internal to the lexical level are not too strong. Moreover, evidence was adduced from four languages showing that Bracket Erasure must *not* apply internal to the lexical level in all languages. These arguments led to the conclusion that Bracket Erasure and Plane Conflation can be equated as long as both are restricted to apply only at the end of the lexical derivation. I suggested that in the end, it may not be appropriate to relate Plane Conflation with Bracket Erasure: the facts of Tiberian Hebrew and Ci-Ruri seem to require allowing Plane Conflation to apply to the morphologically complex stem, before other affixes are added. Thus, Plane Conflation may be a process which is subject to language-particular ordering constraints.

The discussion of the role of the BEC in phonology led us to consider how locality constrains morphological and phonological rules. I claim that such rules always apply in a strictly local fashion, but that the explanation for this constraint does not derive from allowing the BEC to apply within the lexical level, as has been previously argued. Instead, constraints on morpho-phonological parsing require that morphological and phonological elements involved in a rule be adjacent. Adjacency must be defined as a linear relation for phonological elements, but for morphological elements, adjacency is defined in terms of morphological c-command and peripherality. The proposed Adjacency Constraint correctly allows formulation of the rules which are counterexamples to the BEC, while disallowing non-attested, long-distance rule types.

Lastly, it was shown that features on different morpheme planes can be ordered with respect to one another, independent of their association to the skeleton. In particular, the analysis of tonal systems requires that floating tonal features on one plane be ordered with respect to tonal features on another plane. This ordering is necessary in order for Plane Conflation to collapse planes with floating features. The relative linear order of floating features on different morpheme planes derives from the ordering relation defined between the morphemes they belong to in morphological structure.

Chapter 6

Case Studies in Planar Phonology

In this chapter, I present a morpheme-plane analysis of four phonological processes from four languages. The first two examples are from Fula and Malayalam, where a morpheme at one end of a word triggers a phonological change in a segment at the opposite end. These two languages provide further support for the notion of m-adjacency defined in Chapter 5. The third example comes from Dakota, where a phonological distinction between compound and reduplicative structures can be explained by differences in the planar representations of these morphological operations. The fourth example concerns an interesting tonal phenomenon in Hausa, where the tonal melody of certain suffixes is realized on the stem, causing an underlying tonal melody to be deleted. I argue that the association of the suffix tonal melody is most simply achieved by allowing the suffix tones to occupy a distinct plane.

6.1 M-Adjacency in Fula and Malayalam

If the analysis of the Adjacency Constraint in Chapter 5 is correct, then we should expect to see more examples of languages like Ci-Ruri, in which a morpheme at one end of a word can trigger a phonological change in a segment at the opposite end. Fula and Malayalam present two such examples, which are reviewed here.

6.2 Fula Consonant Mutation

Fula, a West Atlantic African language, exhibits a complicated set of consonant mutations which are manifest, among other places, in the noun-class morphology.[1] Each noun in Fula is assigned to up to seven noun classes, where each class marks a particular singular, plural, or diminutive form of the noun. The noun class is marked by the presence of a suffix, and by a mutation in the initial consonant of the stem. The consonant mutations serve to distinguish three consonant grades: continuant, stop, and prenasalized stop. Each of these three consonant grades is distinguished for every place of articulation, as in (1).

1)

	Labial	Alveolar	Palatal	Velar/Glottal
Continuant	w f	r s	y	y w h
Stop	b p	d sh	j	g g k
Prenasalized stop	mb p	nd sh	nj	ŋg ŋg k

Each noun class selects one of the three consonant grades for the stem-initial consonant. Within a noun class, all nouns will appear with an initial consonant of the same grade.[2] For example, Class 1 nouns have initial stop consonants, while Class 2 nouns have an initial continuant consonant.

In addition to the stem consonant mutation, which is governed by a noun's class membership, the class suffixes also display a mutation of their initial consonant. The suffix mutations are determined by the noun stem. Thus, a particular noun will appear with up to seven class suffixes—each suffix determining the grade of the stem-initial consonant—but every class suffix appearing with the noun will have an initial consonant of the same grade. The pattern is one of cross-selection: the noun determines properties of the class suffix, and the selection of class suffix determines properties of the noun. The suffix mutations include the continuant, stop, and prenasalized forms of the stem mutations (2), but in addition, there is a zero form in which

---

[1] The data in this discussion of Fula is taken from Lieber (1984, 1987). She cites Arnott (1970) as the source of her data.

[2] This is a simplification. Some nouns show invariant initial consonants, and others show only partial alternations, or alternations which differ from the ones shown in (1). These variations can be accomodated within the analysis sketched here, which is essentially the analysis of Lieber (1987) with the addition of morpheme planes. Lieber argues that nouns which have an invariant or partially variant initial consonant are prespecified for all or some of the mutation features. See analysis below.

the initial consonant is deleted. The table in (2) illustrates the four
consonant grades on several class suffixes.

2)

Class	Grade A	Grade B	Grade C	Grade D
3	-el	-yel	-gel	-ŋgel
4	-al	-hal	-kal	-kal
5	-um	-yum	-gum	-ŋgum

Seven noun class forms for three different noun roots are illustrated
in (3), from Lieber (1984, ex. (2)).[3]

3)

		a.	rim- 'free man'	b.	wor- 'man'	c.	waa- 'monkey'
Suffix grade:			A		C		D
Class	1		dim-o	1	gor-do	11	waa-ndu
	2		rim-be	2	wor-be	25	baa-di
	3		dim-el	3	gor-gel	3	baa-ŋgel
	5		dim-um	5	gor-gum	5	baa-ŋgum
	6		ndim-on	6	ŋgor-kon	6	mbaa-kon
	7		ndim-a	7	ŋgor-ga	7	mbaa-ŋga
	8		ndim-o	8	ŋgor-go	8	mbaa-ko

Lieber (1987) provides an analysis of consonant mutations in the
noun-class paradigms using the formalism of autosegmental phonology. She claims that the initial consonants of the stem and suffix
are unspecified for the features [continuant] and [nasal]—they bear
only the features indicating place of articulation. The noun class is
marked by two morphemes: a prefix which contains the floating features [αcontinuant] and [βnasal], and a suffix with an underspecified
initial consonant. The floating features of the prefix link to the initial
consonant of the stem, accounting for the stem consonant mutations.
Lieber does not extend her analysis of the stem consonant mutation
to the suffix consonant cases, but we may assume that since the suffix
consonant mutations are dependent on the lexical noun stem, these
noun stems provide the floating features [αcontinuant] and [βnasal]
which link to the suffix-initial consonant. When the noun stem selects
a Grade A suffix, we may say, following Lieber, that the noun stem

---

[3]The symbols ḍ, ḅ represent the implosives [ɗ], [ɓ]. Note also that the suffix
consonant mutations in Classes 1, 2, 6, 8 and 25 deviate from the regular pattern.
These are Class suffixes with specified initial consonants.

contains no floating features, and that the suffix initial consonant is deleted by a special rule.[4]

Departing slightly from Lieber's analysis, we will say that the sole morphological marker for noun class is a suffix which contains the floating features [αcontinuant], [βnasal]. These floating features associate with the initial consonant of the stem by the rule in (4).

4) Stem Consonant Mutation:

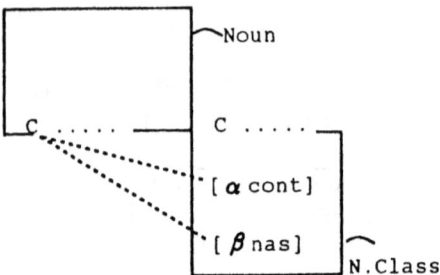

We cannot assume that the association in (4) is the result of an automatic association convention that links floating segments to empty skeletal positions, one-to-one and left-to-right because of our analysis of the suffix consonant mutations. In order to explain how the stem governs the mutation of the suffix-initial consonant, I suggested above that the stem be lexically represented with the floating features [continuant] and [nasal], which will link to the suffix-initial consonant. Consider the representation of the form *waa-ndu* 'monkey' (3c) in (5), which contains a noun stem that selects a Grade D suffix.[5]

---

[4]Marantz (1985) presents a different analysis of the suffix mutations which does not involve a consonant deletion rule. The differences between his analysis and Lieber's are not essential to the focus of this section.

[5]This analysis assumes that the assimilation of [+nasal] to an underlying oral stop results in a prenasalized stop. The details of this aspect of the analysis are not crucial to the question of morpheme planes, but pose an interesting problem for future research.

Case Studies in Planar Phonology

5)

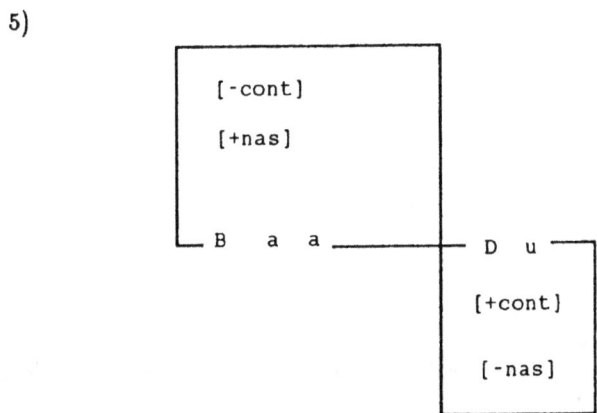

If floating features were linked automatically at all stages in the derivation, then the floating features associated with the noun stem would incorrectly link to the underspecified stem-initial consonant, instead of linking to the suffix consonant, as in (6).

6)

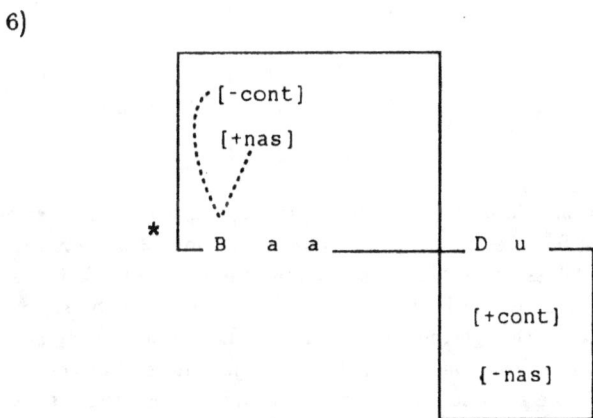

What is needed is two special association rules: one linking the floating features of the suffix to the stem-initial consonant (4), and one linking the floating features of the stem to the suffix-initial consonant, as in (7).

7)

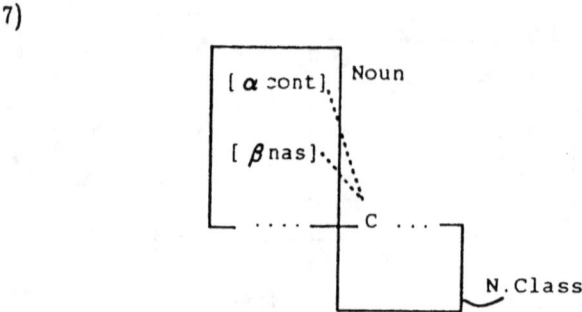

With these two rules, the derivation of *waa-ndu* proceeds as in (8).

8)

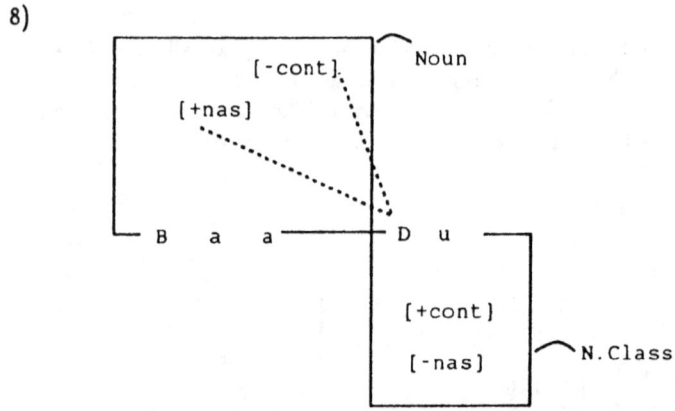

By adopting the Morpheme Plane analysis, we are able to say that the floating features causing stem consonant mutation actually originate in the Class suffix. The association rule that spreads these features is governed by the Noun Class suffix and targets the stem-initial consonant. Although the Noun Class suffix is not linearly adjacent to the stem-initial consonant, it is m-adjacent to that consonant, which is at the periphery of the morphological constituent that is c-commanded by the Noun Class suffix. If we did not assume the Morpheme Plane Hypothesis, then we would be forced to say that the floating features that cause stem consonant mutation originate in a prefix, and that the Noun Class morpheme consists of two parts: a prefix and a suffix, as in the representation of *dim-o* 'free man' from (3a).

Case Studies in Planar Phonology   183

9)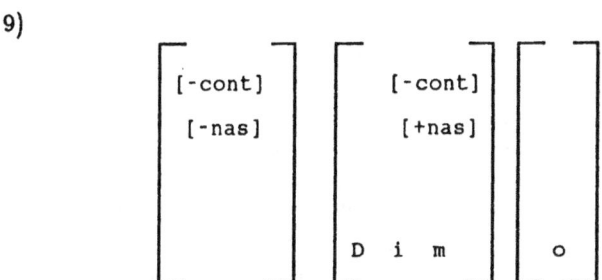

It is clear from (9) that if the floating features that cause stem consonant mutation were to originate in the suffix, then under the uniplanar theory, they would not be able to link to the stem-initial consonant without crossing over the [-cont, +nas] features of the final stem consonant /m/. This ill-formed derivation is illustrated in (10).

10)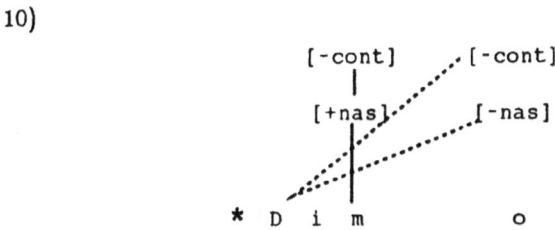

I conclude that the morpheme plane analysis is more perspicuous, since it posits only one morpheme for the Noun Class marker. The fact that the Noun Class suffix causes a phonological change on a remote segment is not surprising, since, given the Adjacency Constraint proposed in Chapter 5, the affected segment is in a m-adjacent relation to the suffix.

6.3 Malayalam Nominal Derivation

Mohanan (1982) describes a derivational process which converts adjectives into nouns by the application of two phonological rules to the noun stem: one rule inserts an /a/ at the beginning of the first rime, and the other rule inserts a /y/ at the end of the last onset, as in (11).

11) anukuulam ⟶ aanukuulyam *'support'*
    cañcalam ⟶ caañcalyam   *'fickleness'*

alasam	⟶ aalasyam	'laziness'
wikalam	⟶ waikalyam	'distortion'

In this example, there is no overt affix which can be said to trigger the phonological rules of /a/-insertion and /y/-insertion; however, both rules are invoked only in this particular process of nominal derivation, and so are morphologically governed rules. Mohanan argues for an analysis in which both the morphological category changing rule and the two phonological rules are just separate components of the morphological nominalizing operation, as in (12).

12) A ⟶ N Rule:
  a. $]_A \longrightarrow]_N$
  b. $\emptyset \longrightarrow a\ /\ [$
$$\begin{array}{c}\sigma\\|\\R\\|\\V\\|\\—\end{array}$$

$\emptyset \longrightarrow i$
$$\begin{array}{c}\sigma\ ]\\|\\O\\|\\C\\|\\—\end{array}$$

Mohanan claims that the facts of nominal derivation can best be accomodated within the theory of Lexical Phonology, where morphology and phonology are interwoven processes. He states,

> If the categorial change from A to N, and the phonological changes of /a/ and /y/ insertion were not directly associated, and the phonological rules applied to the output of the syntactic or morphological component, the facts would become less amenable to description. We would have to postulate an abstract morpheme which changes A to N, and triggers the rules of /a/ and /y/ insertion. The disadvantage of this solution is that we would have to allow the abstract morpheme...attached at one end of

the stem, to effect a phonological change at the other end:

$$R \longrightarrow R \: / \: [[\: \sigma \: Q]_A \: \emptyset \:]_N$$

The only way to formulate such a rule is by resorting to the use of variables (Q), which is unmotivated in phonology. *p. 135*

I am not so much concerned with Mohanan's point regarding Lexical Phonology. What is interesting is that the Malayalam example involves a single morphological rule that is reflected in a phonological change occurring at opposite ends of the morphological constituent that is input to the rule. Given the Adjacency Constraint and the definition of m-adjacency formulated in Chapter 5, it would be possible to present an analysis of this morphological process in which a zero suffix governs the application of the two phonological rules in (12), without relying on the variables that Mohanan argues would be necessary. The target of the /y/-insertion rule is the syllable that is linearly adjacent to the zero suffix, while the target of the /a/-insertion rule is the syllable rime that is m-adjacent (but not linearly adjacent) to the zero suffix.

The formulation of the Adjacency Constraint and the definitions of Adjacency and M-adjacency in Chapter 5 assume that there is always an overt morpheme present in morphologically governed processes. However, this is not a necessary assumption. It would be possible to reformulate these definitions to constrain all morphological processes regardless of whether or not they involve affixation. The revised constraint would allow a morphological process to govern a phonological rule only if the target of the rule were at the periphery of the constituent that is input to the rule. Similary, a morphological process applying to some morphological constituent could only be sensitive to the presence of a morpheme within that constituent if the morpheme were at the periphery of the constituent. With these changes in the Adjacency Constraint, it would not be necessary to assume that Malayam nominal derivation involves a zero affix.

6.4 Dakota

In her analysis of the Lexical Phonology of Dakota, Shaw (1985) argues for a distinction between two cyclic lexical strata. She notes that both Reduplication and Compounding trigger the cyclic stress rule of Dakota, as seen in the following examples.

13) a- phé   "sharp"
         phe-phé
     b- mní-kį   "the water"
         mni-skúya   "salt"

The Dakota stress rule assigns stress to the second syllable of a word. (13a) shows that the stress on the final vowel of a root shifts rightward under (cyclic) reduplication. (13b) illustrates that the stress that appears on a monosyllabic root when it is followed by a (non-cyclic) clitic shifts rightward when the root is part of a lexical compound.

Shaw notes that reduplicative words and lexical compounds show different behavior with respect to two phonological rules. Consider first the rule of Coronal Dissimilation, which neutralizes underlying /t,č,n,d/ with [k] or [g] before another [+coronal] segment. The forms in (14a) show that Reduplication feeds Coronal Dissimilation, whereas (14b) shows that Coronal Dissimilation does not apply after Lexical Compounding:[6]

14) a- /sut/   *sutsuta   suksuta   "strong"
         /žat/   *žatžata   žagžata   "curved"
         /theč/   *thečtheča   thektheča   "be new"
     b- [phet] [nakpa-kpa]   phednakpakpa   "sparks"
         [sdot] [čhi-ya]   sdodčhiya   "I know you"

The second way in which Reduplication differs from Lexical Compounding is with respect to the rule of Degemination. Degemination applies after Reduplication, merging two identical obstruents into a single obstruent, as in (15a). Degemination does not apply to the output of Lexical Compounding, as in (15b):

15) a- [[xux]xux]   xuxuγa   "be broken; to thunder"
         [[sus]sus]   susuza   "be cracked"
         [[khak]khak]   khakhaka   "to rattle"
     b- [čhap][phat]   čhapphata   "butcher beavers"
         [wat][thete]   wadthete   "gunwale"
         [thok][k'u]   thokk'u   "to give over an enemy"

Shaw's analysis of these facts involves assigning Degemination and Coronal Dissimilation to Stratum 1, where Reduplication takes place, and assigning Lexical Compounding and the cyclic stress rule to Stratum 2. I argue that there is a reinterpretation of this data that

---

[6] Shaw notes that in (14b), the final coronal consonant of the first member of a lexical compound undergoes regular Coronal Lenition.

does not require reference to ordered strata, but instead relies on differences in the planar representations of Reduplication and Lexical Compounding.

Adopting the Morpheme Plane Hypothesis, both Reduplication and Lexical Compounding will introduce new morpheme planes into the phonological representation. In the case of Lexical Compounding the resulting structure will appear as in (16):

16)

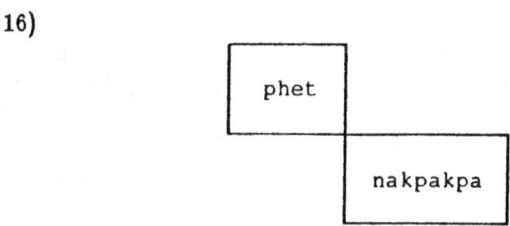

However, the picture for Reduplication is a little different. Following Marantz (1982), I assume that reduplication involves adding an affix which consists of bare skeletal positions, and then copying the melody of the stem and associating this copied melody onto the reduplicative affix, as in (17):[7]

17)

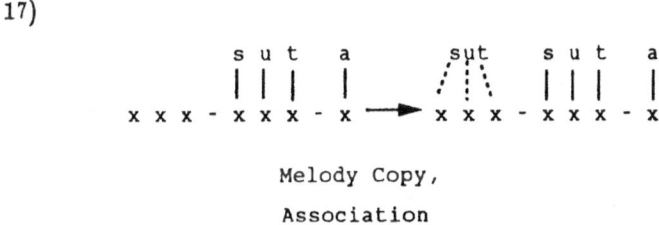

Melody Copy,
Association

Note that in (17) I have copied the melody onto the stem plane. This seems like a reasonable move, if feature specifications on distinct morpheme planes are independent of one another, it is not clear what mechanism could take features from one plane and insert them on another plane. In any case, adopting this approach to Melody Copy provides us with an important distinction between the Lexical Compound in (16) and the Reduplicative structure in (17) — only the

---

[7] The details of this analysis can be reformulated in light of the proposal in McCarthy & Prince (in press) that reduplication always involves a template defined prosodically in terms of the mora and syllable. A prosodic definition of the reduplicative prefix will not affect the points being made here.

two morphemes involved in the compounding structure will actually be represented on two distinct planes. We can say that Reduplication does introduce a morpheme plane, but since the affix consists only of skeletal positions, there is no material on this plane.

Now, if we interpret both Coronal Dissimilation and Degemination as processes which are sensitive to sequences of identical, or partially identical segments *on the same plane*, we can achieve the result that neither rule will apply to the compound structures, in which the sequences in question lie on distinct planes. The reformulated rules are given in (18) and (19), with derivations in (20) and (21). In the formulation of Coronal Dissimilation (18), I am assuming that a consonant with no specified articulator node is interpreted as a dorsal consonant in Dakota, by a rule of default Dorsal insertion. The statement of Degemination (19) employs subscripts to indicate two nodes which dominate an identical set of features.

18) Coronal Dissimilation

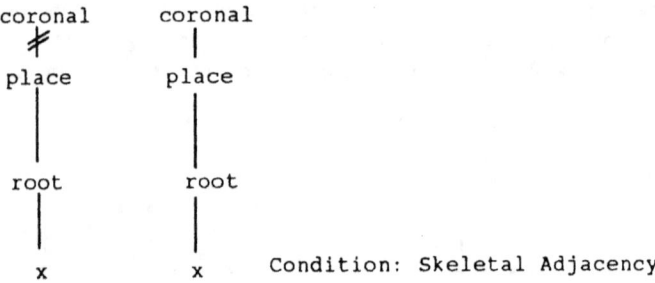

19) Degemination

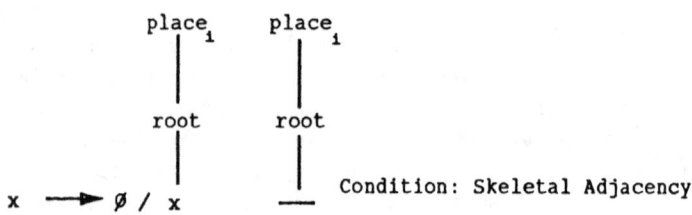

20)

CORONAL DISSIMILATION:
Reduplication:

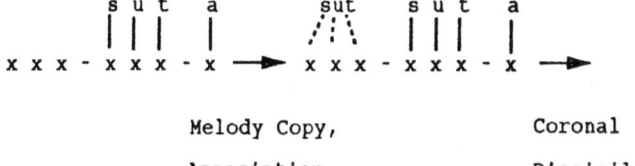

           Melody Copy,   Coronal

           Association   Dissimilation

           Default
           Dorsal Insert.

••

Lexical Compounding:

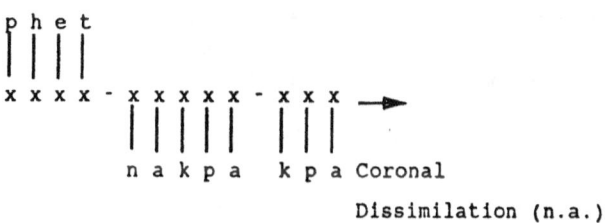

                             Coronal

                             Dissimilation (n.a.)

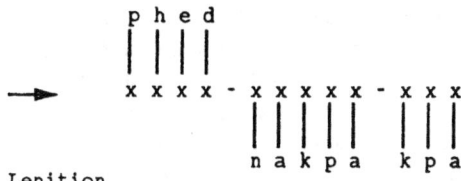

Lenition

21)

DEGEMINATION

Reduplication:

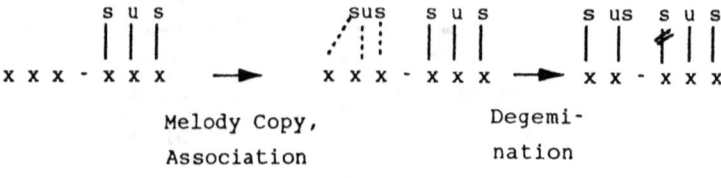

→ susuza

other rules
••

Lexical Compounding:

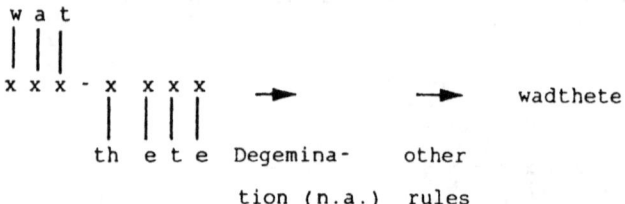

The implication of this analysis is that only one cyclic lexical stratum is necessary for Dakota. This is an important result in light of recent proposals which suggest that Lexical Phonology needs to be weakened to allow multiple cyclic and non-cyclic lexical strata (Halle & Mohanan (1985), Mohanan & Mohanan (1984)). In Dakota, the motivation for positing two cyclic lexical strata is reanalyzed under the Morpheme Plane Hypothesis; if the remaining data presented in support of the weaker version of Lexical Phonology were also subject to reanalysis, then it would be possible to maintain a stronger version of the theory—one in which there is only one block for cyclic rule application and one block for non-cyclic rule application within the lexical domain.

6.5 Hausa

Hausa presents a very interesting tonal phenomenon that is subject to a simple analysis under the Morpheme Plane Hypothesis.[8] As described by Newman (1986), Hausa contains a class of suffixes that have the property of determining the tonal melody of the stem. Newman calls such suffixes *Tone Integrating Suffixes*.

Noun and verb stems are represented underlyingly with a tonal melody consisting of a High or Low tone marked on each syllable (though we may suppose that one of these two tones is supplied by a default rule). The only contour tone is HL. When a stem is combined with a Tone Integrating Suffix, the underlying tonal melody of the stem is replaced with the tonal melody specified by the suffix. The suffix tonal melody is linked to stem and suffix vowels by a right-to-left association rule, followed by leftward spreading. Examples of Tone Integrating Suffixes are given in (22).[9]

22) i- /-ii/ *nominalizer*, tone: HL
  gínà - ii ⟶ gínìi *'building'*
  hàr̃bí - ii ⟶ hár̃bìi *'shooting'*

  ii- /-e/ *adverbial stative*, tone: LH
  záunà - e ⟶ zàuné *'seated'*
  dáfà - e ⟶ dàfá *'cooked'*

  iii- /-aCCee/ *adjectival past participle* tone: LHH
  gàagágà - aCCee ⟶ gàagàrárrée *'unmanageable'*
  dáfà - aCCee ⟶ dàfáffée *'cooked'*

  /-∅/ *imperative* tone: LH
  táashì - ∅ ⟶ tàashí *'get up!'*
  sùnkúyà - ∅ ⟶ sùnkùyá *'bend down!*

I suggest that the tone replacement phenomenon associated with the Tone Integrating Suffixes results from adopting the Morpheme Plane Hypothesis. The tonal melody of the Tone Integrating Suffixes is introduced on the morpheme plane created by suffixation. What is special about these suffixes in Hausa is that the suffix tones are al-

---

[8] Thanks to Morris Halle for directing my attention to this example.
[9] A rule of Vowel Deletion applies in (22i-iii), deleting the final stem vowel before a vowel-initial suffix. Also, long vowels or diphthongs are represented as sequences of adjcent vowels, whose shared tone is marked on the first vowel only.

lowed to link to stem vowels that are already linked to tonal features. When a tone from the Tone Integrating Suffix links to a stem vowel, any tones linked to that vowel will automatically delink. In other words, the spreading tone takes precedence over the existing tone. (23) illustrates the derivation of example (22ii) under this analysis.

23)

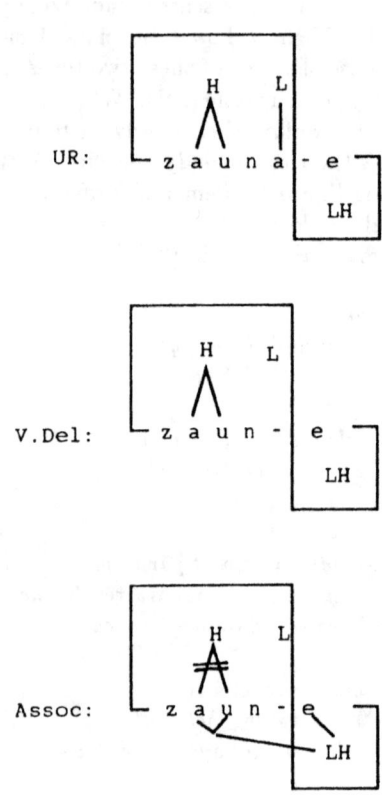

Case Studies in Planar Phonology   193

There is an alternate analysis of this phenomena that can be considered here. For many of the forms in (22), it would be possible to argue that all tones are specified on one plane, and the stem tones simply link and spread in a right-to-left direction, causing all linked stem tones to delink, as in (24).

24)

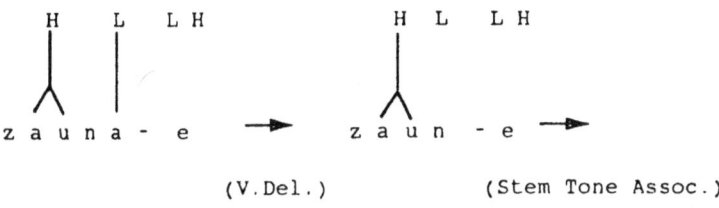

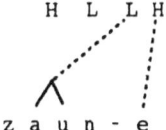

There are, however, forms for which this particular uni-planar analysis will not work. Consider the derivation of the word *jimínúu* (LLH) 'ostriches'-pl. from the root *jimínda* (LHH) 'ostrich' and the plural suffix *-uu*, which is a Tone Integrating Suffix with the tone melody LH.

25)

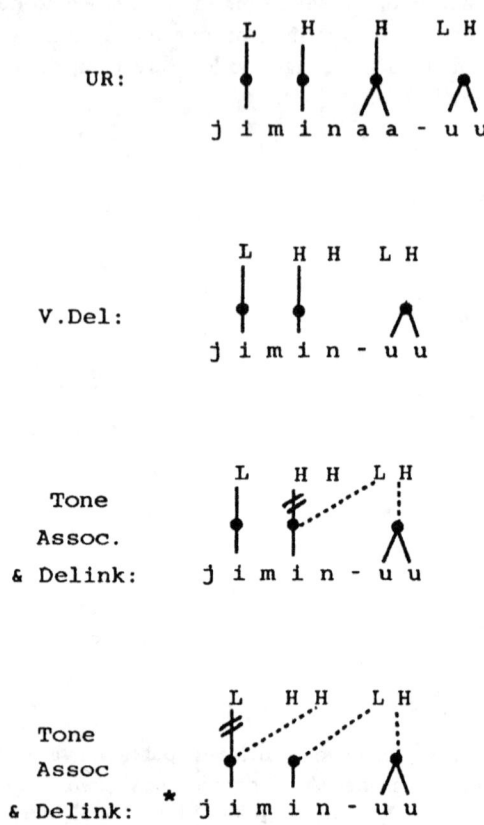

The Association Convention, applying one-to-one, right to left, will link the two suffix tones to the final and penult vowels. But in this example there is still a toneless syllable. By the Association Convention, the rightmost free tone should link to the initial syllable, but in this form the rightmost free tone is part of the stem tone melody (the final H). The crucial part of the correct derivation of this form is that *only* suffix tones are realized on the surface. What is needed is a rule of Stem Tone Deletion, ordered before the association of the suffix tones. Tone Deletion would have the effect of Deleting all stem tones in the context of Tone Integrating Suffixes. The application of Tone Deletion and suffix tone association under the uni-planar analysis is illustrated in (26).

26)

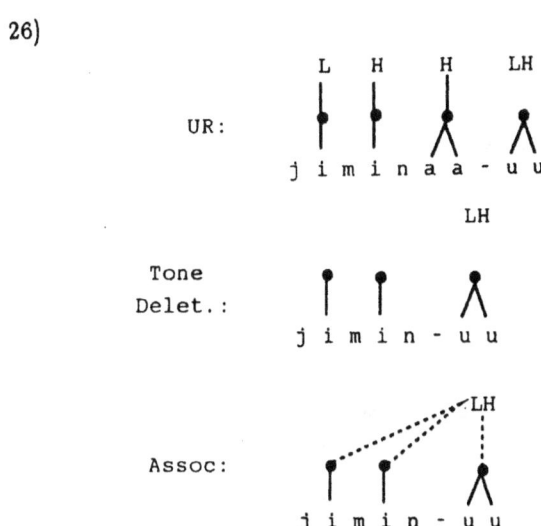

Note that the required tone deletion rule would not be formulatable under the Adjacency Constraint of Section 5.4.2. Since tone deletion does not occur with every affixation process (see discussion of Tone Non-integrating Suffixes below), it is necessarily a morphologically governed rule. But under the Adjacency Constraint, a morphologically governed phonological rule can target only segments that are linearly adjacent or m-adjacent to the conditioning morpheme. This would mean that a tone deletion rule governed by a Tone Integrating Suffix should only be able to target the initial and final tones of the stem to which the suffix attaches. All stem tones delete from stems up to four syllables long, therefore, the deletion rule must be able to affect non-adjacent stem segments. Since the uni-planar analysis requires a tone rule that violates the Adjacency Constraint, we reject it here in favor of the morpheme-plane analysis.

It is interesting to note what happens when two Tone Integrating Suffixes follow a stem. In this case it is only the tones from the tonal melody of the outer suffix that surfaces. This fact indicates that both Tone Integrating Suffixes are represented on separate morpheme planes, and that the association and spreading conventions apply at each cycle. (27) illustrates the derivation of dàkàkkúu 'pounded'-pl. from the stem dákà and the Tone Integrating Suffixes -aCCee 'adj. participle' (LHH) and -uu 'plural' (LH).

27)

CYCLE 1:

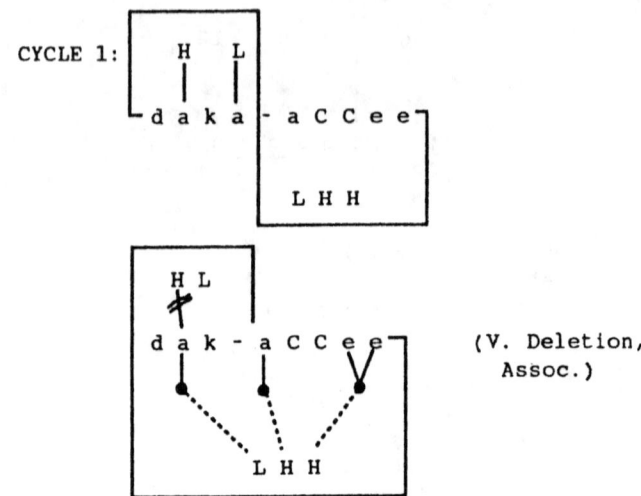

(V. Deletion, Assoc.)

CYCLE 2:

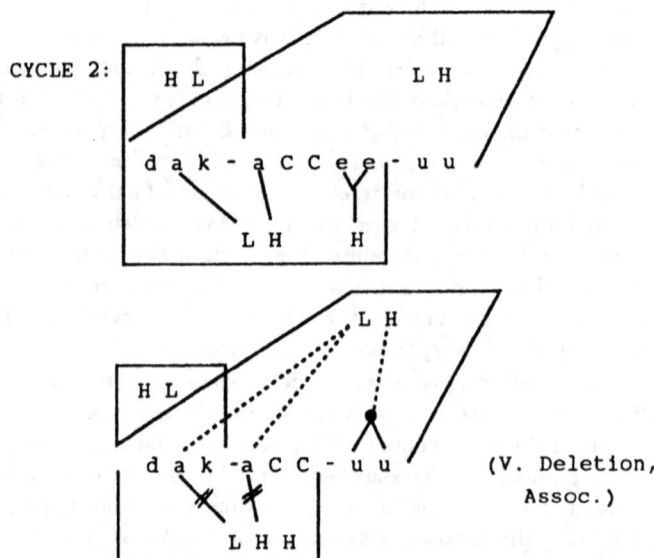

(V. Deletion, Assoc.)

The Tone Integrating Suffixes can be contrasted with what Newman calls *Tone Non-integrating Suffixes*. The latter class of suffixes also contain a tonal melody, but this melody does not displace the melody of the stem. Rather, the suffix tone melody links to suffix vowels, and any extra tones are either deleted or merge with the final stem tone to create a tonal contour. Consider the following examples of Tone Non-integrating Suffixes.

28) i- /-n/ *referential marker* tone: L
   jàakíi - ǹ ⟶ jàakîn 'the donkey'
   hársúnàa - ǹ ⟶ hársúnàn 'the languages'

   ii- /-Vwaa/ *progressive particle* tone: LH
   dáfà - V̀wáa ⟶ dáfàawáa 'cooking'
   kóomóo - V̀wáa ⟶ kóomôowáa 'returning here'

Clearly, the Tone Non-integrating Suffixes demand a different treatment than the Tone-Integrating Suffixes presented above. There are three points to the explanation of the dominance of the tone melody in the Tone Integrating Suffixes: (i) the suffix tones are placed on a separate morpheme plane, (ii) the association convention and spreading were allowed to apply automatically to link and spread the suffix tones to stem vowels, and (iii) stem tones were said to delink by convention when a stem vowel becomes associated with a suffix tone. We could potentially account for the differing behavior of the Tone Non-integrating Suffixes by changing any one of these three points. Lets consider first point (iii). One account of the Tone Non-integrating suffixes would be to stipulate that stem tones only delink under association of a tone from a Tone Integrating Suffix. We might in this case say that since the stem tones cannot delink in the presence of a Tone Non-integrating Suffix, the tones from such a suffix cannot link to the stem vowel. The problem with this solution is that the Tone Integrating Suffix should not be able to govern a delinking rule which applies to all stem vowels. The Adjacency Constraint would limit this morphologically governed delinking rule to the final and initial stem vowels only.

Another possible solution would be to change point (ii) above. We might argue that association of tones from Tone Integrating Suffixes does not follow from an automatic association convention, but is effected by a special morphologically governed rule. This special association rule would say that tones link and spread in a right-to-left direction only if they belong to a Tone Integrating Suffix. It's not clear that this rule could be formulated without violating the Adjacency Constraint, but even if it could, this would be an undesirable solution. Newman presents some evidence that the convention of right-to-left association followed by leftward spreading applies throughout the tonal phonology. But if we can't restrict the association conventions to apply only to Tone Integrating Suffixes, then we must prevent them from applying to the Tone Non-integrating Suffixes. It seems unsatisfying to make a number of lexical exceptions to a process that is supposed to apply automatically at all stages in the derivation.

A third solution would be to make a change in point (i) above. This is in fact what Halle (1987) does in his analysis of the Non-tone Integrating Suffixes. He suggests that the Tone Non-integrating Suffixes differ from the Tone Integrating Suffixes in their planar representation; instead of introducing a new morpheme plane, the Tone Non-integrating Suffixes get added to the stem plane. Adopting this solution, one could say that the association convention applies only once on each plane. When a Tone Non-integrating Suffix is added to the stem plane, the association convention will not reapply to link tones from the Non-tone Integrating Suffixes to linked stem vowels: no stem tones will ever be displaced in this analysis, although by special rule, a suffix tone may link to a stem vowel to create a contour tone, as illustrated in (28). The representation of a word with a non-planar Tone Non-integrating Suffix is illustrated in (29).

29)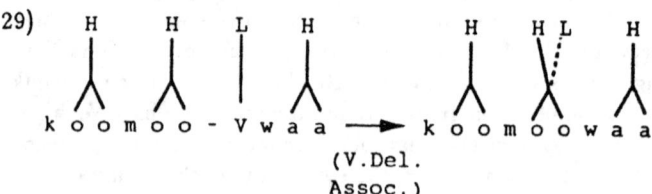
(V.Del.
Assoc.)

This analysis of the Tone Non-integrating Suffixes suggests an interesting extension of the Morpheme Plane Hypothesis, namely that affixes may differ in their planar properties. Halle & Vergnaud (1987) argue for such an extension in their analysis of stress, which employs morpheme planes. Halle (1987) develops this analysis in his discussion of the Hausa phenomena. In the framework of that discussion, the Tone Non-integrating Suffixes would be non-cyclic (attached without creating a new phonological cycle), and the association and spreading conventions would be constrained to apply cyclically. As mentioned earlier, I have no evidence that bears on the cyclicity of these tonal processes to test this particular aspect of Halle's analysis.

There is yet a fourth, and much simpler alternative to consider. One might argue that the convention on association and spreading applies only to floating tones, and only the Tone Integrating Suffixes have floating tones. Tone Non-integrating Suffixes could be said to bear lexically prelinked tones, which will not undergo any further linking or spreading (except in the local process that creates tonal contours). This analysis, like the above three, involves a degree of stipulation, yet in its favor lies the fact that it does not involve formulating any rules which violate the Adjacency Constraint, nor does it involve increasing the power of the theory by allowing the planar representation of individual morphemes to vary within or across languages. Thus, the fourth solution is compatible with a more constrained theory of planar morphology and phonology.

Bibliography

Abney, S. and J. Cole (1985) "A Government-Binding Parser," in *Proceedings of NELS 16*, GLSA, Amherst, Massachusetts.

Allen, M. (1978) *Morphological Investigations*, Doctoral dissertation, University of Connecticut, Storrs.

Archangeli, D. (1984) *Underspecification in Yawelmani Phonology and Morphology*, Ph.d. dissertation, MIT, Cambridge, Massachusetts.

Archangeli, D. (1988) "Aspects of Underspecification," *Phonology* 5.2

Archangeli, D. and D. Pulleyblank (to appear) "The Content and Structure of Phonological Representations," ms., University of Arizona, Tuscon, and University of Southern California, Los Angeles, to be published by MIT Press, Cambridge.

Arnott, D.W. (1970) *The Nominal and Verbal Systems of Fula*, Oxford University Press, Oxford.

Aronoff, M. (1976) *Word Formation in Generative Grammar*, MIT Press, Cambridge, Massachusetts.

Aronoff, M. and R. Oehrle, eds. (1984) *Language Sound Structure*, MIT Press, Cambridge, Massachusetts.

Aronoff, M. and S.N. Sridhar (1983) "Morphological Levels in English and Kannada, or Atarizing Reagan," in J. Richardson, M. Marks, A. Chukerman, eds. (1983).

Baker, M. (1985a) "The Mirror Principle and Morphosyntactic Explanation," *Linguistic Inquiry*, 16, 373-416.

Baker, M. (1985b) *Incorporation: A Theory of Grammatical Function Changing*, Ph.d. dissertation, MIT, Cambridge, Massachusetts.

Barton, E. (1985) "The Computational Complexity of Two-Level Morphology," A.I. Memo No. 856, MIT Artificial Intelligence Laboratory, Cambridge, Massachusetts.

Bever, T. (1967) *Bloomfield and the Phonology of the Menomini Language*, Ph.d. dissertation, MIT, Cambridge, Massachusetts.

Bliese, L.F. (1981) *A Generative Grammar of Afar*, Summer Institute of Linguistics, Arlington, Texas.

Bloomfield, L. (1962) *The Menomini Language*, Yale University Press, New Haven, Connecticut.

Bloomfield, L. (1975) *The Menomini Lexicon*, Milwaukee Public Museum Press, New Haven, Connecticut.

Bosson, J. (1964) *Modern Mongolian*, Indiana University Publications, Uralic and Altaic Series, vol. 38, Bloomington, Indiana.

Chomsky, N. and M. Halle (1968) *The Sound Pattern of English*, Harper and Row, New York.

Chung, S. (1983) "Transderivational Constraints in Chamorro Phonology," *Language*, 59, 35-66.

Clements, G.N. (1976) "The Autosegmental Treatment of Vowel Harmony," *Phonologica*, ed. by W. Dressler and O. Pfeiffer, Innsbruck.

Clements, G.N. (1981) "Akan Vowel Harmony: a Non-Linear Analysis," in G.N. Clements, ed., *Harvard Studies in Phonology*, vol. 2, Indiana University Linguistics Club, Bloomington.

Clements, G.N. (1985) "The Geometry of Phonological Features," *Phonology Yearbook*, 2, 223-252.

Clements, G.N. (1986) "Syllabification and Epenthesis in the Barra Dialect of Gaelic," in K. Bogers, H. van der Hulst, and M. Mous, eds., *The Phonological Representation of Suprasegmentals: Studies Offered to John M. Stewart on his 60th Birthday*, Foris, Dordrecht.

Clements, G.N. (1989a) "A Unified Set of Features for Consonants and Vowels," ms. Cornell University, Ithaca, New York.

Clements, G.N. (1989b) "On the Representation of Vowel Height," ms. Cornell University, Ithaca, New York.

Clements, G.N. and J. Goldsmith, eds. (1982) *Autosegmental Studies in Bantu Tone*, Foris, Dordrecht.

Clements, G.N. and E. Sezer (1982) "Vowel and Consonant Disharmony in Turkish," in H. van der Hulst and N. Smith, eds. (1982).

Cole, J. (1987) "The Interaction of Phonology and Morphology in Seri," *Proceedings of NELS 17*, GLSA, Amherst, Massachusetts.

Cole, J. (1986a) "Vowel Harmony and Coalescence in Menomini," ms., MIT, Cambridge, Massachusetts.

Cole, J. (1986b) "Harmony within Linked Structures," paper presented at LSA Annual Meeting, New York.

Cole, J. and L. Trigo (1987) "On the Representation of Neutral Segments in Harmony Systems," ms., MIT, Cambridge, Massachusetts.

Cole, J. and L. Trigo (1988) "Parasitic Harmony," in H. van der Hulst and N. Smith, eds., *Features, Segmental Structure and Harmony Processes*, part II, Dordrecht, Netherlands.

Fabb, N. (1984) *Syntactic Affixation*, Ph.d. dissertation, MIT, Cambridge, Massachusetts.

Fabb, N. (1988) "English Suffixation is Constrained Only by Selectional Restrictions," *Natural Language and Linguistic Theory* 6.4.

Gensler, O. (1986) "Wiyot," ms., University of California Berkeley.

Goldsmith, J. (1976) *Autosegmental Phonology*, Ph.d. dissertation, MIT Press, Cambridge, Massachusetts; published by Garland, New York, 1979.

Goldsmith, J. (1982a) "Accent Systems," in H. van der Hulst and N. Smith, eds, (1982).

Goldsmith, J. (1982b) "Accent in Tonga," in G.N. Clements and J. Goldsmith, eds., (1982)

Goldsmith, J. (1984) "Meeussen's Rule," in M. Aronoff and R. Oehrle, eds., (1984).

Goldsmith, J. (1986) "Tone in the Ci-Ruri Present Continuous," in K. Bogers, H. van der Hulst and M. Mous, eds., *The Phonological Representation of Suprasegmentals*, Foris, Dordrecht, 95-108.

Goldsmith, J. (1985) "Vowel Harmony in Khalkha Mongolian, Yaka, Finnish and Hungarian," *Phonology Yearbook*, 2, 253-275.

Gregersen, E. (1967) "The Palatal Consonants in Hausa," *Journal of African Languages*, 6, 170-184.

Hall, B. and E. Yokwe (1980) "Bari Vowel Harmony: the Evolution of a Cross-Height Harmony System," in *Proceedings of NELS 9*, GLSA, Amherst, Massachusetts.

Halle, M. (1986) "Speech Sounds and their Immanent Structure," ms., MIT, Cambridge, Massachusetts.

Halle, M. (1987) "Why Phonological Strata Should Not Include Affixation," ms., MIT, Cambridge, Massachusetts.

Halle, M. (1990) "An Approach to Morphology," *Proceedings of NELS 20*, GLSA, Amherst, Massachusetts.

Halle, M. and K.P. Mohanan (1985) "Segmental Phonology of Modern English," *Linguistic Inquiry*, 16, 57-116.

Halle, M. and J.-R. Vergnaud (1980) "Three Dimensional Phonology," *Journal of Linguistic Research* 1, 83-105.

Halle, M. and J.-R. Vergnaud (1981) "Harmony Processes," in W. Klein and W. Levelt, eds., *Crossing the Boundaries in Linguistics, Studies Presented to Manfred Bierwich*, Reidel, Dordrecht.

Halle, M. and J.-R. Vergnaud (1987) "Stress and the Cycle," *Linguistic Inquiry*, 18, 45-84.

Halle, M. and J.-R. Vergnaud (1987) *An Essay on Stress*, MIT Press, Cambridge.

Hargus, S. (1985) *The Lexical Phonology of Sekani*, Ph.d. dissertation, University of California Berkeley, Berkeley, California.

Harris, J. (1983) *Syllable Structure and Stress in Spanish: A Nonlinear Analysis*, MIT Press, Cambridge, Massachusetts.

Hayes, B. (1980) *A Metrical Theory of Stress Rules*, Ph.d. dissertation, MIT, Cambridge, Massachusetts.

Hayes, B. (1986) "Inalterability in CV Phonology," *Language*, 62, 321-252.

Hayes, B. (1989) "Compensatory Lengthening in Moraic Phonology," *Linguistic Inquiry*, 20.2.

Hyman, L. (1988) "Underspecification and Vowel Height Transfer in Esimbi," *Phonology* 5.2.

Itô, J. and R.-A. Mester (1986) "The Phonology of Voicing in Japanese," *Linguistic Inquiry*, 15, 505-513.

Iverson, J. (1980) "On the Category Supralaryngeal," *Phonology* 6.2.

Jacobs, M. (1931) *A Sketch of Northern Sahaptin Grammar*, Publications in Anthropology, Washington University Press, Seattle.

Kartunnen, L. (1983) "KIMMO: A Two Level Morphological Analyzer," Texas Linguistic Forum, 22, Austin, Texas.

Kaye, J. (1982) "Harmony Processes in Vata," in H. van der Hulst and N. Smith, eds., Vol. II (1982).

Kean, M.-L. (1974) "The Strict Cycle in Phonology," *Linguistic Inquiry*, 2, 179-203.

Kenstowicz, M. (1985) "Multiple Linking in Javanese," in *Proceedings of NELS 16*, GLSA, Amherst, Massachusetts.

Kiparsky, P. (1973) "Phonological Representations," in O. Fujimura, ed., *Three Dimensions of Linguistic Theory*, Holt, Rinehart and Winston, New York, 171-202.

Kiparsky, P. (1981) "Vowel Harmony," unpublished ms., MIT, Cambridge, Massachusetts.

Kiparsky, P. (1982a) "Lexical Morphology and Phonology," *Linguistics in the Morning Calm*, Hansin, Seoul, 3-91.

Kiparsky, P. (1982b) "The Lexical Phonology of Vedic Accent," ms., MIT, Cambridge, Massachusetts.

Kiparsky, P. (1982c) "From Cyclic Phonology to Lexical Phonology," in H. van der Hulst and N. Smith, eds., (1982).

Kiparsky, P. (1983) "Word Formation and the Lexicon," in F.A. Ingeman, ed., *Proceedings of the 1982 Mid-America Linguistics Conference,* University of Kansas, Lawrence, 3-29.

Kiparsky, P. (1984) "On the Lexical Phonology of Icelandic," in C.C. Elert, I. Johansson, and E. Strangert, eds., *Nordic Prosody III: Papers from a Symposium,* University of Umeå.

Kiparsky, P. (1985) "Some Consequences of Lexical Phonology," *Phonology Yearbook,* 2, 85-138.

Kisseberth, G.W. (1969) *Theoretical Implications of Yawelmani Phonology,* Ph.d. dissertation, University of Illinois, Urbana, Illinois.

Koskenniemi, K. (1983) *Two-Level Morphology: A General Computational Model for Word-Form Recognition and Production,* Ph.d. dissertation, University of Helsinki, Helsinki.

Kuipers, A. (1967) *The Squamish Language,* Mouton, The Hague.

Levergood, B. (1984) "Rule Governed Vowel Harmony and the Strict Cycle," in *Proceedings of NELS 14,* GLSA, Amherst, Massachusetts.

Levin, J. (1983) "Reduplication and Prosodic Structure," paper presented at the GLOW colloquium, York, England.

Levin, J. (1985) *A Metrical Theory of Syllabicity,* Ph.d. dissertation, MIT, Cambridge, Massachusetts.

Lieber, R. (1981) *On the Organization of the Lexicon,* Indiana University Linguistics Club, Bloomington, Indiana.

Lieber, R. (1984) "Consonant Gradation in Fula: An Autosegmental Approach," in M. Aronoff and R. Oehrle, eds. (1984).

Lieber, R. (1987) "An Integrated Theory of Autosegmental Processes," SUNY Press, New York.

Lumsden, J. (1984) "Round and Back Harmony in Mongolian," ms., MIT, Cambridge, Massachusetts.

Marantz, A. (1982) "Re-Reduplication," *Linguistic Inquiry,* 13, 435-82.

Marantz, A. (1985) "Fula Class Suffixes and Autosegmental Theory," ms., University of North Carolina at Chapel Hill, North Carolina.

Marlett, S. (1981) *The Structure of Seri,* Ph.d. dissertation, University of California San Diego, California.

Marlett, S. (1983) "Empty Consonants in Seri," *Linguistic Inquiry*, 14, 617-639.

Mascaró, J. (1976) *Catalan Phonology and the Phonological Cycle*, Ph.d. dissertation, MIT, Cambridge, Massachusetts.

Massamba, D.P. (1982a) "Tone in Ci-Ruri," in G.N. Clements and J. Goldsmith, eds., (1982).

Massamba, D.P. (1982b) *Aspects of Accent and Tone in Ci-Ruri*, Ph.d. dissertation, Indiana University, Bloomington, Indiana.

McCarthy, J. (1981) *Formal Problems in Semitic Morphology and Phonology*, Indiana University Linguistics Club, Bloomington, Indiana.

McCarthy, J. (1983a) "Phonological Features and Morphological Structure," in J. Richardson, M. Marks, A. Chukerman, eds. (1983).

McCarthy, J. (1983b) "Consonant Morphology in the Chaha Verb," in M. Barlow, D. Flickinger, and M. Westcoat, eds., *Proceedings of the West Coast Conference on Formal Linguistics*, Stanford Linguistics Association, Stanford, California.

McCarthy, J. (1984) "Theoretical Consequences of Montañes Vowel Harmony," *Linguistic Inquiry*, 15, 291-318.

McCarthy, J. (1986) "OCP Effects: Gemination and Antigemination," *Linguistic Inquiry*, 17, 207-263.

McCarthy, J. (1988) "Guttural Phonology," ms. UMASS, Amherst.

McCarthy, (1989) "Linear Order in Phonological Representation," *Linguistic Inquiry* 20.1.

McCarthy, J. and A. Prince (in press) *Prosodic Morphology*, MIT Press, Cambridge.

Mohanan, K.P. (1982) *Lexical Phonology*, Indiana University Linguistics Club, Bloomington, Indiana.

Mohanan, K.P. (1986) *The Theory of Lexical Phonology*, D. Reidel, Dordrecht.

Mohanan, K.P. and T. Mohanan (1984) "Lexical Phonology of the Consonant System in Malayalam," *Linguistic Inquiry*, 15, 575-602.

Nash, D. (1979) "Warlpiri Vowel Assimilations," *MIT Working Papers in Linguistics*, 1, 12-24.

Nash, D. (1980) *Topics in Warlpiri Grammar*, Ph.d. dissertation, MIT, Cambridge, Massachusetts.

Newman, P. (1986) "Tone and Affixation in Hausa," to appear in *Studies in African Linguistics*.

Newman, S. (1941) *The Yokuts Language of California,* Viking Fund Publications in Anthropology 2, New York.

Nichols, J. (1971) "Diminutive Consonant Symbolism in Western North America," *Language,* 47, 826-848.

Odden, D. (1986a) "On the Role of the Obligatory Contour Principle in Phonological Theory," *Language,* 62, 353-383.

Odden, D. (1988) "Anti Antigemination and the OCP," *Linguistic Inquiry* 19.3

Odden, D. (1990) "Phonology and its Interaction with Syntax and Morphology," ms., Ohio State University, Columbus.

Pesetsky, D. (1979) "Russian Morphology and Lexical Theory," unpublished ms., MIT, Cambridge, Massachusetts.

Pesetsky, D. (1983) "Morphology and Logical Form," *Linguistic Inquiry,* 16, 193-246.

Pike, E. (1975) "Coatzospan Mixtec," in R.M. Brend, ed., *Advances in Tagmemics,* North Holland Linguistics Series, Holland.

Piggot, G. (1989) "Parameters of Nasalization," McGill Working Papers, Montreal.

Poser, W. (1982) "Phonological Representations and Action-at-a-Distance," in H. van der Hulst and N. Smith, eds., Vol. II (1982).

Pulleyblank, D. (1986) *Tone in Lexical Phonology,* Reidel, Dordrecht.

Rappapport, M. (1984) *Issues in the Phonology of Tiberian Hebrew,* Ph.d. dissertation, MIT, Cambridge, Massachusetts.

Reichard, G. (1938) "Coeur d'Alene," in F. Boas, *Handbook of American Languages,* Bureau of American Ethnology, Bulletin 40, Washington.

Reichard, G. (1939) "Coeur d'Alene Stem List," *International Journal of American Linguistics,* vol. 10.

Reichard, G. (1925) *Wiyot Grammar and Texts,* University of California Publications in American Archaeology and Ethnology, 22.

Richardson, J., M. Marks, and A. Chukerman, eds. (1983) *Papers from the Parasession of the Interplay of Phonology, Morphology, and Syntax,* Chicago Linguistic Society, Chicago, Illinois.

Sagey, E. (1987) "On the Ill-Formedness of Crossing Association Lines," *Linguistic Inquiry* 19.1.

Sagey, E. (1987) "Non-Constituent Spreading in Barra Gaelic," ms., University of California, Irvine.

Sagey, E. (1986) *The Representation of Features and Relations in Non-Linear Phonology,* , MIT, Cambridge, Massachusetts.

Shaw, P. (1985) "Modularisation and Substantive Constraints in Dakota Lexical Phonology," *Phonology Yearbook* 2.

Siegal, D. (1974) *Topics in English Morphology,* Ph.d dissertation, MIT, Cambridge, Massachusetts.

Schein, B. (1981) "Spirantization in Tigrinya," in H. Borer, and Y. Aoun, eds., *Theoretical Issues in the Grammar of Semitic Languages,* MIT Working Papers in Linguistics, 4, MIT, Cambridge, Massachusetts, 32-42.

Schein, B. and D. Steriade (1986) "On Geminates," *Linguistic Inquiry,* 17, 691-744.

Schlindwein, D. (1986) "Tier Alignment in Reduplication," in *Proceedings of NELS 16,* GLSA, Amherst, Massachusetts.

Schlindwein, D. (1987) "P-Bearing Units, a Study of Kinande Vowel Harmony," *Proceedings of NELS 17,* GLSA, Amherst, Massachusetts.

Shaw, P.A. (1985) "Modularisation and Substantive Constraints in Dakota Lexical Phonology," *Phonology Yearbook,* 2, 173-202.

Sloat, C. (1975) "Vowel Harmony in Coeur d'Alene," *International Journal of American Linguistics,* 38, 234-239.

Spagnolo, L. (1933) *Bari Grammar and Dictionary,* Verona Missioni Africane.

Spagnolo, L. (1960) *Bari-English-Italian Dictionary,* Museum Combonianum, no. 9, Verona Editrice, Nigrizia.

Speas, M. (1984) "Navajo Prefixes and Word Structure Typology," *MIT Working Papers in Linguistics,* 7.

Speas, M. (1986) *Adjunctions and Projections in Syntax,* Ph.d. dissertation, MIT, Cambridge, Massachusetts.

Sproat, R. (1985) *On Deriving the Lexicon,* Ph.d. dissertation, MIT, Cambridge, Massachusetts.

Steinberger, J. and R. Vago (1986) "A Multi-leveled Autosegmental Analysis of Vowel Harmony in Bari," to appear in D. Odden, ed., *Current Approaches to African Linguistics,* vol. 4, Foris, Dordrecht.

Steriade, D. (1987a) "Locality Conditions and Feature Geometry," to appear in *Proceedings of NELS 17,* GLSA, Amherst, Massachusetts.

Steriade, D. (1987b) "Redundant Values," *Proceedings of CLS 23* vol. 2, Chicago Linguistics Society, Chicago.

Steriade, D. (1986a) "Vowel Tiers and Geminate Blockage," ms., MIT, Cambridge, Massachusetts.

Steriade, D. (1986b) "Yokuts and the Vowel Plane," *Linguistic Inquiry*, 17, 129-146.

Steriade, D. (1985) "A Note on Coronal," ms., MIT, Cambridge, Massachusetts.

Steriade, D. (1982) *Greek Prosodies and the Nature of Syllabification*, Ph.d. dissertation, MIT, Cambridge, Massachusetts.

Steriade, D. (1981) "Parameters of Metrical Harmony Rules," ms., MIT, Cambridge, Massachusetts.

Teeter, K. (1964) *The Wiyot Language*, University of California Publications in Linguistics, vol. 37.

Trigo, L. (1987) "Mixtec Nasal Harmony," ms., MIT, Cambridge, Massachusetts.

Tucker, A.N. and J.T.O. Mpaayei (1955) *A Maasai Grammar*, Longmans Green and Co.

Vago, R., ed., (1980) *Issues in Vowel Harmony*, John Benjamins B.V., Holland.

Vago, R. (1985) "Morpheme Level Harmony in a Multi-level Autosegmental Framework," ms., Tel-Aviv University, Tel-Aviv.

van der Hulst, H. (1988) "The Geometry of Vocalic Features," in H. van der Hulst and N. Smith (1988).

van der Hulst, H. and N. Smith, eds. (1982) *The Structure of Phonological Representations*, Vols. I-II, Foris, Dordrecht.

van der Hulst, H. and N. Smith (1985) "Vowel Features and Umlaut in Djingili, Nyangumarda and Warlpiri," *Phonology Yearbook*, 2, 277-303.

van der Hulst, H. and N. Smith (1986) "On Neutral Vowels," in *Studies on African Language Offered to John M. Stewart on his 60th Birthday*, Foris, Dordrecht.

van der Hulst, H. and N. Smith (1988) *Features, Segmental Structure and Harmony Processes*, part II, Dordrecht, Netherlands.

Wallace, B. (1981) "The Morphophonemics of the Maasai Verb," in T.C. Schadeberg and M.L. Bender, eds., *Proceedings of the First Nilo-Saharan Linguistics Colloquium*, Foris, Dordrecht, 75-88.

Whitney, W.D. (1889) *Sanskrit Grammar*, Harvard University Press, Cambridge, Massachusetts.

Williams, E. (1976) "Underlying Tone in Margi and Igbo," *Linguistic Inquiry* 7.3.

Williams, E. (1981) "On the Notions 'Lexically Related' and 'Head of a Word'," *Linguistic Inquiry,* 12, 245-274.

Yokwe, E. (1978) "Bari Phonology," Master's thesis, Institute of African and Asiatic Studies, University of Khartoum.

Younes, R. (1983) "The Representation of Geminate Consonants," ms., University of Texas, Austin, Texas.

Zsiga, E. (1989) "Underspecification and Vowel Harmony in Igbo," *Proceedings of NELS 19,* GLSA, Amherst, Massachusetts.

For Product Safety Concerns and Information please contact our EU
representative GPSR@taylorandfrancis.com
Taylor & Francis Verlag GmbH, Kaufingerstraße 24, 80331 München, Germany

www.ingramcontent.com/pod-product-compliance
Lightning Source LLC
Chambersburg PA
CBHW051058230426
43667CB00013B/2350